Television Studies After TV

Understanding Television in the
Post-Broadcast Era

Edited by Graeme Turner and Jinna Tay

Routledge
Taylor & Francis Group

LONDON AND NEW YORK

First published 2009
by Routledge
2 Park Square, Milton Park, Abingdon, Oxon, OX14 4RN

Simultaneously published in the USA and Canada
by Routledge
270 Madison Ave, New York, NY 10016

Reprinted 2010

Routledge is an imprint of the Taylor & Francis Group, an informa business

Editorial selection and material © 2009 Graeme Turner and Jinna Tay;
individual chapters © 2009, the Contributors

Typeset in Bembo by
Taylor & Francis Books
Printed and bound in Great Britain by
CPI Antony Rowe, Chippenham, Wiltshire

1006264406

British Library Cataloguing in Publication Data
A catalogue record for this book is available from the British Library

Library of Congress Cataloging in Publication Data
Television studies after tv : understanding television in the post-broadcast era /
edited by Graeme Turner and Jinna Tay.
    p. cm.
Includes bibliographical references and index.
    1. Television broadcasting. 2. Television broadcasting–Developing countries.
I. Turner, Graeme. II. Tay, Jinna.
    PN1992.5.T372 2009
    302.23'45–dc22
                        2008047611

ISBN10: 0-415-47769-7 (hbk)
ISBN10: 0-415-47770-0 (pbk)
ISBN10: 0-203-87831-0 (ebk)

ISBN13: 978-0-415-47769-7 (hbk)
ISBN13: 978-0-415-47770-3 (pbk)
ISBN13: 978-0-203-87831-6 (ebk)

Contents

Contributors

Mark Andrejevic is a postdoctoral researcher at the University of Queensland's Centre for Critical and Cultural Studies. He is also Assistant Professor in the Communication Studies Department at the University of Iowa. He is the author of *iSpy: Surveillance and Power in the Interactive Era* (2007) and *Reality TV: The Work of Being Watched* (2004), as well as numerous articles and book chapters on surveillance, popular culture and digital media.

Adrian Mabbott Athique teaches Media and Communications in the Department of Sociology, University of Essex in the United Kingdom. His research interests include the social practice (and malpractice) of film exhibition, the impact of new media technologies on media distribution and the transnational reception of media content. To date, Adrian's work has focused on South Asia and Australia, and has been published in leading journals, including *Media, Culture and Society*, *Continuum*, *South Asia*, *South Asian Popular Culture* and the *European Journal of Cultural Studies*. He is currently completing a co-authored book on the phenomenon of the multiplex cinema in India.

Stuart Cunningham is Professor of Media and Communications, Queensland University of Technology, and Director of the Australian Research Council Centre of Excellence for Creative Industries and Innovation. He is author or editor of several books and major reports, most recently *The Media and Communications in Australia* (with Graeme Turner, 2006), *What Price a Creative Economy?* (2006), *Beyond the Creative Industries: Mapping the Creative Economy in the United Kingdom* (with Peter Higgs and Hasan Bakhshi, 2008) and *In the Vernacular: A Generation of Australian Culture and Controversy* (2008).

Michael Curtin is Professor of Communication Arts at the University of Wisconsin-Madison and director of the Global Studies program at the UW International Institute. His books include *Redeeming the Wasteland: Television Documentary and Cold War Politics*, *Playing to the World's Biggest Audience: The Globalization of Chinese Film and TV*, *The American Television Industry* (co-author), *Making and Selling Culture* (co-editor) and *The Revolution Wasn't Televised: Sixties Television and Social Conflict* (co-editor). He is currently writing *Media Capital: The Cultural Geography of Globalization*. With Paul McDonald, he is co-editor of the 'International Screen Industries' book series for the British Film Institute.

Stephanie Hemelryk Donald is Professor of Chinese Media Studies at the University of Sydney. She researches the politics of media and culture, and the intersection of social history and visual media, with a particular focus on children and young people. Her publications include *Public Secrets, Public Spaces* (2000), *Little Friends* (2005), *Tourism and the Branded City: Film and Identity on the Pacific Rim* (2007), *The State of China Atlas* (1999, 2005, 2008) and *Branding Cities: Cosmopolitanism, Parochialism, and Social Change* (with Eleonore Kofman and Catherine Kevin, 2008). She is currently working on memory aesthetics, mobile media, and class and taste in China and the Australasian region.

Anthony Y.H. Fung is an Associate Professor in the School of Journalism and Communication at the Chinese University of Hong Kong. He received his PhD from the School of Journalism and Mass Communication at the University of Minnesota. His research interests include the political economy of popular music and culture, gender and youth identity, cultural studies and new media technologies. His new books include *New Television: Globalization and East Asian Cultural Imaginations* (with Michael Keane and Albert Moran, 2007) and *Global Capital, Local Culture: Localization of Transnational Media Corporations in China* (2008).

John Hartley, Australian Research Council Federation Fellow, is Research Director of the ARC Centre of Excellence for Creative Industries and Innovation at Queensland University of Technology, where he is a Distinguished Professor. He was foundation Dean of the Creative Industries Faculty (QUT) and previously inaugural head of the School of Journalism, Media and Cultural Studies at Cardiff University in Wales. He has published 20 books, translated into a dozen languages, including *The Uses of Digital Literacy* (2009), *Television Truths* (2008), *Creative Industries* (2005), *A Short History of Cultural Studies* (2003), *The Indigenous Public Sphere* (with Allan McKee, 2000), *Uses of Television* (1999) and *Popular Reality* (1996). He is editor of the *International Journal of Cultural Studies*.

P. David Marshall is Professor and Chair of New Media and Cultural Studies and Head of the School of Social Sciences, Media and Communication at the University of Wollongong. He is the author of *Celebrity and Power* (1997), *New Media Cultures* (2004), the co-author of *Fame Games: The Production of Celebrity in Australia* (with Graeme Turner and Frances Bonner, 2000), *Web Theory* (with Robert Burnett, 2003), and editor of *The Celebrity Culture Reader* (2006), along with many articles on the media, new media and popular culture. He is currently working on a book-length project considering the transformation from representational to presentational regimes via new media.

Toby Miller chairs the Department of Media and Cultural Studies at the University of California, Riverside. He is the author and editor of over 30 books, and his work has been translated into Swedish, Japanese, Chinese and Spanish. He edits the journals *Television & New Media* and *Social Identities*. His last book was *Cultural Citizenship* and his next is *Makeover Nation: The United States of Reinvention*.

Albert Moran is a Professor in the School of Arts at Griffith University, Brisbane. He has published more than 20 books with Australian and international presses on topics within film and television studies. Recent publications include *New Television: Globalization and the East Asian Imagination* (with Michael Keane and Anthony Fung, 2007), *Understanding the Global TV Format* (with Justin Malbon, 2006) and *Television Across Asia: Globalization, Industry and Formats* (edited with Michael Keane, 2004).

Naomi Sakr is a Reader in Communication at the Communication and Media Research Institute (CAMRI), University of Westminster, and Director of the CAMRI Arab Media Centre. She is the author of *Arab Television Today* (2007) and *Satellite Realms: Transnational Television, Globalization and the Middle East* (2001), and has edited two collections, *Women and Media in the Middle East: Power Through Self-Expression* (2004, reprinted 2007) and *Arab Media and Political Renewal: Community, Legitimacy and Public Life* (2007).

John Sinclair is Australian Research Council Professorial Fellow in the Australian Centre at the University of Melbourne. He has followed a research interest in Latin American television since the late 1970s, and is the author of *Latin American Television: A Global View* (1999). He has given guest lectures and held visiting professorships at universities in Mexico, the United States, Portugal and Spain, where he was UNESCO Professor of Communication. His record of internationally published books and articles includes a book in Spanish, *Televisión: Comunicación Global y Regionalización* and *Contemporary World Television* (edited with Graeme Turner, 2004).

Wanning Sun is Professor of Chinese Media at University of Technology, Sydney. She was Visiting Professor at the State University of New York (2005–6). She researches on media, migration and social change in China and its diaspora. Her works include *Leaving China* (2002), *Media and the Chinese Diaspora* (ed., 2006) and *Maid in China: Media, Mobility, and a New Semiotic of Power* (2009).

Jinna Tay is a Research Fellow on the Australia Research Council Federation Fellow Project, 'Television in the Post-Broadcast Era' at the Centre for Critical and Cultural Studies, University of Queensland, with Graeme Turner. She is looking at a comparison of the Chinese television markets across China, Hong Kong, Singapore and Taiwan within the research. She is interested in the areas of Asian cities, popular culture, nation, modernity, television, fashion and media. Her doctoral thesis is entitled 'Looking

Modern: Fashion Journalism and Cultural Modernity in Shanghai, Hong Kong and Singapore'. She edited the 'Creative Cities' section in the *Creative Industries Reader*, edited by John Hartley (2005) and has published in the areas of television, fashion, women and journalism.

Serra Tinic is Associate Professor of Media Studies in the Department of Sociology at the University of Alberta, Canada. Her research focuses on critical television studies and media globalization She is the author of *On Location: Canada's Television Industry in a Global Market* (2005). She has published in a range of scholarly anthologies and journals including *Television and New Media*, the *Journal of Communication*, *Social Epistemology* and *The Velvet Light Trap*. She is currently working on a book project, *Trading in Culture: The Global Cultural Economy of Television Drama*.

Graeme Turner is Australian Research Council Federation Fellow, Director of the Centre for Critical and Cultural Studies and Professor of Cultural Studies at the University of Queensland, Brisbane. He has published widely on media and cultural studies internationally. His recent publications include *Understanding Celebrity* (2004), *Ending the Affair: The Decline of Television Current Affairs in Australia* (2005), and the 4th revised edition of *Film as Social Practice* (2006). He is currently working on a book entitled *The Demotic Turn: Ordinary People and the Media*, to be published in 2009.

Zala Volcic is a Postdoctoral Fellow at the Centre for Critical and Cultural Studies, University of Queensland. Her research areas include mass communication theory, international communication, and media and nationalism. She is interested in the cultural consequences of nationalism, capitalism and globalization, with a particular emphasis on international communication, national and ethnic identity, media and cultural identities. Among her recent published works are 'Former Yugoslavia on the World Wide Web: Commercialization and branding of nation-states', in the *International Communication Journal, Gazette* (2008) and 'Yugo-nostalgia: Cultural memory and media', in *Critical Studies in Media Communication* (2007).

Yuezhi Zhao is Professor and Canada Research Chair in the Political Economy of Global Communication at the School of Communication, Simon Fraser University, Canada. Dr Zhao has broad research interests in communication and democratic governance in North American, Chinese and global contexts, and has written extensively on China's media and communication industries during the reform era. She is the author of *Media, Market, and Democracy in China* (1998), co-author of *Sustaining Democracy? Journalism and the Politics of Objectivity* (1998) and co-editor of *Democratizing Global Media: One World, Many Struggles* (2005) and *Global Communications: Toward a Transcultural Political Economy* (2008). Her newest book, *Communication in China: Political Economy, Power, and Conflict* (2008), explores China's rapidly evolving polity, economy and society through the prism of its communication system.

Introduction

Graeme Turner and Jinna Tay

We have probably all seen images like this, in old advertisements and early press reports proclaiming the arrival of TV. The family is gathered in the living room, children sprawled on the floor, mother seated on the couch, all turned expectantly towards the TV. The father is standing next to it, often with his hand on a dial or a knob, taking a proprietor's role in delivering to the family the benefits of modernity. A little later on in its history, we didn't even need to see the TV itself. Instead, typically, the images would just depict the family seated on the couch, rapt faces bathed in the light projected by the screen. TV had become the hearth of modernity. Even when later representations took us beyond the living rooms of the West to less-developed countries where whole communities were gathered around the one TV in the village, their faces were similarly lit by that magically luminous screen. TV's promise of injecting domestic space with 'space age' modernity was reiterated over and over again.

When TV was represented like this, it was a broadcast technology. It was consumed within the home, addressed to a national audience, universally available, articulated to the democratic state as part of its communications infrastructure, and a leading edge in post-war representations of the consumer society. Now, much of this has changed. At varying points, depending on the location but certainly increasingly from the mid-1970s onwards, TV escaped the confines of domestic space: platforms of delivery proliferated, and TV screens began to appear everywhere – in shops, in malls, in subway cars, in cars, buses, trains, and on the sides of buildings. Giant TV screens became an everyday component of the spectacle of urban public space. Later on, still more screens became smaller, radically privatized, as they shrank to fit the mobile phone, the portable DVD player, or the dashboard of the car. As TV mutated, its solid normativity – probably one of its most fundamental original attributes – began to unravel. For television studies, too, some of its certainties about the histories and understandings of television unravelled as well. It is to this situation, the situation of contemporary television studies, that the contributions in this collection primarily address themselves.

The title of this book acknowledges its debt to Spigel and Olsson's important collection, *Television After TV: Essays on a Medium in Transition* (2004). In that book, the editors introduced a distinction between 'television' and 'TV' in order to draw attention to the ways in which the medium of television was reinventing itself. While their contributors focused primarily on the situation in the United States and Europe, Spigel and Olsson's collection highlighted the need for television scholars to recognize that the television industry worldwide was in the process of fundamental change. If we respond to their lead and look at what has happened to television around the world over the first decade of the twenty-first century, this process is nothing short of dramatic. Globalizing media industries, deregulatory (even reregulatory!) policy regimes, the multiplication and convergence of delivery platforms, the international trade in media formats, the emergence of important production hubs in new 'media capitals' outside the United States/United Kingdom/Europe umbrella (particularly in East Asia), and the fragmentation of media audiences – as what were once national audiences slice up into more and more taste fractions – are all changing the nature of television: its content, its production, how and where it is consumed.   ← *volatile setting*

Television's family audience in the living room has now dispersed – into the kitchen, into the den, study or computer room, into the home theatre, into the bedroom and, finally, out of the home altogether: into the street and onto their mobiles. Just about all of these shifts have responded to the arrival of, or have created markets for, new platforms of delivery and new technologies of reception, production and interactivity. Over the last decade, worldwide, television has been widely deregulated, in many cases disarticulated from the state through privatization, and become increasingly commercial. Content has migrated onto the web through the conventional media's branded websites, but more significantly through video aggregators like YouTube; the circulation of television increasingly occurs through viral, rather than broadcast, networks such as those available through blogs or the social networking sites MySpace and Facebook.

easier to consume
) adaptation

As these mutations proliferate, people start to ask: How is this still television? (Green 2008). As significant fractions of the audiences in Japan and Korea take to watching video content on their mobile phones, the question is asked again: How is this still television? What makes these questions especially legitimate is that in some situations now television has begun to lose a fundamental component of its earlier character: once the prime medium of mass communication, it can now also be discussed (as it is by Hartley and by Marshall in this volume) as a highly personal medium of individualized, privatized consumption.

Of course, all of these changes are in fact significantly varied in practice, with many national systems still dominated by broadcast media and national regulatory regimes, while others are framed by subscription services and multichannel, transnational, commercial environments. Despite the assumptions built into the many early accounts of globalization, which saw the local almost inevitably losing out to the global, it remains the case (as Moran's chapter demonstrates) that local, national or regional conditions are still powerful determinants of how these changes play out in particular markets: while free-to-air audiences are declining steadily in the United States, they are multiplying dramatically in India; the use of mobiles as television receivers is minimal in Australia, but it has emerged as a major platform in Japan. It is easy to get carried away by what seem to be the overwhelming trends in Western markets, but one of the aims of this volume has been to qualify that kind of enthusiasm by introducing competing accounts of other, equally significant markets. As the chapters in this volume dealing with China (by Fung, Tay, and Sun and Zhao) make abundantly clear, the rise of the global market for television does not necessarily require the nation-state to relinquish its control over the structure and content of its media industries; some of the more optimistic projections of a deregulated and open market for China may have misunderstood the determining influences in what is now the largest television market in the world. Furthermore, in the midst of all this diversity and volatility, it is important to recognize that, even though so much current academic and public discussion about the evolution of the contemporary media focuses on the rise of new digital media, the 'old media' such as television remain dominant in most locations – even, as Toby Miller's chapter on the representation of politics suggests, in the United States. That said, it is evident that, at the very least, new media are recontextualizing television, changing what it is that television can do, for whom it can do it, and under what conditions.

Consequently, where once broadcast television was the fundamental format that television studies had to address, now we need also to address what Michael Curtin's chapter describes as a media 'matrix': a much more complex environment in which change has been vigorous but uneven, and where local and national conditions vary significantly. The similarity of many of the factors influencing the discussion of changes in the West has perhaps encouraged Western scholars to underestimate the contingency of their effects in other locations. While it was always true that what individual communities consumed as television was highly specific to the national, regional or transnational environment in which the media systems operated, much academic work on television was happy to overlook that. Now it is absolutely clear that we can no longer talk about 'TV' as if it were a singular entity, if we have any chance of adequately understanding the contemporary social, cultural and political functions of the media.

Acknowledging the need to think beyond the Anglo-American nexus that has overwhelmingly driven the field of television studies, the contributors to this collection not only discuss national and transnational markets in the customary anglophone locations – the United States (the chapters by Curtin, Andrejevic, Marshall, Miller), the United Kingdom (Donald, Cunningham, Hartley) and Canada (Tinic) – but also focus on key regional and geo-linguistic markets in

Asia (Athique, Sun and Zhao, Tay, Fung, Moran), Central Europe (Volcic), Latin America (Sinclair) and the Middle East (Sakr). In addition, most of the contributions adopt a comparative and transnational approach rather than providing self-contained accounts of individual markets. The objective has been to work towards a recontextualization of the default settings for Anglo-American television studies. As a result, the television landscape presented in this book is not dominated by the usual topography – that of the United States, the United Kingdom and Europe – although many of the essays develop their arguments in the context of changes in these markets and the work of television scholars dealing with them. Rather, the wider global context in which this book's account of television situates itself is aimed at shifting the focus of television studies towards recognizing the highly varied stories – local, national and regional – to be told about the production and consumption of contemporary globalizing television.

Implicit in this project is not only a shift in the locations of interest to television studies, but also a shift in its theoretical focus. In general, media and cultural studies has built its theories of television upon the model of a broadcast television system that addresses a national culture, and is in one way or another fundamentally connected to the governance of the nation-state. Few would disagree that such a model, emphasizing television's informational, national and democratic institutional role, is looking a little anachronistic in some markets today. In its place, typically, are the convergent media, addressing and creating different kinds of audiences. On the one hand, the notions of mass communication which underpinned the earlier model and, on the other hand, the expectations of a homogenizing process of globalization both need to be revisited if we are to develop an accurate map of the contemporary television landscape. Alternatively, there is also plenty of evidence in this book of the capacity for the national culture, in other markets, to reclaim the traditional role of television, and of the durability of the uses to which it can be put for the nation-state.

The contributions to this book reflect a wide range of the available theoretical and analytical positions in contemporary television studies. Hartley, Marshall and Andrejevic, for instance, present very different readings of the dramatic changes wrought by the new media as television reinvents itself as a highly interactive medium of interpersonal communication and social networking. Curtin helps us understand the framework for the US industry after broadcasting has lost its dominance, and Cunningham acquaints us with the strategies being developed by public broadcasters to 'reinvent' television for another generation of users by drawing on theories of 'innovation'. Against those who hold that the nation is no longer a relevant factor in mapping global television, there is Turner's critique of such positions, Moran's adroit understanding of the processes through which global formats are localized and Volcic's account of a new form of commercial nationalism in the Balkans. Whereas there may be something of an orthodoxy in the new media end of television studies which is happy to regard television as categorically post-broadcast, post-national and post-digital, the various accounts of regional or geo-linguistic markets (Adrian Athique's chapter on India, for instance) high-light the specificity of the histories of television around the world, and thus work against the unreflective application of those categories. Finally, as a strong counter-discourse to the dominance of Anglo-American television studies, this book has deliberately foregrounded accounts from what might be described as the peripheries of television studies (Tay's chapter on the Chinese geo-linguistic markets, or Sakr's discussion of Arab satellite television, for instance) as holding important lessons not only about the contingency of the specific contexts for these television industries but also about the contingency of the theoretical perspectives used to direct television studies.

The objective of this book is to explore new ways of understanding the form, content and function – the place – of television in the post-broadcast era. It is divided into four parts. Each part begins with a short contextualizing introduction from the editors. There is an aggregated list of references at the end of the book, but notes to individual chapters will appear at the end of each chapter. Part One asks what might be collected under the label of tele-vision today: with television content travelling across so many platforms in so many varied ways, the question of 'What is television?' needs to be addressed. Part Two asks another fundamental question: if television no longer categori-cally performs the public sphere function once assumed to be the role of national broadcasting systems, then what are the functions it now serves – socially, culturally and politically? Indeed, can we any longer claim a char-acteristic socio-cultural function for the medium at all? Part Three focuses this issue more directly by examining the part that television now plays in gen-erating, mediating or resisting social change. Finally, given the importance we have attached to understanding the formations of television in various markets around the world, it makes sense for us to provide in Part Four some com-parative transnational accounts of television content. These accounts are quite varied, with the local, national and regional contexts and the socio-political conjunctures pertaining to each location leading to very specific cultural and industrial formations.

As a number of our contributors suggest, the task for television studies is today far more complicated than it would have been 20 years ago. Not only are there fundamental technological questions to do with formats and plat-forms of delivery that affect our understanding of the production of television, but the modes of consumption have proliferated in ways that challenge our capacity to find a common link between them that might justify the applica-tion of an approach like television studies. Rather than an exercise in policing the boundaries of television studies, however, the project for this collection is to more accurately acknowledge its complexity as a first step towards locating key points for analysis and examination, towards better recognizing the varied histories that contribute to so-called 'global television', and towards setting the

agendas for a rethinking of the media and representational theory that under-
pins so much of what has been done within the field.

This book is the outcome of a 'scoping symposium' held at the Centre for
Critical and Cultural Studies at the University of Queensland in 2007, as part
of Graeme Turner's Federation Fellowship Post-Broadcast Television project, in
which many of the current volume's contributors participated. We would like
to thank all those who attended and who generated the ideas and the enthusiasm
for putting it all together. We also owe our thanks to a number of others
whose assistance has been important in completing this project: to Sue Jarvis
for her impeccable work on the manuscript, to Natalie Foster at Routledge for
supporting the project, and finally to our contributors for coming in (well,
mostly) on time.

Part One

What is television?

Introduction

MTU big on this (handwritten)

Television is no longer a stand-alone medium. The major ratings successes of
the twenty-first century have been multi-platform, multimedia events. One
significant example is *Big Brother*, with its websites, chat-rooms, live video
streaming, and its key narrative moments – the evictions, for instance – turned
into public events by being performed before a live audience. The decline of
the broadcast era in the West has seen increasing industrial and technological
convergence as telecommunications, information technology and the electronic media coalesce under the same corporate umbrellas, and as technologies
themselves interact more directly than ever before. Broadband is now the
coming thing in the US industry, as the internet develops new forms of access,
new modes of interaction and new media products for a youthful, innovation-
seeking audience. This has produced an environment where the demand for
content has exploded as media companies try to keep pace with the proliferation of new media formats and distribution channels – both in terms of
providing content and in terms of working out how to 'monetize' these new
platforms.

Within this climate, of course, television continues – even if 'TV' may not.
As Spigel and Olsson's collection (2004) demonstrates, the model of 'TV' can
no longer be regarded as normative. Now, in many developed media markets,
broadcast television must compete for its audiences against new media formats – not just subscription television, print and radio, but the attractions of
the online and mobile environment as well. Admittedly, in such markets as
Australia, New Zealand and to a lesser extent the United Kingdom, the free-
to-air networks still dominate and continue to address a national audience for
much of the time. Even in these markets, however, the situation has changed
such that we cannot think of television networks in the way we once did: as
merely competing for their slice of the national mass audience. In other locations, such as Latin America, the situation is different again in that there is a
transnational, regional audience built upon a transnational language, Spanish,
rather than solely upon the citizenship of a territorial state or membership of a

BBC (handwritten)

KEY (handwritten)

Inbetweeners works exactly because it harks back to old traditions, therefore proving difficult to replicate (handwritten) national community (Sinclair 1999). Further, and as we will see in Part Four, outside the major markets of the West, the national political contexts in which television is produced and consumed exercise a major influence over what kinds of markets are constructed, and what kinds of experiences are offered to television viewers. Notwithstanding the internationalization of the media industries, these days the answer to the question 'What is television?' very much depends on where you are.

Although one of the objectives of this book is to present evidence that might help to problematize the 'end of broadcasting/rise of broadband' narrative referred to above, the task of Part One is to focus upon the undeniably dramatic changes – technological, industrial and cultural – that have motivated such a narrative. Michael Curtin's essay presents a highly nuanced discussion of how these changes have affected the shape and structure of the American television industry as it moves into what he describes as an era of 'matrix media' – where the earlier patterns of dominance no longer work, and where the television platform can no longer stand alone. John Hartley's chapter plots the displacement of the traditional forms of television by the growth of social networking sites and further develops his signature argument that the changing patterns of media consumption implicated in this shift constitute an intrinsically democratic development. For television studies, he argues, there is a significant lesson to be learnt about the importance of examining the productivity of the television/online audience with as much attention as we have previously given to representations in television texts.

Mark Andrejevic also approaches the issue of the productivity delivered by the interactive capacities of digital media, but in a very different way. Rather than focusing on the opportunities that interactivity provides for the active consumer, Andrejevic focuses on the opportunities it provides for the advertiser and marketer. Andrejevic's version of the politics of the new interactivity is far less optimistic than Hartley's: rather than empowering the audience, he sees interactivity as providing another avenue through which they are articulated to commercial interests. Finally, David Marshall's chapter describes the migration of television content away from the television screen, with the rise of internet television, mobile television and television on DVD. This migration, he argues in ways that complement Hartley's analysis, has had the consequence of changing television from a mass medium of exhibition into what Marshall calls an 'intermediary form of interpersonal communication'.

Chapter 1

Matrix media

Michael Curtin

As the world's leading programme exporter, the American television industry has for decades been a trendsetter in the development of the medium worldwide. American TV exports not only entertain and inform audiences in far-flung locales, they also influence local production practices, programme formats, institutional behaviours and audience tastes. As key assets of the world's largest media conglomerates, the US TV companies appear to be both prosperous and powerful. Yet the latest trends in the industry are somewhat foreboding, as new competitors, restless advertisers and empowered audiences agitate for change. The network oligopoly of the 1960s that confidently controlled the most powerful mass medium in US history has morphed into a constellation of huge multimedia conglomerates that seem far less confident of their abilities to manage audience behaviours and advertiser needs. Consequently, television companies seem to be undergoing a historic shift in their organizational structures, industry strategies and programming practices. US television, which was founded on principles of broadcast networking, is now moving into the matrix era – a shift that is emblematic of transformations taking place at media institutions around the world.

Several developments during the 2007 season seemed to herald this change. The season began with an agreement between national networks and advertisers to include DVR audiences in their ratings reports, basing calculations for each show on the number of live viewers plus those who watch within three days via DVR. At the time, close to a quarter of all US households owned a DVR and the major networks had been pressing advertisers to acknowledge some of these viewers, since they comprise a substantial share of the audience. In return, the networks accepted advertiser demands for ratings of TV *commercials* as well as programmes. The agreement represented a fundamental change in the ways in which audiences are measured and interpreted. It allowed networks to claim larger audiences for their shows, but it also intensified accountability for the commercial minutes they sold to sponsors. Both parties saw it as an important innovation aimed at coping with dramatic changes in media technologies and audience use patterns.

Yet these weren't the only issues troubling the television industry. Executives also expressed concern about growing competition from video games. On 9 March 2008, Nintendo released *Super Smash Bros Brawl*, updating the enormously popular *Super Mario* and *Super Smash Bros* franchises. That evening, television ratings among 18- to 24-year-old males dropped 8 per cent. The following day, they dropped 14 per cent (Fritz 2008: 1). Furthermore, studies showed that young people spent 25 per cent more time online than viewing television. Just as worrisome, an increasing number of Americans were turning for video entertainment and information to the internet, a medium that Google dominates with 38 per cent of all video streaming (ComScore 2008a). Although television companies remained the leading producers of video content, their historic control of distribution seemed increasingly uncertain.

As these changes unfolded, another daunting challenge emerged as Hollywood writers voted to strike on 5 November 2007 in the very heart of the television production season. Late-night talk shows were most immediately affected, and in December drama series were forced on hiatus as well, leaving gaping holes in the prime-time schedule. Ratings plummeted and, by the time a strike settlement was reached in early February 2008, it proved unexpectedly difficult to lure audiences back to network television. Many executives declared the season a washout and nervously shifted their attention to the upcoming (US) fall schedule. Some struck a more contemplative posture, arguing that it was time to reassess the foundational assumptions and practices of the industry. As if to emphasize the point, all four networks announced that they would transform their upfront sales presentations in May, seeking to demonstrate that, despite the apparent slide in ratings, the national networks remained leaders of the overall television economy and that, along with their corporate siblings, they could attract substantial audiences across a range of electronic media, including the internet.

Interestingly, intermedia rights were the key point of disagreement between the networks and the writers during the strike, with the latter arguing for a share of revenues earned via new delivery systems. During the classical network era, when three companies dominated American television, writers were compensated for prime-time showings and syndicated reruns, a formula that carried over easily into the cable era. Yet that compact became subject to debate during the 1980s, due to the development of VCR technology. At the time, writers tried to convince the studios to share a percentage of video revenues, but executives claimed it was too early in the development of video to establish a revenue-sharing formula and that high royalty rates might smother the nascent industry. After a bitter strike in 1988, the two sides settled on 0.3 per cent royalty on reportable gross sales. As video took off and became a multi-billion-dollar industry, the formula was earning writers only pennies from each sale and it therefore became a bitter point of contention, since royalties are often the only source of income for writers during inevitable stretches of unemployment.

In 2007, screenwriters were determined not to let the video rights formula established 20 years earlier become the basis for internet royalties, but media executives countered that rising costs and growing competition made it difficult for them to surrender internet revenues at a time when the income from online sources was minimal and tenuous. Executives for the media conglomerates seemed to be speaking out of both sides of their mouths, however. To advertisers at the upfront sales events, network executives presented their companies as powerful multimedia providers, while only months before they had told the writers exactly the opposite. Although seemingly duplicitous, their position pointed to a momentous transformation of the American television industry as it moved from the network era into the matrix era.

During the 1950s, when American television was in its infancy, executives confronted the challenge of building a durable and prosperous industry, despite the enormous capital costs of production and distribution. At the time, most agreed that television would be ten times as expensive as radio, a prospect that encouraged industry leaders and policy makers to advocate for a centralized commercial system in the hope of realizing economies of scale. By the time television took off, three networks were solidly entrenched and would remain so for more than 20 years, a system based on principles of national mass production, distribution and consumption – what Michele Hilmes (2007) refers to as the classical network era.

With the arrival of cable, these mass media logics were challenged, as the number of channels multiplied and the audience began to fragment. Joseph Turow (1998) has shown how advertisers fuelled this transition, as they sought to undermine the network monopoly and to pursue greater efficiencies in the delivery of advertising messages to targeted audiences. Amanda Lotz (2007) portrays this period as the multichannel transition, suggesting that the fundamental logic of the network system remained in place, even though audience behaviours were changing. That is, programme development, scheduling and advertising practices remained largely the same, even as hints of a more profound transformation began to emerge in the 1990s.

Unlike the mass television era, when the industry churned out inoffensive mass-appeal programming, executives during the multichannel transition began to pursue groups of viewers who were passionate about particular ideas, topics and interests. These niches were constituted as much by their audiences' shared world-views as they were by their sense of difference from other viewers. To serve these audiences, producers began to pitch programmes with 'edge', meaning both programmes that pushed up against the boundaries of mass taste and programmes that hailed their viewers as self-consciously distinct from others. These niche programmes were not for everyone. Indeed, they offended some viewers while catering to the passions of others (Curtin 1996).

Observing these changes, executives came to believe that they needed to compensate for the erosion of network ratings by investing in niche cable channels as well as mass-appeal network services. Furthermore, they needed to anticipate the emergence of new digital media offerings and internet services. This led to a period of mergers and empire building during the 1990s, resulting in the formation of huge media conglomerates premised on the notion that content might successfully be exploited across a range of media. Proponents argued that successful corporations would be those that could control multiple sites of creativity and diverse modes of distribution, and could operate them in synergistic harmony.

Yet synergy was easier to imagine than to execute, largely because the various components of each conglomerate were too accustomed to operating as distinct units: as network broadcasters, cable channels, internet portals, and so on. Moreover, line executives were compensated on the basis of the performance of their respective divisions, not on the health of the overall corporation. In the very top echelon of the media conglomerate, synergy seemed a logical objective, but down in the trenches executives and creative talent often fought bitter battles with their corporate cousins. When the merger bubble burst shortly after the dawn of the new millennium, many executives became openly critical of the huge conglomerates, which they averred only made sense to investment bankers who pocketed fat fees for putting them together. Consequently, the promise of synergy began to fade as media executives more or less went back to their old ways. Despite such resistance, changes in the media industries continued to unfold, driven largely by the fact that audiences and advertisers were increasingly engaging with television as part of a multimedia environment.

The 2007–8 TV season therefore proved to be something of a tipping point for the industry, a moment of crisis when executives and creative talent were again forced to revisit the issues of synergy and intermedia strategy. In part, they needed to recalibrate daily practices, audience-measurement techniques and revenue-sharing formulas, but at a deeper structural level they needed to rethink the spatial logic of electronic media. Both the radio and television eras in the United States were premised on the notion of broadcasting: the dispersal of information and entertainment from a central source to a diverse audience, limited only by the reach of electronic transmission waves. Radio did not discriminate among its listeners; indeed, as Roland Marchand (1985) argued, it played upon the ambiguity of second-person address, beckoning 'you', the mass audience, and 'you', the individual listener at home, while also massaging the two into an 'us'. Advertisers paid to become part of that circle of mutual recognition, and the most powerful among them would underwrite the interconnection of transmitters across the country so that they might deliver their messages from highly centralized facilities in New York and Hollywood to a vast, networked nation. By the 1960s, each of the three major television networks regularly drew close to 25 per cent of all television households to their prime-time schedules. Yet during the 2007 season, prime-time audiences for each of the four leading networks averaged roughly 5 per cent of television households, only a fraction of what they had attracted during the classical era. Interestingly, daily television viewing hours remained high – in fact, higher than the 1960s, at 4 hours 35 minutes – but it was coming from more centres and flowing through more circuits than ever before: via DVD, cable, satellite and broadband; via Telemundo, Spike, Netflix and YouTube (Nielsen Media Research 2006). It was no longer a broadcast medium or a network medium, or even a multichannel medium; television had become a matrix medium, an increasingly flexible and dynamic mode of communication.

According to the *Oxford English Dictionary*, 'matrix' was first employed with reference to social life during the late nineteenth century, when biological metaphors spawned conceptions of human societies as comprising complex, dynamic and interconnected elements. In the 1960s, managerial experts began to invoke the term with respect to flexible organizational structures, as opposed to linear or hierarchical institutions. This emphasis on complexity and flexibility was seemingly picked up by the telecommunications industry as it developed the matrix switch, which is an array of circuits laid out in a grid so that paths can be established between any input port and any output port. A matrix switch can, furthermore, provide full bandwidth to multiple transmissions. When confronted with traffic congestion, it allows signals to be broken down and rerouted, only to be reassembled at their destination. These basic principles of electronic design prevailed during the late twentieth century, but just as important, they governed the development of vast telecommunication systems, which were often portrayed as large-scale iterations of the matrix switch: a field of paths and possibilities for multiple users.

If the classical network era was characterized by centralized production and transmission to an undifferentiated mass audience, the matrix era is characterized by interactive exchanges, multiple sites of productivity, and diverse modes of interpretation and use. Although huge corporations continue to shape and influence the media environment, they can no longer presume to deliver a national mass audience at an appointed hour, and they can no longer market the attention of that audience to eager advertisers at the upfront presentations each spring. For media industries, the matrix era suggests emerging new structures and practices as well as changing conceptions of advertising, which remains the single most important source of media financing.[1]

It is always difficult to lay a confident finger on watershed moments of significant historical change, but the 2007–8 season seemed to offer stark evidence that the television industry was undergoing a profound transformation. CBS saw its viewership plummet by almost 30 per cent, from a 7.9 rating to a 5.6 average for the season. ABC and Fox experienced a similar slide, and NBC brought up the rear with a 4.8 rating (Simons 2008). In response to its changing fortunes, NBC announced that it would substantially alter its upfront sales presentation in May, transform its marketing practices and reconfigure its season schedule. Instead of a conventional fall premiere, NBC said it would introduce new series throughout the year, giving more attention to the promotion of each new show. Instead of a 23-week season anchored by autumn premieres and summer reruns, it would shift to a 52-week schedule that would constantly be adapted and reinvigorated by the addition of new series. And, rather than presenting the entire season's schedule at the upfront market in New York, NBC executives began to travel the country, consulting with advertisers about programme ideas and multi-platform content.

NBC's weak network ratings no doubt motivated this change in strategy, but company executives were also seizing the opportunity to direct attention to their best-performing assets: cable and internet enterprises. Remarkably, while NBC's prime-time line-up was faltering, its cable channels were flourishing – and even more important, its advertising sales remained strong largely because it was presenting itself less as a broadcasting network and more as a multi-platform operator. As if to emphasize the point, top management at NBC mandated that every television programme must develop intermedia strategies for programming and advertising.

Among NBC's divisions, Bravo is one of the most successful practitioners of what the company now refers to as 360-degree programming. For example, *Top Chef* – a popular cooking competition presided over by head judge Tom Colicchio – features a cable show and a robust website that extends the brand via recipes, games, blogs and dedicated mobile video content. Most popular is Colicchio's blog, where he provides commentary on the show and related topics, and where fans can engage in online deliberation. Most of the show's judges and contestants (including both winners and losers) maintain blog sites as well. In addition to these social networking services, the site delivers broadband video programming and promotes products such as the *Top Chef* cookbook. Furthermore, Bravo has a talent management company that represents chefs whose careers take off after they have appeared on the show. These 'brand extension' strategies aim to deepen the viewer experience by delivering content in a variety of formats so it is available to audiences wherever and whenever they wish to engage with it. As Bravo President Lauren Zalaznick puts it: 'Our value comes from super-serving a niche of passionate customers' (Whitney 2007: 1). Unlike the network era of weekly prime-time scheduling, or even the daytime practice of stripping, *Top Chef* develops and delivers content in rolling time-frames on multiple platforms, while striving to retain a coherent brand identity.

Bravo serves one of the youngest and most affluent audiences in cable television, and has scored notable success with its intermedia strategies. It targets an upscale, educated and metro mindset – primarily viewers living in the top 30 television markets. It designs programmes aimed at affinity groups that organize around food, fashion, beauty, design and pop culture. Zalaznick says that women comprise some 60 per cent of the audience, but she claims that is less a matter of targeting by gender than one of building a brand around topics that attract passionate customers. In addition to Bravo, Zalaznick presides over NBC's recently acquired Oxygen channel, which describes itself as being 'on a mission to bring women (and the men who love them) the edgiest, most innovative entertainment on television'. Claiming to air more original series than any other women's channel, Oxygen promotes itself as a slightly younger and hipper version of the industry leader, Lifetime.

In 2006, NBC also acquired the iVillage website, dedicated to 'connecting women at every stage of their lives'. Claiming 31.4 million unique visitors per month, iVillage.com touts itself as the number one destination on the web for women seeking information about health, parenting, pregnancy, beauty, style, fitness, relationships, food and entertainment. The site's interactive features include thousands of message boards and a variety of social networking tools, allowing women around the world to share information and advice. By assembling this collection of enterprises, NBC is able to present advertisers with a matrix of media opportunities that include Bravo, Oxygen, iVillage and the *Today* show. It can package spots according to age, interest, psychographic profile and socio-economic background. It can provide access to broadcast viewers of *Today*, cable fans of the *Bad Girls Club*, and online customers with a passion for cheese. Rather than assembling a mass audience, these NBC services *accumulate* a very substantial base of users via the multiple circuits of matrix media.

Strategies such as multi-platforming, repurposing and cross-promotion became important tools of network news divisions during the 1990s. The most successful organizations expanded into cable and web services, spreading the cost of the news-gathering infrastructure and branding their content in multiple formats. NBC was the most ambitious practitioner of this strategy, which not only extended its presence across the media matrix but also strengthened its core properties, helping to sustain the leadership of *NBC Nightly News* and *Today*. The news division's strategy was largely driven by a desire to control costs and secure new markets. No doubt similar concerns spurred recent changes in the entertainment division, but these more recent innovations also seem to be motivated by the fact that advertisers are now asking for more than 30-second TV spots when they purchase commercial time. Instead, they are looking for product placement opportunities, internet click advertising and pre-roll ad spots on mobile video devices. As a result, NBC altered its 2008 upfront presentation, focusing less on prime time and more on the company's ability to package advertising opportunities across media (Adalian and Schneider 2007: 28). NBC furthermore conducted a series of smaller meetings with advertisers to solicit their input regarding plans for the upcoming season. Emphasizing partnership, NBC is responding to advertisers' growing desire to break out of the box that defined American network television for more than 50 years. The flexible, dynamic and horizontal qualities of these services suggest a matrix-media strategy rather than a conventional network strategy.

In interviews with more than 100 senior media executives worldwide, researchers for Accenture found that, between 2005 and 2008, opinions began to coalesce regarding corporate strategy in the new media environment. Almost two-thirds said multi-platform distribution would be the key driver of future growth. New types of content were the second most commonly mentioned (24 per cent) and new geographies of operation were third (10 per cent) (Accenture 2008). These results suggest that media companies are beginning to focus on the meaningful execution of matrix strategies. Although rivalries and differences within conglomerates persist, the erosion of revenues among the discrete media divisions as well as the further development of broadband and mobile delivery systems have encouraged companies to revisit the complementarities of various media platforms and the advantages of cumulative audiences.

Some television series are now viewed millions of times after they are broadcast, via Fancast, Veoh, Hulu and dedicated network sites. For example, in (US) spring 2008, MTV's most popular show, *The Hills*, premiered to 3.7 million 'live' viewers. Within the next three days it added almost a million DVR viewers and over the next few weeks episodes and excerpts of the show were streamed 32 million times (Stelter 2008a: C1). Although some overlap is likely, MTV seemingly generated many more advertising opportunities outside of conventional telecasting. *The Hills* episodes also generated other revenue streams, as it scored among the top ten downloads on iTunes and among the top five videos in the 'teen scene' television category on Amazon, where one can also buy licensed merchandise that includes books, wall calendars and soundtrack albums. On the MTV website one can find *The Hills* music, news, games and message boards in addition to the episodes themselves. This not only reflects changes in audience use patterns, but also points to changes in the ways that programmes are conceived, financed and executed. As one executive put it: 'We have to manage for profit margin and not for ratings' (Adalian and Schneider 2008: 14).

Mobile telecommunications is another medium of growing interest to television executives. At its 2007 upfront presentation, ESPN executives lavished attention on new programmes designed to appear exclusively via mobile devices, including *Mayne Street* (featuring *Sports Center*'s Kenny Mayne), a mixed martial arts series, and *POV*, a compilation of clips submitted by viewers and fans. According to one ESPN executive, these mobile services are a strategic attempt to broaden and deepen the network's relationship with sports fans (Steinberg and Elliott 2008: C6). ESPN isn't alone in its enthusiasm for mobile delivery. It is estimated that content delivered over cell phones could generate $50 billion in revenue worldwide. Alert to the music industry's success with the multi-billion-dollar ringtone trade, television executives are adding mobile video services to their media matrix (Halper 2006: 19).

With all these changes afoot, the scheduling, distribution and financing of TV programming pose significant challenges for media executives. Just as challenging are the creative decisions associated with the production of online and mobile video content. Seventy-five per cent of US internet users view online video regularly, streaming an average of 85 videos per month (Fulgoni 2008). Google (the corporate parent of YouTube) delivers more than a third of all views, most of it amateur content. Initially the service grew popular as a site for sharing video clips from TV shows; however, the major television companies soon protested about copyright infringement and pressured YouTube staffers to remove the offending videos.

Interestingly, the major television companies not only complained, they soon launched services of their own – many of them quite successful. In fact, the major television companies as a group now deliver well over half of all advertiser-supported video streams (Garrett 2008: 16). Their success seems in part attributable to the quality of their content. A Pew Foundation study found that 62 per cent of internet users prefer professional video, while only 19 per cent prefer amateur material (Madden 2008). Just as important, advertisers are more willing to place their messages alongside professional video because they find the content more compelling and less likely to engender controversy. Rather than posing a threat, online video may represent a grand opportunity for television companies, but executives are nevertheless aware that they cannot simply recirculate broadcast programming onto the web. They must develop dedicated material that is conducive to web viewing.

The potential for online video seems enormous, as suggested by Will Ferrell's and Adam McKay's brief series about a foul-mouthed two-year-old landlord that was streamed more than 50 million times on funnyordie.com. Within months, their company added more than 25 employees and expanded its website into a robust buffet of comedy videos that reportedly generates more than $50 million in annual revenues.[2] Backed initially by Sequoia Capital – one of the most successful venture capital firms in Silicon Valley – funnyordie.com soon attracted HBO as a minority partner interested in securing cable television products that could complement the online service.

Online producers such as Ferrell and McKay are experimenting with the emerging conventions of online video genres. In order to make their work commercially viable, they are tinkering with formats and formulas, hoping to come up with generic conventions that will bring viewers back on a regular basis. For example, even though most creatives agree that online videos should be short, successful videos range from two to seven minutes in length. Producers also debate about the frequency of episodes, the length of 'seasons' and strategies for promotion. These challenges may seem manageable, but many video ventures – some with very big budgets and strong institutional backing – have nevertheless failed miserably, such as Budweiser's bud.tv site and *Quarterlife*, a melodrama series sponsored by Pepsi and Toyota that was directed by Marshall Herskovitz and Edward Zwick of *thirtysomething* fame.

Producers are also experimenting with interactive features, hoping to mine their fan bases for feedback and creative input. In May 2007, Mindshare, an advertising agency in the WPP Group, launched a series on MSN called *In the Motherhood*. Mindshare executives initially came up with the series while brainstorming with executives from Sprint and Unilever, both of which appear as prominent sponsors on the site. Billing *ITM* as a series 'for moms, by moms, and about moms', producers solicit story ideas from the audience and then set about fashioning episodes featuring Jenny McCarthy (formerly of MTV), Leah Remini (*King of Queens*) and comedian Chelsea Handler. The production values are professional, but the budgets are modest. *In the Motherhood* has a homey, 'let's put on a show' quality to it. Visitors to the site are immediately invited to write a story or to read and comment on stories that others have written. More than a thousand script ideas are submitted for every show that is ultimately produced, and more than 13,000 fans regularly vote for the top candidates. The value of the series resides in its ability to tap the millions of stories that mothers have to tell about their lives, their children and their families. The producers and the cast (all of them mothers) then bring the stories to life using the generic formulas of the domestic television comedy. Each episode runs for five to seven minutes and is supported by online discussions, games and recipes, as well as interviews with the cast and out-takes from the series. By the US spring of 2008, the audience had grown to more than 20 million streams per month, encouraging ABC executives to pick it up and develop *ITM* as a prime-time network offering as well.

Unlike the classical network era, when three dedicated television companies exercised oligopoly control over production, distribution and exhibition, the matrix era is characterized by the formation of huge multimedia conglomerates. Although constituted more than a decade ago, these conglomerates are finally beginning to pursue the strategies and practices that are appropriate to this new media environment. Accordingly, their conception of television has

Table 1.1 Top video sites, May 2008

Property	Unique viewers (000s)	Average videos per viewer
Total internet	141,657	85.3
Google sites[a]	83,828	50.2
Fox Interactive[b]	60,760	12.8
Yahoo! sites	40,197	8.6
Microsoft sites	29,471	8.3
Time Warner	24,612	5.9
AOL	21,670	4.8
Viacom	21,260	9.7
Disney	12,385	8.7
ESPN	8,425	8.9
ABC	7,747	16.3
Hulu (NBC)	6,800	13.0

Source: ComScore (2008c).
Notes: a Includes YouTube.
 b Includes MySpace.

changed from that of a highly centralized mode of transmission to a more flexible field of electronic media. Rather than indifferently transmitting a line-up of shows each evening, television companies now operate in an interactive, asynchronous intermedia milieu. They build brands and render them accessible to audiences in a range of formats across rolling time horizons. Still financed primarily by advertising sales, television companies no longer rely solely on ratings as a measure of their success, but rather have begun to embrace the importance of intermedia reach, as they attempt to target and accumulate audiences in a cost-efficient manner. Anxious to please advertisers who are demanding accountability and input, networks have opened their doors, infusing their clients' messages into the media matrix rather than selling them gross lots of commercial minutes.

These changes have been motivated in part by new competitors and new technologies, but just as important, they are spurred by the changing beha-viours of audiences that now navigate a growing universe of entertainment, information and interactivity. No longer restricted to a menu of 'least offen-sive' mass-appeal programming, audiences make use of a diverse repertoire of mass, niche and micro-niche content. Accordingly, television companies are complementing their investment in capital-intensive studios with multiple modes of production and creative input. This is partially a cost-cutting assault on unionized labour, as they pursue lower-cost and non-union production opportunities, but it is also part of what Tiziana Terranova (2000) refers to as a broadening out of media production into society as a whole. Quoting the Italian autonomists, she observes that 'work processes have shifted from the factory to society, thereby setting in motion a truly complex machine' (2000: 821). The media matrix increasingly thrives in an environment where dis-tinctions between production and consumption blur, where television seasons give way to an evergreen cavalcade of content that is made use of by audi-ences on flex-time schedules. It is perhaps remarkable that it took television companies so long to adapt to these changes and to acknowledge the funda-mental transformations of the matrix era. One can only hope that their increasing enthusiasm portends a more open media future rather than the more ominously imagined matrix of Baudrillard and the Wachowski brothers.

Notes

1 This analysis focuses specifically on the implications of matrix media for commercial institutions. The authors are nevertheless aware that it could be extended with respect to debates regarding the dystopian visions of the matrix, as suggested by the Wachowski brothers' eponymous feature film, William Gibson's novel *Neuromancer*, and Jean Bau-drillard's critique of *Simulacra and Simulation*.

2 See www.alexa.com/data/details/main/funnyordie.com (accessed 22 August 2008).

Chapter 2

Less popular but more democratic?

Corrie, Clarkson and the dancing *Cru*

John Hartley

Cultural climate change

The central cultural experience of modernity has been *change*, both the 'creative destruction' of existing structures, and the growth – often exponential – of new knowledge. During the twentieth century, the central cultural platform for the collective experience of modernizing societies changed too, from page and stage to the screen – from publishing, the press and radio to cinema, television and, latterly, computer screens. Despite the successive dominance of new media, none has lasted long at the top. The pattern for each was to give way to a successor platform in popularity, but to continue as part of an increasingly crowded media menu. Modern media are supplemented, not supplanted, by their successors.

Broadcast television has proven to be no exception. What constitutes 'television' now is quite different from how things appeared when its broadcast form emerged in the 1950s. As the internet, Web 2.0 and mobile devices shift from their open, 'generative' stage (Zittrain 2008), towards a stabilizing phase of adoption and retention through market-based 'affordances', it has become clear that 'television' has been transformed radically. What counts as television is diversifying, across technology, mode of production, viewing experience, programming, production base and geography:

- *Technologically*, TV includes non-broadcast technologies (DVDs, TiVo, BitTorrent files), and it can be viewed on computers (YouTube) and mobile devices (phones, iPods) as well as via traditional TV sets, which have evolved to flat-screen technologies.
- Television has physically *migrated* out of the domestic living room and is now integrated into bedrooms, offices, shops, cars, clubs and cafés. It is personalized and portable, integrated with clothes, phones and music platforms.
- Its *mode of production* has also been transformed: the giant studios that were once the unarguable sign of a powerful broadcaster are now largely empty, industry production having migrated to naturalistic settings or just-in-time facilities.

- It is a different *viewing experience*. Broadcast TV can be used as an adjunct to other activities (e.g. a TV stream on the office computer). You can customize TV by decoupling viewing from transmission (e.g. collecting DVDs or files and wallowing in a favourite series for a weekend).
- *TV entertainment* has evolved to take user participation into the heart of programming – plebiscitary TV (Hartley 2008a: 126–62). The fragmentation of platforms, many of them associated with a specific demographic segment, has fed back into the evolution of television forms, resulting in both format repetition (e.g. clones of a given format like home-improvement shows) and creative innovation (repurposing a traditional genre for a specialized audience, e.g. *Skins*).
- Most radically, the *production base* has broadened to include, in principle if not (yet) in practice, everybody with access to a computer. You can make TV yourself or with others, and you can 'redact' existing content. Either way, you can publish your efforts to family and friends and to the world at large. And then, the restlessness of imaginative creativity being what it is, some bright spark can turn that DIY format into a brilliant new type of 'TV' drama (online internet video log) – *lonelygirl15* and *KateModern*.
- *Spatially*, television has diversified from its origins in national and city-based communications systems to overlapping personalized and social networks that may be next door or global. Migrants, taste constituencies, communities of interest (around identities, sport, politics, pastimes) and enterprising creatives can exploit the 'long tail' characteristics of the internet to find content or an audience from anywhere.

Broadcast TV: a representational regime

Broadcast television was always a mixed blessing, displaying at once the positive and negative aspects of a regime of semiotic and political representation in which common, generalized experience was represented on screen and in legislatures by professional expert elites (actors and politicians, *mutatis mutandis*). So *everyone was represented* – ordinary life and everyday choices were the real 'platform' of mass media – but simultaneously *no one spoke for themselves*. Everything was realist but nothing was real.

On the plus side, television's domestic setting, live immediacy, leisure-time availability, casual continuity, operational simplicity (two knobs) and the human scale of its screen were all suited to the context in which it thrived best: private life and family building in conditions of expanding consumer affluence, otherwise known as the suburban experience. On screen, broadcast television excelled at head-to-head dramatic conflict, both fictional and factual: drama, comedy, news, sport and kids' shows. While encouraging people to stay at home, it taught neighbourly comportment, and experiential and national togetherness, and it continuously brought new information and experience to all sections of the public. It could also coordinate population-wide (sometimes planet-wide) attention to, and emotional investment in, periods of excitement and high uncertainty, as during sporting finals, end-of-season cliffhangers, elections and political crises. It was the bellwether of change for a population living through change.

But at the same time, television was a worry. The high capital cost of production and highly regulated distribution networks resulted in an extreme 'division of labour' between corporate expertise and lay audiences, who seemed to be at the mercy of powerful persuaders, commercial marketing and political manipulation. 'Network' television came to mean the universalization of corporate will, encapsulated in advertising that reduced audiences to consumers, agency to behaviour, and modernity to an endless pipeline of products, carried from manufacturers and retailers to waiting, willing, wanting housewives, whose job it was to buy the things that were advertised, serve them up to the family (slouched on the couch watching TV), then clean up the house and the bodies in it using more TV-advertised products. Broadcast television perfected its role as the purveyor of what was needed to sustain domestic life by reducing it to a flow of consumption – products came into the house, went through the alimentary system and then safely out again, chased by cleansing agents from toothpaste to Toilet Duck. No wonder they called it the Tube.

'That sign needs changing': representational semiotic democracy

Fifty years later and trillions of tissues down the toilet, some things have changed – for instance, the mode of TV production, the domestic context, the content (and the study) of television, not to mention the identity, lives and general outlook of all the people involved on both sides of the screen. But there is continuity too. Some things have stayed very much the same; for instance, the world's longest-running soap opera, first broadcast (live) on 9 December 1960 and still going strong – the United Kingdom's *Coronation Street*. Ena Sharples (Violet Carson) uttered *Coronation Street*'s first line, 'That sign needs changing.' She was referring to a shop sign (a new owner was moving into the corner shop), but perhaps this was a prophetic assertion of semiotic futures more generally. Either way, whether you were watching at the time or not yet born, there is a recognizable sense of continuity in *Coronation Street* from that day to this, and also in television more generally, as a cultural form.

The essence of that continuity is in the *viewing experience* of broadcast television, including generic realism onscreen in news and serial drama, which from the point of view of the audience is not about change or difference so much as stability and recognition, both at home on the couch with the biscuits and sisters and in the diegetic world of the characters with their unfolding dilemmas about relationships. Continuous over half a century is a *representative model* of the *broadcasting relationship*, based on one-way transmission of narrative entertainment from a centralized corporate industry to a receptive but unproductive domestic audience. Another, matching continuity is that much of the disputation in television studies has pivoted around this relationship and how it should be explained or evaluated. While there were undoubtedly negative aspects to the 'powerful producer/purposeless consumer' model, there was also something positive in it for both sides:

- *Economically*, the media industries burgeoned and became influential beyond their scale during the century of mass media.
- *Culturally*, the 'imagined community' of very large populations was coordinated into semiotic unity when 'we' all watched the same programmes.
- *Individually*, the experience of TV was cheap, open, sociable and full of emotional immediacy.

Broadcast TV proved to be better than the press, cinema or even radio at *riveting* everyone to the same spot, at the same time – in fear, laughter, wonderment, thrill or desire. Television's emblematic moments – the shooting of J.R. Ewing in *Dallas* or J.F. Kennedy in Dallas; the moon landings; the twin towers; Princess Diana's wedding and funeral; the Olympics and football World Cup finals – the cliffhangers, weddings, departures and finales gathered populations from across all demographic and hierarchical boundaries into fleetingly attained but nevertheless real moments of 'we-dom', a simultaneous commonalty of attention that could sometimes aggregate to the billions.

Less popular?

Because audience choice is increasingly fragmented across more channels and platforms, it is unlikely that any single fictional TV show will ever again achieve the audience numbers of *I Love Lucy*'s top-rating episode (1953), Elvis Presley's *Ed Sullivan* debut (1956), the 'Who Shot JR?' episode of *Dallas* (1980) or the series finale of *M*A*S*H* (1983). Even so, it is still possible to experience *live community* through television – *Survivor, Lost, Idol*, the Super Bowl, the Olympics, and occasionally the news. Sometimes television is still used to experience the *live polity*. For instance, according to the *New York Times* TV Decoder blog, the telecast of Senator Obama's acceptance speech at the Democratic National Convention in August 2008 reached 38.3 million viewers (plus millions more on PBS, C-Span). This was the highest rating in history for a convention speech – until Senator McCain's 38.8 million the following week (Serjeant 2008). Both were also watched by unknown millions worldwide, many of them also tuning in to a live feed. For once, politics out-rated sport and reality TV: 'Mr Obama's speech reached more viewers than the Olympics opening ceremony in Beijing, the final *American Idol* or the Academy Awards this year' (Stelter 2008b). Such a result is all the more surprising when compared with the 'tiny' ratings achieved by routine network programming:

> Sen. Barack Obama may have earned record-breaking ratings for his acceptance speech on Thursday ... but *network television attracted otherwise tiny audiences during prime time.* According to Nielsen's final ratings, CBS led the night with *Big Brother*, which drew 6 million viewers at 8 p.m. ... CBS broadcast a rerun of *CSI* at 9 p.m. (5.3 million).
>
> (Toff 2008)

Even more surprisingly, perhaps, during that convention week the subscription news channel CNN out-rated all three free-to-air broadcast networks (ABC, CBS, NBC) in head-to-head competition, again for the first time in history:

> In nearly three decades, CNN has never beat all three broadcast networks in viewership when competing directly ... This year, CNN had 5.38 million viewers, while NBC had 5.36 million, ABC had 3.48 million, CBS had 3.46 million, Fox had 2.7 million and MSNBC had 2.3 million.
>
> (*New York Times* 2008)

Even as they show how television can still bind a nation around an exceptional event, these figures also record some epic changes. The ratings for regular US network entertainment, topped at a mere 6 million for *Big Brother*, are pitiful compared with TV's heyday. By comparison, the 1994–2004 sitcom *Friends* routinely rated between 20 million and 30 million viewers; its range was from a low of 15 million to a high of over 50 million (Dan n.d.). Meanwhile, pay TV has begun to beat network broadcasting, albeit with figures lower even than those scored by *Big Brother*. Thus has the proliferation of platforms destroyed the unity of the imagined community. It is a long way from the finale of *M*A*S*H* in 1983, when 105 million Americans tuned in (Wikipedia n.d.).

However, it would not be entirely true to say that the millions are abandoning *television*, only that they are choosier about when they watch and what platform they watch 'TV' on. The audience has migrated to subscriber, online and mobile platforms. As a result, global popularity may significantly outpace even US prime-time audiences, and yet not register in traditional broadcast ratings. For example: 'It is popularly believed that the British TV show *Top Gear* is one of the most watched shows around the world. It is ... purportedly watched by up to one billion people' (Wikipedia n.d.). Admittedly, the evidence for a billion viewers is shaky, precisely because no ratings system can follow a show's multi-platform career, but nevertheless such global reach is possible. Let *AutoTrader* explain how:

> From Australia to Albania, Kazakhstan to Vietnam, travel abroad and you're never far from the show. It's licensed to 117 countries via BBC

World and BBC Prime ... More than 1.3 million hotel rooms have access to the show, 37 airlines use it and you can watch it on 29 mobile phone platforms ... It's licensed to 48 cruise ships. Before it was wiped off, one Clarkson clip had received almost a million views on YouTube ... *Top Gear* magazine's Michael Harvey claims *the show is the planet's most pirated programme.* Since its re-launch in 2002, the show has been a worldwide phenomenon.

(Hearn 2007)

Top Gear remains a favoured piratical prize. A September 2008 search of YouTube yielded 52,000 *Top Gear* videos, headed by Jeremy Clarkson's test drive of the Ariel Atom, with nearly 4 million views, 8,000 ratings, 20 video responses and 4,000 text comments. Further comment will be needed on the extent to which increasing decentralization – *distributed popularity* if you like – seems to entail increasing silliness, or at least dancing, for this may turn out to be an important theoretical, or at least taxonomic, principle of post-broadcast television.

More democratic?

But before that, it is necessary to consider a couple of conceptual paradoxes: first, what might be thought to be *democratic* about old-style popular television, given the extreme asymmetry in a representative system between the corporate, expert makers and the domestic viewers of broadcast communications; and second, why the *declining* ratings of mainstream broadcast television might nevertheless entail a *more democratic* television system. How on earth, in short, did we get from Ena Sharples to Jeremy Clarkson? The answer lies in the *model* of the *broadcasting relationship.* In the heyday of live, broadcast, expert-made, choice-restricted television, the model is that of *representation* (both semiotic and political). This is what has changed. Now, with streamed, downloaded, mobile and DIY/DIWO or consumer co-created TV, the model is that of *productivity.* And to cap it all off, the increasingly democratic system of viewer choice and participation seems also to require increasing silliness.

During the heyday of representational broadcasting, popular TV was hailed as democratic, both politically (it reached most people) and semiotically (it represented ordinary folk on screen). What, for instance, could be more democratic than *Coronation Street*? It was a popularization of a radical spirit on the British left of the 1950s that sought authentic expression for ordinary people's lives, in the spirit of Richard Hoggart's *The Uses of Literacy* (1957), which included a sympathetic and influential portrait of working-class communities in the back-to-back terraces of northern England's industrial cities. *Coronation Street* was Richard Hoggart incarnate – the British architectural critic Reyner Banham dubbed it 'Hoggartsborough' at the time (Banham 1962; see also Whiteley 2003: 94ff; and Turner 2003: 41). Richard Dyer (1981) makes the same point, as has Maroula Joannou more recently (2000: 69).

Not only was *Coronation Street* enormously popular among working families, it also represented their strongest character traits, sometimes giving the show an emancipationist edge despite the street brawls and class sentimentality. It is 'character led' rather than 'issue led'; its democratic spirit lay in the overall representativeness of the drama, not in the demographic proportionality of the characters. Instead of finding a place for each minority identity or social issue, its writers from Tony Warren onwards have wanted to share good stories about ordinary life among ordinary people. That they are consistently good at this has been recognized well beyond the reaches of any remaining working-class district – as, for instance, when Melvyn Bragg's highbrow *South Bank Show* named *Coronation Street* the 'best drama' of 2005 (Henderson 2007: 32–3). *Coronation Street*'s model of democratic inclusion is typical of broadcasting: not to identify separately but to enfold narratively; not to speak for but to speak to. It wants to encompass its audience and entertain them, but it doesn't want them to do very much in return, except watch.

From *Coronation Street* to *Corrie*

How things have changed! One look at *Corrie* on the web will suffice to illustrate how different is the *representative mode* of broadcasting from the *productivity mode* of broadband. Developments in technology, globalization and consumer activism have challenged the broadcasting model of a nationally bounded, vertically integrated, monopolistic, expert paradigm TV industry dedicated to leisure entertainment. Instead, a new model is emerging, based on social networks, consumer-created content, multi-platform publication and a semiotic long tail. These changes, wrought in and by media technologies and the uses of Web 2.0, have altered the way television is produced, distributed and consumed, even the way it might be imagined. The medium has transformed from mass to DIY, from 'read only' to 'read and write', and from network TV to social networks – in short, from a regime of *representation* to one of *productivity*.

On the net, *Corrie* is a quite different animal from *Coronation Street*. For a start, it becomes what consumers want it to be, and beyond that the distinction between producer and consumer becomes very uncertain. So, for example, since 1999 Corrie.net has been 'a website *by Coronation Street* fans *for Coronation Street* fans'; its pages of profiles and updates are 'the work of many *Coronation Street* fans from all over the world'. It is distinct from the show's 'official' ITV website, although it credits people from the production company. Corrie.net is information rich and archival, a classic user co-created site. However, it is much less 'consumerist' than the show's own site.

Meanwhile, Corrie Blog is produced by Shiny Media, a commercial stable of technology, fashion and lifestyle blogs. Corrie Blog is edited by Sue Haasler, herself a successful romance author. On the day I visited, she had posted a news item about a new *Coronation Street* scriptwriter, which prompted the following exchange of comments:

I'd seriously love to write for *Corrie*. That's what i plan on doing when i am older. After completing my A levels i plan to head on up to Manchester uni and hopefully get a job doing anything at Corrie, just so i have my foot in the door. It's my dream :) *Posted by: Clare*
> Clare – Good luck with your plans! It would be fantastic if you became a *Corrie* writer. Hope you achieve your ambitions. [Sue H] *Posted by: Sue*
> Thank you very much Sue, it's much appreciated. *Posted by: Clare*
> (www.corrieblog.tv/2008/09/so_you_want_to.html)

Although this is a commercial site, Sue Haasler responds directly to the wishful thinking of young, hopeful Clare. A quick Google search reveals why – perhaps fellow feeling?

> Sue Haasler was born and brought up in Co. Durham and studied English Literature & Linguistics at Liverpool University. After graduating she moved to London and worked for three years as a residential social worker.
> (www.hilaryjohnson.demon.co.uk/SueHaasler.htm)

This bio is one of the success stories listed on the site of a professional authors' advice service, which seems to have assisted Haasler towards her own debut as a published author. This string of links is typical of what any internet search exposes: a *social network* of both fans and professionals, readers and authors, newbies and experts – people who are more than willing to share their stories with each other, using *Corrie* literally as a pretext for social networking in the name of what used to be called the 'republic of letters'.

Over on YouTube, *Corrie* blossoms. Thousands of clips have been posted, in which fans classify 'The Street' according to their own tastes and interests, whether these are prompted by the show (vintage episodes, favourite scenes) or by external criteria ('Gay *Coronation Street*', '*Coronation Street* Babes Past & Present'). Spoofs abound, both DIY and pirated professional (e.g. Victoria Wood as Ena Sharples). Comments and tribute videos continue the conversation and extend the network.

But there is no need to extend these examples further. The point is that 'television' online takes on the open and productive characteristics of the internet, while maintaining intricate relations with its broadcast form and audience. There is one issue that should be mentioned, however: episodes of *Coronation Street* are highly protected properties, especially if you are using a computer located outside the United Kingdom. The clips available to UK viewers on the official site won't play; lawyers crawl across YouTube issuing take-down orders; you can't get whole episodes through torrent streaming. From the corporate perspective, knowledge shared is knowledge lost, so *Corrie* is treated by *Coronation Street*'s owners as a virus to be controlled, Viacom style, not a mode of propagation to be encouraged, viral style.

The more democratic – and the sillier?

Jonathan Gray, Jeffrey Jones and Ethan Thompson introduce their book *Satire TV* (2009) by observing the 'unique ability of satire TV to speak truth to power' (2009: 12), and not only in the anglophone countries – they cite examples from China and Iraq too. They conclude:

> Gradually satire TV has crept up on the news as one of the pre-eminent genres used to understand varied political realities, rendering it an ideal entry point for a study of politics, audiences, television, comedy, entertainment, and citizenship in the early twenty-first century.
>
> (Gray et al. 2009: 47)

Now, all this may be true – and it is a substantial claim on behalf of 'damn funny' TV (2009: 46) – but turning audiences into activists requires something stronger than old-style US network TV. Shows like *The Colbert Report* and *The Daily Show with Jon Stewart* know from the outset that the polity is partisan, the audience is fragmented and the platforms have proliferated. They thrive on subscription TV (Comedy Central); they rely on viral propagation (clips on YouTube; fan sites like ColbertNation); and they relish a mainstream adversary, trading (mercilessly) on the failings of Fox News and CNN.

The success of 'satire TV' is a measure of the extent of popular disaffection with both mainstream politics and mainstream TV – political and semiotic representation alike. But such shows are only the tip of the iceberg. The extension of television's productive and distributive base via the internet reveals infinite demand for an alternative to the regime of representation. The demand is for 'just anyone', if not everyone, to do it themselves (or with others). DIY and DIWO give the population formerly known as the audience something to do; it makes real what was meant to be a contradiction in terms, the 'productive consumer'.

However, concomitantly it seems, the more productive 'we' get, the sillier we become. Elections are now marked not only by online citizen journalism (Bruns 2008a: 69–99), but also by homemade spoofs, satire, parody and take-offs, some of which out-rate the official campaigns – for instance, Hugh Atkin in Australia and Obama Girl in the United States (Hartley 2008b: 687–8). The collapse of long-held (but always wobbly) distinctions between public and private life, power and entertainment, politics and celebrity, television and viral video, was spectacularly evidenced by the entry of Paris Hilton into the 2008 US presidential campaign. Posted on the 'Funny or Die' site, her reply to a negative comment by John McCain soon attracted over 7 million views, 2,000 responses and 500 favourites. Tagged as both 'political ad, president' and 'hot swim suit photo', the uncanny attraction of the parody was that, while it was knowing, sly and funny, Paris's energy platform was also quite plausible: as one response put it: 'She's right, though. The offshore drilling thing?

Totally hot. Anyway, it's just funny that she's kinda right' (More Cowbell Girl).

Although the official presidential nominees did not take up the Paris challenge directly, it should be noted that much of Barack Obama's early appeal was credited to his easy competence in the protocols of online DIY television. For instance, in a video posted to 'Barack TV' on YouTube in June 2007, Senator Obama is taped on a hand-held camera, in an informal setting with available light, talking directly and apparently unscripted to the camera. Instead of telling viewers what he thinks and wants, he appeals to viewers to 'send us your stories' and to share stories about ordinary people making a difference. Obama uses both the aesthetics and the participatory ethic of Web 2.0 to reach those who have 'turned away' from politics as usual.

How many answered the call is unknown. But there were certainly competing attractions. When silly is 'hot', the serious players get up and dance. One of the most dynamic and popular features of YouTube is dancing, from the original girls in the bedroom miming to favourite songs, such as the classic 'Hey Clip' (24 million views), to more elaborate dance competitions. These have become so popular that they have attracted the participation of celebrities. A good example is Miley Cyrus's *M & M Cru* – responsible for 'the biggest dance battle in YouTube history ... an onslaught of videos packed with celebrity cameos, MTV parodies and more "WTF!?" moments than you can shake a tail feather at' (Watercutter 2008). This was a competitive exchange of dance videos between serious celebrities: 'Pop wunderkind Miley Cyrus and the director and star [Adam Sevani] of *Step Up 2: The Streets* have officially taken the art of the YouTube smackdown to a whole other level.' No matter that Miley and Adam were 15 and 16 at the time, these videos were 'hot', good enough to attract the same number of viewers as *Big Brother* and CNN over on regular TV – 5 to 6 million hits each and many thousands of comments. Naturally the whole thing ended up on prime-time TV as the 'dance off' was decided at the MTV Teen Choice Awards, which Miley Cyrus hosted (and won). Here was cyberdemocracy in full 'party' mode, all difference between user and celebrity erased, and everyone enjoying both making and watching the show. Or as Angela Watercutter (2008) put it: 'The sheer silliness of this exercise (and its overuse of the concept of stepping things up) notwithstanding, what say you?'

Implications for television studies

After a quiet period when everyone wanted to talk about new media, television studies is certainly enjoying a resurgence; the quality, boldness and interest of many new books is remarkable. Perhaps like cinema studies, it will flower most luxuriantly just after the medium to which it is attached has ceased to be popular on a mass scale. At the same time, television studies has begun to taxonomize itself, with ever narrower specialisms. It seems at last to be emerging into a formal order as a discipline in its own right. However, this is no time for coalescence into orthodoxy, because television studies is subject to the same forces of change that beset its object of study. In television evolution, some species are headed for extinction (e.g. network TV, couch potatoes), some look forward to open futures (e.g. social network markets, distributed expertise) and, as old antagonisms decay (e.g. cultural versus scientific approaches), new political struggles emerge (e.g. corporate DRM and copyright enforcement versus knowledge-sharing systems). The changes that affect television also have an impact on television studies. Only recently established and still a contested field, television studies is already being forced to recast some basic assumptions, metaphors and methods. It needs to shift from explanations based on structures of power to ones based on the mechanics and dynamics of change. Such a shift brings into sharp focus the most important innovation in television as the TV industry migrates out of the boardroom, and the TV experience out of the sitting-room – the *democratization of productivity*.

The problem faced by television studies is not simply one of how to *account for* distributed expertise among the general population. Such an approach would only confine it further within the regime of representation, where the purpose of scholarship is to encompass the whole object of study and to represent it in knowledge. Rather, the problem is how to take the risk of *releasing television studies itself into the evolving system* of networked productivity, using the affordances of Web 2.0 in ways that were not available in the broadcast environment. Integrating scholarly and 'vernacular' knowledge systems is itself productive, and can lead to new forms of professional expertise, just as amateur efforts like the Hey Clip get recoded into M&M Cru's dance-off. But as television studies chases DIY TV into its participatory reaches, won't it too get silly? Can it survive the participatory turn? We may look pretty silly for a while, but that's the challenge: academic expertise will have to learn some nifty new steps if it doesn't want to end up looking like an Ena Sharples trying to do a Miley Cyrus.

Chapter 3

The twenty-first-century telescreen

Mark Andrejevic

In 2008, the NEC Corporation took the occasion of an annual TV conference in Tokyo to introduce a commercial version of what George Orwell dubbed the telescreen – a TV that watches you while you watch. The device came complete with a set-top camera that captured the images of viewers, assessed their ages and genders, and modified advertisements accordingly. As one account put it: 'If the device finds viewers are predominantly female in their 20s, it will show cute miscellaneous items sold by Fuji Television for young women or an NEC cellphone designed for the demographic' (*Times of India* 2008). It is perhaps a misnomer to call NEC's device a telescreen: its mission is not authoritarian discipline, but surveillance with a commercial face. This shinier, happier telescreen captures an emerging trend in the development of commercial TV: an attempt to harness the interactive capability of digital media to the ends of marketers. NEC's TV doesn't just respond automatically to viewers, it also exploits the participatory character of interactivity to provide more detailed information to them. The TV includes a device that downloads internet links, promotional coupons and other product information to the mobile phones of interested viewers. It then allows advertisers to 'tell whether the promotion has been effective by checking whether viewers visited their stores or made purchases' (*Times of India* 2008).

Experiments like NEC's announce television's entrance into the digital enclosure – that virtual space within which content of all kinds converges into the universal medium of the bit. As other media are demonstrating, the digital enclosure is a space that allows not only for convergence, flexibility and interactivity, but also for increasing customization and powerful forms of audience monitoring and targeting. As newspapers go online, for example, they are able to update their content throughout the course of the day with interactive features that combine audio, text and video. They are also able to devise new business models that package and sell groups of readers to advertisers based on reading preferences, demographics and geographic information. News outlets can also 'monetize' their archive, making past articles available with updated, digitally inserted advertising – and much the same thing is happening with online delivery of television content.

The implications of television's move into the digital enclosure for content and consumption may be many, but the monitoring aspect is clear. As one TV executive predicted: 'You know the old John Wanamaker saying, "Half of what I spend on advertising is wasted, I just don't know which half"? I think we'll know which half ... And we'll charge double for the other half!' (Mandler 2007). Digital interactivity promises to deliver the elusive Holy Grail of advertising: to provide an accurate, direct measure of so-called 'return on investment' – the amount of sales generated by an advertising campaign.

There are myriad ways to approach the fate of TV, many of which are presented in other contributions to this volume. The goal of this chapter is the narrower one of exploring one aspect of the emerging logic of TV in the interactive era: the increasingly important role of consumer monitoring. For the moment, the commercial exploitation of interactivity is being pioneered by the internet model, from which other media – including TV – are borrowing. It is an information-intensive model that deploys the interactive capacity of the medium to put audiences to work generating detailed data not just about their viewing behaviour, but about their social networks and their consumption patterns. Although the model is still in its early stages of (uneven) development, its three main interconnected elements can already be discerned: the monitoring of consumers, the customization of content, and advertising. The model is reliant on two important shifts in the media environment: the development of interactive, digital technology and the resulting proliferation of content. It is an approach that relies on an information 'glut' in a twofold sense: not just to give consumers a chance to differentiate themselves by navigating a wealth of choices, but to capture and exploit the information they generate in so doing. Both consumers and advertisers are faced with more information than ever before, but of different kinds: content for the former and demographic information for the latter.

For the time being, commercial TV is a very different medium from the internet, but it is coming under increasing pressure to refine its audience-measurement techniques and to adapt the forms of targeting and mass customization pioneered online. In the interactive era, advertisers are increasingly coming to rely on the ability to monitor and track consumers for the purposes of targeting and 'accountability' – determining whether ads were viewed or interacted with and whether they led to purchases. In this regard, interactivity is helping to further blur the distinction between the two major forms of financing commercial television: subscription and advertising. Both satellite and pay TV providers are currently developing ways to use their infrastructure and set-top boxes to capture data about viewing behaviour and serve customized content. Even for pay TV, the interactive model of custom targeting is emerging as an important aspect of financing. Convergence, in this regard, suggests that the monitoring-based advertising model will increasingly supplement subscription-based financing. The remainder of this chapter explores some of the implications of the turn to interactivity as a technique for audience monitoring.

Monitors that monitor us

One of the first signs of the emerging TV economy was provided, suggestively, by a perennially top-rated media event in the United States: the football championship Super Bowl. In 2002, the fledgling digital video recorder (DVR) company TiVo revealed that its installation in some quarter of a million households in the United States allowed the company not only to provide viewers with a range of recording features, but to record how these features were used. Increased functionality results in more detailed data. During the 2002 Super Bowl, for example, TiVo revealed that Britney Spears' Pepsi ads and a last-minute field goal by the New England Patriots received the most replay attention off and on the field respectively – with Britney winning overall (Wong 2002). In 2005, the company received even more press attention when it issued a news release revealing that the Janet Jackson 'wardrobe malfunction' was the most replayed moment in TiVo's (admittedly short) history (CNN.com 2004).

The real news, however, was the quantum leap in the ability of interactive digital technology to track viewer behaviour. Against the background of TiVo, the sampling method of traditional ratings companies looked clunky and crude – a relic of the pre-interactive era. Pay TV systems have been quick to embrace the model – and to search for ways of bypassing intermediaries like TiVo. In the United States, for example, a consortium of cable operators is collaborating on an initiative, named 'Project Canoe', to deliver targeted advertising. The goal, as the project's leader put it, is to place 'dog food commercials only in front of people who own dogs' (Fitzgerald 2008). In the United Kingdom, Multi Channel Networks is working with BSkyB on a scheme to provide targeted advertising via DVR, and in Australia, Foxtel and Austar intend to capture detailed information about 10,000 households for marketing purposes: 'In each of these houses, every single button press of the remote will be saved in the set-top box, the data captured and reported daily' (Fitzgerald 2008).

Satellite providers are also working out ways to make their set-top delivery of advertisements interactive, targeted and addressable. Google has teamed up with satellite provider EchoStar to incorporate interactivity into a formerly one-way, top-down (as it were) platform. Google plans to serve ads (that will become increasingly targeted) and monitor 'which ads were watched or skipped, with a second-by-second breakdown' (Stelter 2007: 4). So far, cable networks have been unwilling to give Google access to their viewers, relying instead on the potential of their own interactive advertising initiative. Free-to-air television poses its own problems when it comes to addressability and monitoring, but has relied on websites and mobile phones to gather information about viewers, target markets, and promote its offerings.

The efforts of Project Canoe, Austar, BSkyB and others to track the behaviour of viewers can trace their lineage back to the efforts of early ratings researchers to find a two-way channel for monitoring the audience, first over the phone and then via journals and people meters. In this respect, the story of the future of TV is one of continuity rather than rupture: the lifeblood of both the marketing industry and commercial broadcasting has been, from their inception, information about audiences. Insofar as the promise of interactivity is revolutionary in the literal rather than political sense, it is to complete the 'circle' of monitoring from ad exposure to consumer behaviour. The goal of the surveillance-based, digitally enhanced, scientific management of consumption looms on the digital horizon.

The audience auto-commodity

Through the lens of surveillance, focused by political economy, the audience manifests itself to marketers in the form of a commodity to be bought and sold. Such a perspective is an admittedly narrow view of audiences and their behaviours, which it reduces to aspects with economic salience: size, disposable income, tastes and any other characteristics or behaviour that might help boost sales in the foreseeable future. To acknowledge this perspective is not to downplay other aspects of viewers' behaviour – their creativity, their pleasures, and so on – but to consider them in the same way marketers do, and thereby to anticipate the role that surveillance-based marketing is likely to play in the digital era. Audiences can be sold to advertisers, Gandy argues, because of the 'labour' they perform which, following Smythe (1981), he describes as 'the work of watching commercials, making sense of them, and ultimately behaving as consumers appropriate to their social position' (1981: 228).

The notion of audience labour has been a vexed and contested one, not least because of the difficulty in specifying what it produces. In a digital environment, however, where information can be captured about users as they engage in networked forms of communication and consumption, interactivity renders the formulation more precise. As audiences interact with the technology, they generate data about themselves: information commodities that can be bought and sold. Internet companies are pioneering the model, but the various approaches to interactive TV are following closely. Consider the example of Facebook, which was valued at about $15 billion by Microsoft during a time when its annual profits were, by comparison, only about $30 million (Guth and Delaney 2007). It seems fair to conclude that much of this valuation was based on the anticipated value of the tremendous quantity of information about users collected by the site. More generally, part of the economic labour performed by interactive audiences is the generation of information about themselves – the auto-production of audience commodities. In the case of a social networking site like Facebook, prospective advertising audiences are doubly productive: they create both the content that draws them to the site and detailed information about their tastes, behaviour and patterns of social relations.

If information glut and audience fragmentation posed a threat to mass advertisers, for mass-customized advertisers, by contrast, they provide the opportunity for greater specification of individual viewers. To the extent that it can be monitored and managed, viewer 'mobility' – individual patterns of viewing, channel surfing, and so on – allows audience members to create more detailed portraits of themselves for the use of marketers and providers of customized content. As TV moves into the digital enclosure, some of the monitoring-based trends whose implications will be developed in the following sections include advertising tied to particular viewers rather than shows (enhanced 'addressability'), behavioural targeting of programming and advertising and an increasingly experiment-based approach to market research.

Platform issues: defining TV

The logic of convergence, as Henry Jenkins (2006) has astutely noted, doesn't culminate in the form of some universal device that we will use to consume all our media. It is, rather, a logic of ongoing proliferation, differentiation and reintegration. Take the example of digital music, which can now be played in a variety of formats on a range of devices, from laptops to iPods, mobile phones, DVD players and satellite tuners. A similar future awaits TV, which according to one cultural critic will soon come to 'mean a jumble of professional and amateur short- and long-form content shipped via a variety of platforms to a variety of devices' (Hirschorn 2008: 1). The good news for marketers is that the ability to access content at any time, anywhere, on whatever device necessarily depends upon a two-way signalling system, which also facilitates monitoring and tracking. The 'bad' news, on the other hand, is that total audience transparency via a unified content delivery platform is an unlikely outcome. In the United States, for example, cable providers are not collaborating with satellite providers, and the networks aren't likely to share information about viewing patterns from their online video players. What is more likely is an outcome similar to what takes place online: a series of strategic partnerships and information-sharing agreements between marketers and content providers that facilitate the goals of interactive marketing – tracking viewing behaviour, gathering background information, targeting advertising and monitoring outcomes.

Glut checks

Interactivity rapidly transforms the television medium from one of decreasing scarcity into one of full-on glut. The emergence of video-on-demand – via whatever platform – means no longer having to choose from an expanding array of channels, but from a sea of content. Channel surfing becomes obsolete. Digital cable is already heading in this direction: with several hundred channels to choose from in some markets, scanning through them could easily last longer than a typical prime-time programme. The same goes for online or video-on-demand, with thousands of shows – past and present – to choose from. In the digital enclosure, consequently, the paradigm shift is from user-controlled surfing to algorithm-controlled sorting (or some combination of the two). Online video players like those developed by the major TV networks are developing systems to use information about consumers to provide targeted content based on context, demographic information, past behaviour and collaborative filtering.

The somewhat paradoxical result is that an information glut transfers an element of control over viewing choices from consumers (who, on their own, are left with the thankless task of sorting through thousands of offerings) to those who operate the algorithms subject to their marketing imperatives. The company ChoiceStream, for example – which uses its recommendation technology not just for TV, but for companies including Borders, Overstock.com and Blockbuster video – notes on its website that its goal is to help 'drive sales and increase loyalty by automatically recommending the most relevant content and products to each consumer, whether they're online, reading email, watching TV, or on their mobile' (ChoiceStream 2008). It is tempting to think of these programmes as search algorithms – analogous to the service that Google provides for web surfers, for whom the task of browsing through all the pages on the web is a practical impossibility. Without a unified platform for video, however, these programmes are likely to remain fragmented and subject to the marketing priorities of their various clients, who will claim that the solution is more monitoring.

When there were only a few choices of programming, audiences could be roughly grouped demographically. As choices proliferate and audiences fragment, it is possible to customize programming while at the same time assembling more precise audience profiles. One of the emerging strategies for customizing content delivery is to piggyback on the forms of interactivity and so-called 'crowd-sourcing' (putting the audience to work) exploited by online media. For example, the start-up ffwd.com will draw on relational demographics – information gleaned from webs of social networks – to custom-target TV content. The major TV networks are hoping that, by bundling social networking functions with their media players, they can induce people to register and provide data that will 'give advertisers more immediate, granular ways to measure viewers' (Klaassen and Hampp 2008: 8). Aggregate providers like Hulu and Joost are following much the same model, attempting to use the variety of content they provide as a means of more closely profiling audience members. The goal is not just to gather detailed information about relationship behaviour that might have marketing value, but to exploit the potential of viral marketing. Producers are keeping a close eye on successful online business models. As a Disney/ABC executive put it at the 2007 Future of Television Conference: 'I think another trend to watch is the impact of social network sites ... for a marketer to be able to see that trend and pour some gasoline on it, to optimize it from that spark is going to require some really fancy footwork' (Mandler 2007).

Super crunching in the data mine

The quantum leap in consumer monitoring envisioned by the television industry raises the issue of privacy in the digital era, and developers of interactive platforms will have to negotiate the complex and fast-changing landscape of privacy regulation. Members of the US cable consortium Project Canoe say they are careful to avoid clashes with regulators, but much will hang on the shift in cultural expectations associated with the promised benefits of commercial monitoring. An executive for the US cable provider Cablevision has predicted that audiences are likely to accept targeting as long as it subsidizes their access to content. 'They don't mind being sold if we're delivering them information and entertainment,' he told attendees at the 2007 Future of Television Conference (Frey 2007).

There is an element of blackmail to the industry refrain: if our digital, interactive world is going to be saturated by advertising, wouldn't we prefer it to be relevant to our interests and tastes? The formulation assumes the dominance of advertising as a means of supporting the digital infrastructure for our communication and media networks in the post-welfare state era. It also downplays one of the emerging elements of interactive marketing: the ability to conduct ongoing controlled experiments to determine how to influence consumers most profitably. In his book *Super Crunchers* (2007), Ian Ayres describes how Google optimizes advertising effectiveness: 'Want to know whether your AdWords ad for beer should say "Tastes Great" or "Less Filling"? Well, Google will put both ads in rotation and then tell you which ad people are more likely to click through' (2007: 55). Google has already transposed the model into the realm of TV through a partnership with the satellite provider EchoStar. Advertisers can purchase particular markets and try out different ads to see which are most effective at keeping viewers from switching channels. As the vice-president of one media agency put it: 'It's an interesting way to test your creative. You can run one ad one day and run another the next and see how each did. [Google] has all these different metrics – you can see the length of each tune-in, and you can kind of gauge whether your creative works' (Friedman 2008: 20).

Down the road, the goal will be to link ad impressions with behaviour: to determine whether viewers respond to interactive ads and how advertising exposure influences purchasing patterns. This type of data gathering shouldn't be understood as purely descriptive – simply as a means of capturing information about behaviour that would have 'taken place anyway'. The express goal is to influence behaviour, and to do so in ways based on detailed information gathered not just by monitoring consumers, but by subjecting them to a continuous series of controlled, randomized experiments.

It is this shift from the comprehensive monitoring of a 'super-panopticon' to that of a giant laboratory that is envisioned by what Ayres (2007) describes as the 'super crunching' revolution: 'Academics have been running randomized experiments inside and outside of medicine for years. But the big change is that businesses are relying on them to reshape corporate policy' (2007: 50). The effectiveness of such an approach relies upon asymmetrical forms of information gathering – on the ability to subject entire populations to controlled experiments without their awareness in order to develop marketing campaigns that result in predictable responses. As the head of a United States-based media consulting company put it: 'It's not just about what the audience is going to see, but what [it's] going to do … The Holy Grail is to get to predictive modeling' (Morrissey 2008).

The shift from observation to experimentation is important to emphasize. Members of the public who are willing to accept the explanation that increased monitoring is necessary to create ads relevant to their tastes might nevertheless be reluctant to become unwitting lab rats for an industry attempting to model and modify behaviour. Marketers argue that this type of research merely reflects latent demand. Ayres (2007) claims, for example, that insofar as the use of comprehensive data mining and statistical analysis harnesses marketers to every nuance of consumer demand, it 'empowers the consumer' (2007: 172). In a context in which marketers control the environment and subject the public to constant experimentation so as to determine how best to trigger behaviour, it is worth asking who has the power. The simple fact that consumers might well behave otherwise if they were aware of what experiments were being run and how the findings were being used suggests there is more to the story than simple consumer empowerment. In the super-crunching world, marketers know much more about consumers than consumers know about how this information is being used.

Replacing the proxies

In a rallying cry that hearkens back to the turn of the last century, the TV advertising mantra for the interactive era is monitoring-based rationalization: 'It's no longer going to be this inefficient, unmonitored advertising' (Patel 2007). Another way to describe the shift facilitated by interactive monitoring in the digital era is the gradual replacement of proxy measurement of audiences by more direct forms of data collection. The economic model of advertising is based on determining who watches what ads in an attempt to correlate ad exposure with consumption behaviour. Since getting at this information has been difficult and costly, the industry has relied on various forms of proxy measurement. In the era before time shifting, day parts served as a relatively crude proxy measurement of audiences. The representative sampling of programme viewership practised by the ratings industry provided a slightly more refined proxy for the viewing of advertisements, though the industry has recently made the shift to more direct measurement: from programme ratings to advertisement ratings. These have both been threatened, to some extent, by the advent of time shifting and, more recently, by what might be described as platform shifting. To the extent that these developments result in more flexible viewing behaviour – viewers choosing to set their own schedules and craft their own programming line-ups – advertisers are devising strategies for bypassing the proxies of scheduling, and even content, to get directly at target audiences. The promise of monitoring-based interactivity is to yield up audiences – when and where they are watching.

This is not to say that content drops out of the equation; rather, it becomes one more input into the behavioural marketing equation. Viewers associated with a particular bundle of programming will be separated out from those who choose a different mix and may well receive different ads when they are watching the same show. The US cable network AMC, in partnership with the Neilsen Co., has developed an 'Audience Identity Metric' that traces 'correlations between genre and behavior' in order to determine what type of consumers are likely to watch particular movies (Crupi 2008). As an AMC executive put it: 'Say you're a financial services client, looking to reach men 25–54 who also happen to use the Internet as a primary source for financial information. AIM helps us generate a list of the films that the target is most likely to watch' (Crupi 2008). More detailed correlation information of this kind might influence not only advertising purchases, but also programming behaviour. Thus, for example, AMC has also developed an in-house metric called 'Ad Vantage' that 'lets us take a closer look at the people who actually choose to stick around for commercials and gives us a better sense of how engaged they are' (Crupi 2008).

The implications for programming are suggestive: as the ability to monitor and predict audience behaviour advances, it may be possible to structure programming elements to ensure that the audience they attract are 'high value' in the sense of being more likely to watch advertisements instead of fast-forwarding or tuning out and, down the road, more likely to respond to advertising appeals. To put it somewhat differently, rather than using broad-brush proxies to determine what counts as a 'quality' audience (one likely to respond to particular ads) for marketers, the goal is to measure actual response. This possibility raises the question regarding the impact on content: what types of programming will be privileged because they draw a more 'responsive' audience, and which viewers will consequently end up being under-served or neglected by the increasingly rationalized commercial model? This is not to say that particular programming isn't already favoured by marketing imperatives, but that enhanced audience monitoring and measurement promise to 'perfect' the process.[1]

Unity in fragmentation

Even if it is possible to gather detailed information about viewer behaviour and demographics from individual households, the cost of creating and serving customized advertising based on these ads is likely to remain prohibitive for the immediate future. The more likely strategy is to borrow some of the logic of interactive customization associated with the web and translate it, with practical modifications, into strategies that are workable for broadcasters. Thus, for example, companies like Spot Runner in Los Angeles offer micro-targeted media buys to advertisers based on tightly focused purchases in local cable and broadcast markets. For the 2007 release of the movie *The Painted Veil*, Spot Runner 'targeted ads for the art house film to mature female viewers in the 18 specific neighborhoods where the movies were playing' (Cummings 2008). The company claimed to be able to narrow its target down to 'as few as 500 homes' (Cummings 2008). Similarly, companies like Visible World are developing platforms for flexible advertising that 'swaps in or edits the ad on the fly so it's dynamically customized for the audience' (Whitney 2008a: 8).

The creation of this customized cultural content will rely on the proliferation of attempts to put the audience to work providing information about themselves – in the name of convenience and self-expression. Comcast has already conducted pilot research that suggests 'some viewers would be interested in creating cable customer profiles that would indicate preferences in products and services for which they'd like to see commercials' (Cummings 2008).

At the big-picture level, the appeal of monitoring-based advertising to marketers suggests a rethinking of the logic of digital-era fragmentation. The flipside of what Lotz (2007) describes as 'the increased fractionalization of the audience among shows, channels, and distribution devices' (2007: 28) is the apparent emergence of an underlying shared logic: that of monitoring-based marketing.[2] This shared logic of productive fragmentation provides a slightly different take on the consequences of convergence. Rather than simply asserting the decline of a shared set of content-based reference points (since we all may decide to watch different programming when consumption becomes increasingly flexible), we might trace the emergence of a different cultural 'glue' – that of the pervasive advertising messages that will track us across platforms and shows, from one portable device to the next. These ads will be customized, but the underlying message will retain the very uniformity that fragmentation ostensibly threatened.

Notes

1 It is worth pointing out that one of the other strategies for countering time shifting and ad skipping is product placement. From the perspective of interactive marketing, this is, in certain respects, a retrograde approach because it reduces flexibility rather than enhancing it – at least until the development of technology for customizing product placement in response to changing audiences.

2 It is certainly possible to argue that the more 'natural' model for flexible consumption is a subscription-based service, but as both cell phones and pay-TV suggest, even the subscription model is incorporating target marketing.

Chapter 4

Screens: television's dispersed 'broadcast'

P. David Marshall

This chapter focuses on the television-like industries and viewing practices that have emerged on other screens. Through a discussion of the internet and mobile media, it explores the developing relationships between the existing television industry, the constellation of new media industries that have integrated video, and the new audiences generated by these technologies and practices.

Television and the internet: the emergence of networked video culture

The generational shift: trawling for content

The internet is now used by millions of people for viewing televisual-like content, and a key driver of its take-up is the part played by a new generation of users. Young (relatively affluent) consumers in many countries are now more likely to have a wired or wireless computer than a television – often because it intersects with their education or work needs. Far more individualized than the traditional mode of television consumption, the computer screen for this 'audience' replaces the television screen and it has enabled them to search for content in an internet-delivered format. What is also interesting about this generation of users is their intersection with the flows of television. Although their viewing practices are not connected to the television networks directly, nonetheless their choice of what to watch is driven by their relationship to the content produced by major television production houses and networks. The success of download social networking sites that use BitTorrent, with its peer-to-peer structure of parsing up content among its users and contributors and its reassembling of that content, is very much attached to particular North American and European-produced television series (see Pouwelse et al. 2005). Thus, within minutes of their broadcast, many popular television programmes are available for download through these networks of distribution, creating a secondary audience.

The distinctive quality of this secondary audience is the level of commitment of its members, which has driven them to download and watch programmes in a more user- and time-intensive way. Their fan-ish behaviour is further augmented by their use of the internet for further exchange of information, news and gossip about individual series via other social networks, blogs and in some cases wiki sites. Perhaps an effect of this intense relationship to content that leads to these internet-based viewing practices is the development of more elaborate programme narratives, aimed at attracting those fans who luxuriate in the labyrinthine plots. Programmes such as *Lost*, *Doctor Who*, *Heroes*, *24* and *Prison Break* have attracted this kind of core, 'cult' audience. Jenkins (2006) recognizes the force of this phenomenon by identifying the change in the narrative structure of some American television series as 'transmedia storytelling' (2006: 95–7). The production of the narrative migrates from the actual television programme into other media forms such as websites or games – each providing greater narrative depth. *Lost* has a number of websites generated by the producers themselves to further embellish the story and to intersect with the fan 'chatter' that fills the many other cavities of the internet.

However, BitTorrent television culture describes only one node of intersection between television and internet users. It is very difficult to identify how large or prevalent such practices are, because they skirt close to challenging the intellectual property rights that television networks and production companies work very hard to protect. Easier to identify is the way television has appeared in a transformed format on more prominent websites, where it is watched and used in very different modes. Television news, for instance, is reconstituted for its delivery by the internet, where it does not resemble the structure of a newscast. Instead, stories are organized by textual and still image cues to help users make decisions about which story to watch. A menu of possible video feeds is available at any one time, in conjunction with a transforming web page of pictures, headlines, texts and blogs. The differences between news sites run by the television networks such as Fox News, MSNBC or CNN and those run by newspaper sites or newsradio sites have become progressively unclear. Content deals are shared across these various online news forms; videos generated from traditional television news constitute the core content of a newspaper site such as *The Australian*, much as an aggregator site such as Google News. Augmenting these are further video productions by in-house reporters posted in blog format. The *New York Times* has regular video feeds from its key national and international reporters; they don't necessarily match the quality of television production, but they at least rival the information content that is produced by television. In such cases, video online collapses the distinction between video produced by television and video produced from some other source.

This Balkanization of television content is further accentuated on the most successful video sources on the internet. Nielsen, along with other surveying companies such as ComScore, has now compiled survey information around online video in different parts of the world (see Nielsen Media Research 2008c; ComScore 2008b). For instance, in March 2008 in the United

Kingdom, ComScore calibrated that 48 per cent of online video content is seen through Google and its YouTube subsidiary. The nearest rival to You-Tube was the BBC, with 1.2 per cent. A total of 27 million people in the United Kingdom actually viewed an online video in the month and the total number of videos viewed was 3.5 billion (ComScore 2008b). Similar totals are evident in the United States, where 34.8 per cent of video content was viewed through YouTube in May 2008, with the closest rival, on 6.4 per cent, being Fox Interactive. Some 142 million internet users in the United States viewed an average of 85 videos each, with more than 4.2 billion videos viewed in the month. Similar statistics have been generated from other national markets, and what they identify generally is a different relationship to video content from anything that television has produced in the past. The average length of viewing for online video is three minutes, which indicates a different viewing strategy from that implied by the organization of television schedules into 30-minute and 60-minute shows.

For much of the world, YouTube dominates both the supply of video content online and the prevailing patterns of its distribution. Television content is being 'unbundled' as it is being reconfigured for other screens (Dawson 2007: 139–42). The idea of the television 'segment' Ellis once employed to describe the organization of television has now taken on even greater significance on the internet (Ellis, from Dawson 2007: 232). Fans use YouTube to divide up and distribute less-than-10-minutes segments (the mandated length for the site) of their favourite programmes. Television networks, for their part, routinely strive to have their content taken down. At the same time, television networks themselves have entered into content deals with YouTube to put what they would classify as promotional content for their key properties on the site. Surrounding these industry efforts to deal with the breakdown in their control of content are the users themselves, posting millions of videos – some entirely new, self-produced content, others homages to existing produced content, and still others mash-ups of network-produced content reorganized for their own and other fans' pleasures.

There is a further complicating layer in the movement of online video that differentiates it from the traditional economic models of production and distribution of television. YouTube is a social networking site that encourages the sharing of content among its users. Other social networking sites such as Facebook, MySpace, Orkut and Friendster actively support putting video content from YouTube into the profile spaces of individual users so that the location of a video and its final 'screening' are thus recontextualized into an interpersonal exchange.

There have been several responses from the major television industry players to this changed production and distribution environment. First, as indicated above, the industry has developed alliances with sites such as YouTube where exclusive content deals are struck in exchange for controlling the piracy of television content. Second, the television production industry has moved much more readily than film into a music distribution model for its pro-gramsme. Thus, through iTunes one can pay for the downloading of parti-cular television episodes. Third, and possibly most costly, the network websites have become more elaborate places for the distribution of pro-grammes than in the past. Increasingly, television websites are now designed for 'catch-up' television, where past episodes and/or compilation summary videos of past episodes can be streamed from the site. Catch-up television has become standard for major American networks, and uses what is called pre-roll advertising to pay for its delivery. Some public broadcasters, such as the Australian ABC and the BBC, have made their respective online services sites for the thousands of hours of past programme content, an amount that dwarfs the content that major networks have made available. In all cases, whether commercial or public, broadcasters have worked to make their own sites the portals for their own content through a partial embrace of the internet cacophony via multiple add-on videos to productions and extended capacities for viewers/users to write in or video in their own comments.

ITV and IPTV: the overlaying of screens and the TV putsch

In contrast to the chaotic structure of online video and its often-interpersonal re-mediation by users, there are other developments that overlay television onto the internet. It is difficult to essentialize the pleasures of television as they have developed over the last 60 years, but one of its foundational elements was that it was programmed for you. You could reject the programme and change channels or switch the machine off, but fundamentally television employed what could be described as a paternalistic form of delivery. In industrial metaphors, television's content was pushed at the viewer, and the viewer accepted the pleasures of the flow (and the flow of segments). This pleasure could be summarized in the phrase 'watching television', as opposed to watching a particular programme. Television viewing was and is a state of mind – whether one surfed channels with the remote control, or allowed the programmers of a particular channel to construct formations of pleasure, pro-motion and information for an entire evening.

The limitations of this model are among the reasons for moving television onto the internet through internet protocol television (IPTV) and internet television (ITV). These platforms of delivery have had minor success in most parts of the world, but identify some potential for how other screens could effectively be recolonized by television. IPTV is television delivered through telephone services such as DSL; it is sometimes described as telco television. At least in North America, its emergence coincided with cable companies offer-ing broadband and phone services; telecommunications companies such as AT&T and Verizon, which dominated landline phones, crossed over and began offering similarly bundled television, broadband and telephone services. The actual look of American IPTV resembles cable television, as it is a direct service to the subscriber. Much like current digital cable services, IPTV also offers many interactive features and guides for more agile use of the streamed channels. In other parts of the world, such as Australia, IPTV is used to identify viewing television via the computer but, similar to the American system, it sets up a direct intranet structure that is walled off from the rest of the internet for its delivery to the household.

The take-up of IPTV internationally is determined by a number of factors:

- the speed and reach of broadband and the associated quality of the cable to any endpoint;
- the standardization of technologies of delivery;
- forms, agreements and standards of both regulating content and determining how the content is redelivered and packaged;
- the extent to which there has been a movement of advertising revenue away from traditional media and into internet forms; and
- the record of existing television services operating successfully on their own terms.

The play of these factors varies from country to country. IPTV was developed after the introduction of digital television and digital video recorders, and contemporaneously with add-on technologies such as replay television and TiVo. Often the interactive, on-demand and time-shifting capabilities of these new traditionally delivered television services nullify consumer interest in watching IPTV. Nonetheless, IPTV is expanding and represents a challenge to cable-delivered television in some markets. According to 2008 statistics, IPTV has 15.5 million subscribers worldwide; the greatest presence is in Europe, where there are 8.4 million subscribers (Guevarra and Lee 2008). Other research indicates that there are 900,000 IPTV subscribers in Asia and 1.9 million in North America (*Electronic News Weekly* 2008).

In contrast to IPTV, internet television, or ITV, refers to the packaging of television or video content for direct and open delivery through the public internet. Whereas IPTV can guarantee the quality of its signal and image because it controls the delivery, ITV's quality is dependent on wider internet traffic. Like BitTorrent, ITV can use peer-to peer structures to deliver diverse television/video content. The open-source Miro TV is one of these examples. Similar to YouTube, it allows users to generate channels alongside more commercial or professional channel providers. Unlike YouTube, Miro is a software viewing and retrieval program that can be downloaded onto your personal computer and thereby provides a distinct viewing structure and frame. The format of Miro TV leads the user to structure their video environment as they would for RSS feeds – highly personalized and delivered directly to a desktop environment. The users subscribe to 'channels' and Miro arranges the new content on those channels for potential download through a series of thumbnail images and short title/texts. Joost, similar to Miro TV except that it carries advertising and has a paid subscription model, offers 480 channels and boasts that it has over 28,000 programmes available.

There are two key differences between services such as Joost or Miro and IPTV. First, live content or feeds are just not part of these services as they are with either IPTV or traditional television services; Joost and Miro TV provide a collected and regularly updated archive of available video content. Second, ITV is closely integrated into Web 2.0's emphasis on social networking. Miro and Joost structure their sites to allow for the sharing of material, the collaborative building of channels or personal content, and the general expansion of video from a medium of exhibition, as it was with traditional television, into what I would call an intermediary form of interpersonal communication.

As noted above, the changes in the movement of television onto the internet are occurring at different rates internationally. Nonetheless, some patterns are emerging. South Korea, for instance – the site of the most active online game and social network culture – is migrating to internet video much more rapidly than other parts of the world, perhaps precisely because of its previous embrace of online life and its almost universal access to broadband infrastructure. Australia, on the other hand, is moving slowly into these areas and has a clear urban and regional divide in the take-up of these more video-oriented features of the internet. These differences point to infrastructural variations as well as cost differences. A further significant difference is emerging along language lines. As Mark McLelland's (2008) work has demonstrated, there are geo-linguistic variations in the use and organization of the internet: Asia is leading in the adoption of technology and providing distinctive paths of use that differentiate its activities from those of North America (2008: 611–14). There is not the space here to detail these, but it can be said that a shared language, perhaps more than a shared national identity, is leading to the development of a number of distinctive internet video cultures.

It is important to note the ongoing tension among three competing and overlapping imperatives that are shaping online video. First, there is the continuing emergence of the democratization of the moving image among users, where video, because of its accessibility and deployability, becomes a more everyday and mundane form of communication. Second, the television industry, in its re-mediated form on the internet, is working vigorously to hierarchize the value of images and thereby protect its market through earmarking premium video content that it alone can provide. And third, the new online industries – the Googles, Facebooks and YouTubes of the internet – that have been instrumental in making video just another component of social networking are working just as vigorously to find new ways of generating income. The older economic models, where video as a form of exhibition was used to produce audiences that were sold to advertisers, are now vying with new economic models where video is used to produce communication exchanges that generate richer information about audiences for more targeted and perhaps more valued types of advertising.

Television, DVD and mobile media

In contrast to the uncertain economies of internet television, there has been an accepted and comforting development of DVD production and distribution. Television series' DVDs now are a major element in the video sales and rental market, with worldwide sales by 2005 of 2.6 billion, or 10 per cent of the overall industry (Idato 2005). Due to the capacity to compress episodes into the DVD format, entire annual dramatic series such as *24* or *Sex and the City* can be collected in boxed sets and sold to avid fans and new viewers alike. The pleasures of viewing television series on DVDs have had a subtle but important impact on the migration of television to other screens, as well as breaking the relationship that television programme-viewing had to interspersed advertising.

After the first generation of home DVD players, subsequent production moved to making the player portable. And in the last five years, DVD players have become a regular accessory, with smaller screens embedded in the backseats of SUVs and vans to entertain children. Also, for several years, portable DVD players with attached screens (modelled in the style of slightly larger portable game systems such as Nintendo DS and Sony PSPs) have become a popular North American commuter device for screening television and films. In a similar vein, airlines began providing personal screens for their passengers from the last years of the twentieth century. Most recently, another migratory television practice has emerged: satellite television for cars and airplanes. Modelled on the North American satellite radio systems, these television services are designed for video delivery. Much like ITV, satellite-delivered mobile television is reconstructing content in ways that resemble the models emerging with other mobile media platforms.

Portable DVD players represent a very modest transformation of television that has permitted the traditional television companies to maintain their relative pre-eminence. In contrast, television's move to mobile media forms such as iPods, mobile phones and, to a lesser extent, portable game players articulates a much more concerted effort at building alliances outside the traditional industry. The business structure of mobile video demands that television content providers connect to a software and a technology that can present the video image on a much smaller screen, and to mobile telecommunications companies that can provide the service to their customers. Predating this business alliance is the building of the infrastructure through which large numbers of consumers have access to the latest generation of mobile phones – generally known as third-generation (3G) phones – in order to make any service viable.

The success of this constellation of deals has varied markedly around the world. There are certain markets, such as South Korea, where mobile video is at least as commonplace as internet video, and used in a manner that resembles the mobile satellite television discussed above. The Korean model is broadcast from terrestrial and satellite sources direct to the wireless phone, and thus matches previous television delivery structures. The system called DMB (which has also been adopted in Japan) depends on elaborate government-supported infrastructure and purchase of the phone that can take the signal. In 2007, South Korea had a mobile television audience of 6.3 million (*Economist* 2007), with another 1.2 million watching in-car satellite. The distinctiveness of the Korean approach is that there is no delay in the delivery of pro-grammes: they are simultaneously delivered to satellite, terrestrial and broad-cast receivers.

From 2005, Apple has been developing an iPod that can download videos. Since that time, and progressively in other national and international markets, Apple has worked vigorously on developing content deals with television production companies so that programmes would be available to customers through iTunes. The model of content delivery resembles the successful music download model. As Apple has rolled out the production of iPhones, the move to video delivery on demand has matched its development by certain new industry players. In Europe, the standard developed for mobile video is called DVB-H, and it has had some success in Finland (through Nokia) and in Italy. In the United States, a different technology, called MediaFLO, has been developed. Prior to MediaFLO, and continuing to operate in the United States, is a system called MobiTV that is delivered individually to each mobile phone; this system works well so long as the number of users in a given area does not become overwhelming. There is no question that MobiTV has expanded in the United States. Operating since 2003 with the mobile phone provider Sprint, MobiTV has 4 million subscribers, and it has also established content delivery deals with some of the key networks in the United States, such as Disney, ESPN and NBC, for certain kinds of programmes (Whitney 2008b). MediaFLO is linked with the mobile service provider Verizon, and has similarly expanded its broadcast style service (*Economist* 2007). The IDC research firm projects that, with the shift to video-ready phones, mobile video will expand to up to 10 million subscribers in the United States by 2010 (*Economist* 2007).

Occurring simultaneously with the expansion of mobile providers is content development that recognizes the smaller screen of mobile phones. The most notorious content developed specifically for mobiles was a series connected to *24*, entitled *24: Conspiracy*. The mobile series was a companion to the televi-sion series, but independently produced. It attempted to shoot with a greater number of close-ups and simpler *mise-en-scène* to make sense for the smaller screen of mobile media; however, as Dawson reports, these aesthetics and its separation from the main series actually made *Conspiracy* only a very limited success (Dawson 2007). Other examples of original television content have been advanced, but these developments are still dwarfed by the interpersonal and amateur use of image, sound and video that mobile phone users utilize for simple communication and exchange.

Conclusion

James Bennett has correctly identified that television is already digitalized. As a technology, as an industry and in terms of user practices, television is a digital media form that needs to be studied and taught as such (Bennett 2008). This chapter has identified that there has been a proliferation in the sites and locations of television. Television content has been transposed into the structures and desires of the socially networked world of the internet, as well as reconfigured spatially and temporally so that it fits into the intermittent flows of mobile media use. The 2008 Beijing Olympics is a useful demonstration of how television as a cultural industry now treads a multi-platform line between traditional coverage and alignments with the new screens of digital media.

First, the Olympics is a classic televisual event, as Rothenbuhler (1989) has analysed. It underscores the centrality of television to the understanding of the nation and of what is international. Due to its power in expressing the central ideals and myths of a culture, as well as its capacity to capture large audiences, the Olympics is enormously valuable to major national networks. The Beijing Olympics, through the IOC licensing of television rights, was very similar to past games: national broadcasters paid millions for exclusivity in each of their markets – the American NBC network paid US$3.5 billion (Hoffman 2008). On closer inspection, though, one can see all the new dimensions of how the Olympics was to be delivered to its audience. A total of 2,200 hours of Olympics coverage was allocated to NBC-Online as traditional television tried to control its distribution through blanket multi-platform exhibition. Similar tactics were used by other national broadcasters, such as the Canadian CBC, using online services to multiply the number of events available to viewers. Side-deals with specific phone companies became part of the new exclusivity as it became clear that some sort of information about the Olympics could and would be imparted through mobile media. Indeed, the Olympics was a promotional vehicle for the value of mobile video and television for some companies – in essence, a potential tipping-point to attract users to a new service. In Australia, Telstra Mobile, through a massive rotation of television commercials, promoted its new video-capable mobile phone service where individual events could be streamed live to one's handset for as little as $3 a day. The actual image was heavily branded with the logo of the national network to maintain the exclusive IOC relationship. In the United States, NBC had arrangements with MediaFLO for two channels of Olympics coverage. Similar mobile arrangements were made in other parts of the world, where mobile coverage was twinned with the official broadcast partner in an acknowledgement that mobile video users would be attracted to streaming the short videos that might relate to a particular race or competition – in other words, mobile video allowed the user to unbundle the programming content of traditional television.

The Olympic frenzy of the new television industry, both in terms of its traditional broadcast form and in its different screens' incarnations, demonstrates how an industry is working through a transformed moving-image ecology and economy. Older models of advertising support remain valuable and profitable in their accepted simplicity around audience engagement, and thus broadcast television continues to exercise a weakened but nonetheless forceful pre-eminence. Online cultures have challenged this pre-eminence by flattening the idea of video and its exhibition, where video becomes much more a technology of communication for users rather than predominantly a system of heightened and expensive mediating productions that work to represent national cultures. Emerging delivery systems have their modalities – personal computers translate the televisual experience into individualized and database retrieval experiences and aesthetics, while mobile media not only individualize the experience but also transform the aesthetics of the moving image into smaller screens and different relationships to space and time. Ultimately, the dispersed screens of television are producing an industry and an audience that are forming different alliances as the meaning of television in contemporary culture oscillates between a technology that represents a mythic concept of a culture and a technology that is a further extension of the emerging new, interpersonalized networks of cultural activity that are now both the ground-zero and the default starting point of digital media.

Part Two

The function of
post-broadcast television

Introduction

It would be a simple task to gather together the common sense of much of television studies over the last decade and argue that television no longer serves its traditional function as the prime location for conversations about the nation, or for the operation of a mass-mediated public sphere. There are certainly many who have made this kind of argument. However, among the motivations for this book is our clear view that it is not possible to make such a comprehensive claim about the function of television. Once we extend our horizon beyond the usual locations – the United States, the United Kingdom and Europe – television's functions look too varied to allow for one simple account. In this Part, then, the chapters run slightly against the grain of some of the orthodoxies that have discounted the public dimension of the social function of television, in order to highlight areas where these orthodoxies might benefit from a more comparative, instantiated and evidence-based approach.

That said, of course, it needs to be acknowledged that there have been widespread and important trends in the make-up of the television industries around the world. In many locations, there has been a fundamental shift in the institutional location of television as liberal-democratic governments have embraced the neoliberal programme of deregulation and commercialization. This has dramatically affected the broadcasting and media industries. The results have included the weakening purchase of public service obligations on media industries, as commercial considerations have been increasingly accommodated within the policy structures framing operating environments. Public-interest regulation, widespread during the free-to-air era, has been wound back progressively across Europe, North America and Australasia in the post-broadcast era. Controls on ownership, local content and the provision of news and public affairs programming have all been removed or diminished. Through the 1990s, within governments of all political colours and on all continents, the political support for direct government intervention in the media industries waned; in its place arose a new consensus of support for the principles of privatization – or, as it was sometimes called, market liberalization. This resulted in the full or partial privatization of many public service providers, an expansion in the numbers of new commercial entrants to television markets, and the effective sidelining of the arguments used to justify the introduction of television into most markets in the first place – which focus on its developmental, cultural, informational and educative function.

It has to be said that the consequent changes to the structure of the media industries have made many of the standard regulatory positions developed in relation to earlier models of the mass media untenable and inappropriate. The increase in the number of channels available through the spread of transnational, and often largely unregulated, satellite or cable services has made public-interest regulation look anachronistic. In addition, the sheer number of channels available appears to be able to generate much of the diversity of content and opinion the earlier regulatory structures were designed to ensure.

In those markets that are moving beyond the broadcast era, the role television can play within the imagined community of the nation has changed. In a number of countries now, less than half the audience watches those free-to-air channels that might address the national popular audience. In their place, audiences are watching the various subscription services, many of them originating in other countries entirely. In some countries, the proportion of the television menu that is of local or national origin is a tiny fraction of what is available. The market served by satellite services, in particular, tends to be regional and transnational, as much as national or local. The trends are not all one way, of course. Japan, for instance – once a significant importer of television – now produces 98 per cent of its television content. Local programming, too, continues to attract stronger audiences than imported programmes in just about every market one might care to examine. And in some locations, that preference is still deliberately and programmatically mined for what now look like quite old-fashioned projects of citizen education and nation building.

Given the widespread acknowledgement of all these contextual factors, however, we have taken the view that there is no need to replay accounts of them in this Part. Rather, we have included four chapters that offer challenging perspectives on what has become, it must be admitted, a familiar set of diagnoses, arguments and projections. Graeme Turner's chapter interrogates the limits to projections of a thoroughly globalized, post-national television industry. While acknowledging what he describes as a 'digital orthodoxy' that emphasizes these trends, he also points to factors outside the field of television studies which are informing such positions before suggesting there are aspects of the function of television that still lend themselves to the construction of a national 'co-presence' for the television viewer. Serra Tinic focuses on the conflicting demands made on national public service broadcasters in the current environment. Still required to foster a sense of national community and to assist the growth of a local and independent production industry, public broadcasters are also increasingly being asked to internationalize and to

why Inbw.
worked
well because
it didn't
do this

commercialize aspects of their activity. Using the case of the Canadian public broadcaster, CBC, Tinic approaches these conflicts through a set of case studies drawn from the Canadian experience of developing international co-productions, in order to argue for the importance of the public broadcasting sector's specific contribution to the 'global media ecology'.

In a rousing rebuttal of arguments that broadcast television is now an irrelevance in public debate, Toby Miller compares the audiences for television and for other platforms of delivery during the coverage of the 2008 presidential election in the United States. Provoked by what he characterizes as a hyperbolic debate within television studies between 'television and the internet', Miller draws on the available audience data over the election to make the point that, notwithstanding the rise of the internet, TV 'is more popular than ever'. While revealing the increasing role of other media formats, and their force in particular demographics, he demonstrates that it is certainly too early to suggest that traditional television no longer plays the lead role in hosting the national conversation on the question of who gets to govern next.

Finally, Stuart Cunningham's chapter looks at three examples of how some public broadcasters are responding to the shifting media environment and the looming prospect of their models of operation losing their relevance, significance, and – ultimately – their audience. Cunningham shows, through the work of 'innovation' units, how these institutions are attempting to get ahead of the technological and industrial changes by reinventing not only forms of television but also how audiences of the future might make use of them in ways that still resonate with the social function and public charter of the broadcasters concerned.

Chapter 5

Television and the nation

Does this matter any more?

Graeme Turner

Introduction

For most of its history, in most places where it is available, television has been a national medium. Too expensive to be taken on by an individual or private company, its projected benefits at the outset closely connected to the public good, television broadcasting was introduced by governments for specific national, cultural or developmental policy objectives and addressed to the citizenry of a single nation-state, who were promised more or less universal access. Now the many recent studies of transnational and global television (e.g. Chalaby 2005) suggest that the connection between television and the nation is becoming more attenuated. The hold that national public broadcasting systems had on European television – where their influence possibly was strongest – has been relaxed after several decades of deregulation and privatization. In most other locations, public broadcasting has gone into what might look like terminal decline. Commercial broadcasting is in trouble too. In some of the national markets where it was previously dominant, the introduction of satellite television and the rise of alternative platforms of delivery and aggregation on the internet have pushed national commercial broadcasting into the background. As the consumers of television move ever more fluidly across national boundaries – accessing programming via satellite or the internet – it seems inevitable that the nation must become a more marginal player in the future of the medium.

Given the standard justifications for the nation-state's original investment in the infrastructure of broadcast television, and in many cases in the development of those platforms that have enabled the convergence between the telecommunications and broadcasting systems which has contributed to the current situation, this constitutes a significant historical shift in the function of television.

Nonetheless, there are still plenty of reasons why I would not want to write the obituary of national television broadcasting just yet. For a start, there are significant differences between the industrial histories of television around the globe. Typically, those working on media markets outside the Anglo-American axis point out that the Western enthusiasm for globalizing accounts of television simply ignores the diverse range of conditions obtaining in the various national and regional environments in which it functions today (McMillin 2007; Keane et al. 2007; Straubhaar 2007). Among these scholars, it is by no means agreed that the nation has become irrelevant – or even what that might mean in particular contexts (for instance, how might we imagine that possibility in the world's largest television market, the People's Republic of China?). As a number of the chapters in this book demonstrate, the conditions under which television operates around the globe are still more comprehensively over-determined by national factors than by the influence of the transnational media industries.

In the light of such contrasting evidence – all of it highlighted and debated at some point within contemporary television studies – this chapter sets out to explore how television studies might now think about what must be regarded as an increasingly contingent relationship between television, broadcasting and the nation-state.

Broadcasting and the nation

There is no doubt that there are commercial and technological challenges to television broadcasting in many markets. The United States is merely the most dramatic example of a market where broadcasting is now watched by a minority of its citizens. Broadcasters' share of the market has also declined significantly in, for example, the United Kingdom, Australia and Canada. Demographic trends indicate that it is the over-50s who dominate the remaining broadcasting audience, raising the possibility that the next generation of viewers – the primary consumers of alternatives such as online video – may never acquire that habit. The indicators supporting such a possibility include the patterns of consumer preferences among large sections of the 18- to 34-year-old audience: rejecting 'appointment viewing' and embracing digital media's capacity to personalize their media diet, young people's consumption of 'television' has left the family television set far behind (Rizzo 2007). There are good reasons, then, why television studies has turned to review the medium's original status as a national, often public, broadcasting institution, and to reframe it within a more commercial, multi-platformed and transnational context.

The rise of the internet and the various digital platforms enabling the delivery of video online is the most significant provocation to this revision. The capacity to regulate a national broadcasting system is not easily adapted to the task of regulating a transnational communication system such as the internet. Even though states such as China and Singapore have been able to 'manage' their citizens' access to extra-national sites, it would be very difficult for liberal democratic states to defend the kinds of strategy that have made this possible. It is entirely reasonable to argue that, as the importance of and access to the internet increase, the capacity of the single nation-state to effectively structure the relevant markets or to implement a unilateral regulatory regime is likely to be compromised. Although there is evidence that some regulatory regimes are getting on top of that now (Magder 2006), most commentators recognize that there have to be appropriate multilateral international protocols if any meaningful control over web use and content is to be achieved. That said, it is also the case – as Magder points out – that these international agreements, rather than heralding the death of the nation-state, are still only negotiable between nation-states.

Nonetheless, it is around the complex of issues surrounding the technical capabilities of digital technologies, which are now directly competing with broadcasting, that the debates have been most vigorous in recent years. The strongest arguments against the traditional model of the national television system, and the most optimistic projections of the possibilities inherent in the alternatives, come from those who have focused on the systems of delivery enabled by new media (Gauntlett 2007). Excited by the possibilities for interactivity and for the fracturing of the distinction between the producer and the consumer of television, these accounts focus on user-generated material online and the comparison between the highly personalized choices available through, say, video aggregators like YouTube and those more limited and proscribed choices available through the conventional broadcast or the cable television schedule.

There is an element of the technological sublime colouring some accounts of digital media, it must be admitted, and arguments are sometimes marked by enthusiastic projections into the future rather than historicized accounts of the present (Bruns 2008b). Among the possibilities that attract enthusiasm for new media is what is taken as a shift in power – highlighting the interactivity and agency of the digital consumer, and the grass-roots foundations of many of the media enterprises involved. While in practice such agency may not amount to that much, it is not hard to see why it is welcomed as a distinct improvement on the broadcast television schedule. Ultimately, an explicitly democratizing politics is projected onto these consumer behaviours. This is articulated in various ways – examples include the early DIY model used by John Hartley (1999), the convergence culture described by Henry Jenkins (2006) or David Gauntlett's manifesto for a thorough remaking of media studies around the consumption model exemplified by Web 2.0 (Gauntlett 2007). In the latter two accounts, there is an implicit (sometimes explicit) techno-political hierarchy in play: the traditional media are placed not only as outdated technologies but as the residue of an outdated industrial system that distributed media power in an anti-democratic manner.

Digital technology, according to these most optimistic formulations, has been turned to the purposes of the consumer rather than to those of the industry or the state. The fact that these technologies have transformed previously high-cost industrial activities into twenty-first-century cottage industries runs pleasingly against the grain of the normal political economies of popular culture. It is easy to see why their take-up would be regarded not only as enhancing popular participation and independent enterprise, but also as providing mechanisms of political enfranchisement. It is also easy to see why a degree of technological determinism might accompany this. The distinctive technical capacities of the new technologies are seen as explicitly enabling, they compete directly with the traditional platforms, and their subcultural appeal has only been enhanced by the characteristic media panics about their projected social effects (typically focusing on social networking sites and young people). The political promise of digital media has inoculated its supporters against the criticisms of those who are sceptical about prognoses of the future of television that are based on such limited evidence, and that are dealing with such unpredictable factors as shifts in new technologies, new regulatory frameworks and aspirational 'businesses' that have yet to work out how to sustain their commercial activities (Magder 2006).

The exceptionally warm reception accorded these new technologies has fed into the formation of something of a digital orthodoxy within television, media and cultural studies. This orthodoxy has its negative and its positive dimensions. On the negative side, the digital orthodoxy has the broadcasting industry in terminal decline, broadcast technology out of date, and the national institution of television paternalistic, old-fashioned and anti-democratic. On the positive side, the digital orthodoxy embraces user-generated content, the interactive and democratizing potential of digital technologies, globalization, and the activities of the so-called 'prosumer' or 'produser'. The closer to the global consumer we come, it seems, the further we are from the nation-state, and thus the more categorically the technology liberates the consumer from political and regulatory containment. Henry Jenkins' *Convergence Culture* (2006) is an exemplary location for the digital orthodoxy, and the fact that it was published as a trade, rather than an academic, book reflects its cultural currency.

Not to exaggerate this influence, or its unanimity or comprehensiveness, these are still active debates and have quite some time to run. There is also a growing counter-discourse to do with the limits to the progressive politics that might be read from interactivity (Andrejevic 2004, 2007; Jarrett 2008; Petersen 2008), as well as a critique of democratization as a means of understanding what, in my view, is more accurately described as 'the demotic' (Turner 2006, 2009). There is also, it has to be said, a wealth of evidence to challenge elements of the digital orthodoxy: it is the case that broadcasting remains the dominant platform for television worldwide (Straubhaar 2007: 2); US television viewing has not yet declined as use of the internet has increased – the most recent Nielsen report had it growing by 4 per cent (Nielsen Media Research 2008a); the business of advertising, the key economic driver for all these media, is still focused overwhelmingly on a national audience (Straubhaar 2007: 82); and the evidence from China (to name just one location) will frustrate any attempt to link the take-up of capitalist media – digital or otherwise – with a genuine process of democratic enfranchisement (see Sun and Zhao in this volume). Nonetheless, even while these debates work themselves out, it is clear that the study of television – for so long situated comfortably as an account of television broadcasting within the boundaries of the single nation-state – has fundamentally changed in response to these technological and market developments.[1]

It is important to note, however, that these debates are not confined to the disciplinary territory of television studies. The ready embrace by television studies scholars of what they characterize as the democratizing and post-national cosmopolitanism of television consumption via the internet draws much of its momentum from other areas of social and cultural theory where, in my view (to appropriate Mark Twain), reports of the death of the nation-state have been greatly exaggerated. Contemporary theories of globalization and cosmopolitanism have responded to the history of – particularly European – nationalisms by taking a highly critical view of the nation-state as a political formation. Although some accounts of cosmopolitanism recognize that the nation has often provided fertile ground for the 'bottom-up' development of the hybridizing formations of cosmopolitanism, in other accounts the idea of the nation-state, and especially nationalism as an ideological formation, is regarded as inherently suspect (Morley 2004: 316–17). Consequently, within these accounts, any indicators which might seem to point towards nationalism's eventual obsolescence are eagerly taken up.

Sociologist Craig Calhoun (2007) has argued against the categoric certainty of such positions for some years now. In *Nations Matter: Culture, History and the Cosmopolitan Dream*, he suggests that a key support for the condemnation of even apparently benign formations of the nation is a particular aspect of some social theorists' desire for 'cosmopolitan democracy':

> That is, they embraced not just cosmopolitan tastes for cultural diversity (which too often rendered culture an object of external consumption rather than internal meaning); not just the notion of hybridity with its emphasis on porous boundaries and capacious, complex identities; and not just cosmopolitan ethics emphasizing the obligations of each to all around the world. They embraced also the notion that the globe could readily be a *polis*, and humanity at large organized in democratic citizenship.
>
> (2007: 11)

As he goes on to say, this is an 'attractive but very elusive ideal': 'it is one thing', he warns, 'to seek to advance global civil society and another to imagine democracy can thrive without effective states' (2007: 4).

David Morley (2004) takes a slightly different view by locating the principled dismissal of all forms of national belonging as among the unintended consequences of postmodernist thought. Morley is critical of the absolutist nature of such a position, with the blanket condemnation of nationalism not only producing something of a backlash (producing what he calls 'born-again nationalism'), but also encouraging the mistaken view that 'any search for a sense of place must of necessity be reactionary' (2004: 317). Against such points of view, Morley's work over a long period has demonstrated the value of a much more nuanced analysis of the varied cultural functions performed by such constructions of place and belonging as the 'home' or the nation (Morley 2000). Similarly, Calhoun (2007) insists on the need for a more nuanced historical account of the nation that acknowledges the complexity of its political and cultural possibilities:

> National identities and loyalties and structures of integration are among the many complications of the actual historical world in which moral decisions must be made. Globalization challenges nation-states and intensifies flows across their borders, but it doesn't automatically make them matter less. Because nations matter in varied ways for different actors, it is important to think carefully about how they are produced and reproduced, how they work and how they can be changed.
>
> (2007: 9)

Conversely, Calhoun suggests, the cosmopolitan enthusiasm for globalization needs to be tempered by the lessons that *its* emerging history can teach us; that while globalization does constitute a significant shift in human organization, it is not a shift that is politically or socially neutral: 'it advantages some and disadvantages others':

> And that is in fact a crucial reason for the continuing reproduction of nationalism, and a reason why caution is warranted before suggesting that nationalist projects are inherently regressive and cosmopolitan projects progressive ... The liberal state is not neutral. Cosmopolitan civil society is not neutral. Even the English language is not neutral. This doesn't mean that any of the three is bad, only that they are not equally accessible to everyone and do not equally express the interests of everyone.
>
> (2007: 17)

The nation-state, then, is not so much a fixed ideological category as a historical construction that needs to be examined conjuncturally rather than simply allocated its predetermined politics. If that principle were applied more widely in television studies, we might benefit from analyses of particular television systems within a wider range of national or regional locations than we have at present. This would not run against the grain of the ideal of cosmopolitanism, but it would certainly complicate our synoptic accounts of the global relation between television and the nation.

Television and the reshaping of the public sphere

What counts as television around the world today has come a long way from the Reithian rationales for its introduction – the medium's capacity to educate, inform and entertain. What was once a rationale consistent with liberal constructions of the civilizing purpose of the public sphere has given way to a more thoroughly commercial purpose and ambition. Given the centrality of television broadcasting to the operation of the public sphere in modernized states since the end of the Second World War, the shifts I am describing are actually fundamental changes in the configuration of the public sphere. The privatization of the mass-media economy and the accelerating trend towards the personalization of consumption that have marked changes in its patterns of use have elbowed 'the public' dimension aside as it proliferates private choices for the individual consumer. In what Ellis (2002) calls the 'era of plenty', the mass media in the United States offers such exorbitant choice – of medium, platform and content – that it has surrendered, in a sense, its rationality as a form of 'mass' communication. Indeed, according to Milly Buonanno (2008), the drift away from the US broadcast networks constitutes a choice for 'narrowcasting': television marketed to thinly sliced sub-groups defined by taste, location or demographics. As a consequence, US broadcasters have surrendered their dominance of the public sphere to a diversified, privatized plethora of niche markets.

While this development is certainly welcomed by more than just those who subscribe to the digital orthodoxy, Buonanno (2008) presents an interesting counter-argument. She is highly critical of narrowcasting's restricted circle of consumption and its 'selective communication model'. She compares the politics of narrowcasting unfavourably with those of broadcasting by arguing that narrowcasting is 'divisive and selective' whereas 'broadcasting joins and unifies people': 'the former isolates and separates, the latter unites people and keeps them together'. She is also critical of narrowcasting's tailored address to a particular cultural formation:

> [T]he advent of narrowcasting has … been made possible by the emergence of a strain of social demand, not widespread but diffused to a greater or lesser degree according to the particular case, for 'made-to-measure' television tailored to the specific preferences and interests of a restricted number of viewers (the so-called 'niche' market).
>
> (2008: 25)

This is a very different reading of the politics of proliferating choice; rather than proclaiming the democratization of the public sphere, Buonanno is describing its commercial capture by preferred taste formations.[2]

However television studies might read this situation, the US television industry has its own orthodoxy, which regards the current trends as likely to accelerate, resulting (in the most extreme formulation) in 'the end of broad-casting' (Palmer 2008; Collins 2008). However, there are plenty of reasons to think it will not play out that way. For a start, television now costs more. As content choices, delivery platforms and technological options multiply, the cost of each successive option is likely to become increasingly significant. Straubhaar (2007) has pointed to a number of locations (the United Kingdom and Germany, for example) where consumers have chosen to stay with broadcast networks simply because of the relatively slim margin between the quality of the service provided by paid subscription services and of the free service provided by broadcasters. In the United States, subscription services have a significant competitive advantage in terms of their content, so that behaviour is not being repeated there. However, since we know that cable consumers only use a small fraction of the channels available to them (Bar and Taplin 2007: 72), and that they eventually suffer from 'choice fatigue' (Ellis 2002: 169–70), the continued provision of more choices must ultimately be a risky commercial strategy. On the other hand, it could be a highly successful strategy for free-to-air broadcasters. In the United Kingdom, Freeview is delivering a free-to-air digital broadcast service on a scale (40 channels) com-parable to base-level subscription offerings; in the United States, local broad-casters are arguing that the shift from analogue to digital in 2009, with its attendant capacity for broadcasters to multicast up to four channels each, may finally enable them to compete effectively against the cable networks.

The one area where almost everyone agrees that there will continue to be a market for broadcasting is in live 'event' television – key sporting events, national celebrations and so on. It is still possible for broadcasters to gather enormous audiences for these events, and everyone acknowledges that they should continue. For that to happen, there has to be a platform on which this kind of programming can be mounted. Notwithstanding the fact that there are massive global audiences for events such as the Super Bowl, the Olympics or football's World Cup, the presentation of these events is also the subject of localization through the insertion of (at least) a national broadcaster's com-mentary over the top of a shared video feed. That would suggest that the primary provenance of even these 'global' events is national. However, such events do not happen every day, and this raises the question of how you programme and fund a broadcasting network that only really gathers a national audience when it broadcasts special, high-profile media events.

Some suggest that you don't, with the likely result that broadcasting would be 'scaled down to a mere residual presence' (Buonanno 2008: 26). Others are more hopeful, arguing that there are other aspects of the distinctiveness of broadcast television that remain important: 'the possibility of reaching all citi-zens with important information remains valuable to nation-states, and the need for institutions that can provide some sort of social cohesion has not lessened'; therefore, there will have to be at least 'a few central broadcast TV channels in each country' (Gripsrud 2004: 221). I would also suggest that the 'everydayness' of broadcast television, the embedding of the schedule into the patterns of everyday life (notwithstanding some sections of the audience embracing alternatives to this), as well as the perception of a broader co-presence, the national audience, as we watch remain distinctive and powerful attractions to the broadcast model. While much of our recent attention has been drawn to new capacities which enable the interactivity of the lone consumer, there is no reason to see this as categorically displacing a capacity that is actually substantially different: broadcasting's provision of a 'voluntary point of social cohesion, of being-together while being-apart' (Ellis 2002: 176).

It is important to recognize that what we are witnessing in this era of plenty is a diversification of the media diet, not the simple substitution of one form of consumption by another. As I have argued, how that plays out varies significantly from market to market; these are highly contingent rather than simply over-determined market responses. If we take a global view, there is limited evidence to suggest audiences have decided, categorically, that they no longer require the core public function of the national (public or commercial) broadcaster: that of providing the opportunity for the nation to conduct its conversations with itself, to construct and confirm its national identities, and to populate the symbolic space in which it can play out its 'dramas of nationhood' (Abu-Lughod 2005). While this capacity may not necessarily be uppermost in the audience's mind as they make their choices, it is important to recognize that, more than any other current component of the contemporary public sphere, broadcast television retains the capacity to construct a sense of unity and belonging for citizens of the nation:

> It can link the peripheral to the centre; turn previously exclusive social events into mass experiences; and, above all, penetrate the domestic sphere by linking the national public into the private lives of its citizens through the creation of both sacred and quotidian moments of national communion.
>
> (Morley 2004: 312)

This reasserts the necessary inclusiveness of the public sphere if it is to perform the 'important functions of culture and identity binding within the national collectivity of each country' (Buonanno 2008: 24).

In my view, this remains a fundamental component of what television does, and it is probably worth specifying that it does so through all kinds of programming, not just 'live' event TV. The co-presence of the national audience is implicated in the consumption of news, soap opera, locally produced drama, sport – even, I would suggest, through such favourites of the YouTube audience as *The Daily Show*. The centrality of the television audience's connection to the national community and its acknowledged locations is also implicated in the general preference for local programming over imported programming, in the standardization of the practices used to indigenize international formats

and in explaining why the globalization of television has proven such a powerful force, against all predictions, in reviving local production industries (see
Albert Moran's chapter in this volume). There are limits, then, to the post-
national trends I have spent much of this essay describing – although I'll admit
we probably haven't reached them all yet.

Of course, it may be that these debates are occurring too close to the subject of their attention and we need to step back and take a longer view. Beaty
and Sullivan (2006) remind us, for instance, that television has always straddled
both the public and the private spheres:

> [O]n the one hand [it is] a crucial instrument of nationalism and public
> identity formation, while on the other a distinctly private practice under-
> taken in isolation by atomized citizens who need neither be citizens of the
> nation nor located within its boundaries.
>
> (2006: 14)

Hence the play between these two capabilities may be a constitutive, not
merely a contingent, aspect of what television is. Perhaps, rather than witnessing the end of broadcasting or the beginning of post-national television, we
are simply watching these two constitutive elements renegotiate their particular roles against an unusually volatile background of hyper-commercializa-
tion and emerging technologies.

In my view, then, and responding to the question posed in my title, the
nation still matters in television studies' account of what television does and
what it will do in the future. While it may on its own no longer be a 'sufficient site' (Curtin 2004: 271) for television studies, it remains an unavoidable
site – although for a more internationalized, more comparative and more
conjunctural analysis. Finally, it is important to recognize that whatever results
from the current reconfigurations, it won't simply be the technologies that
determine the outcomes, nor will it be the grass-roots consumers making their
personal choices who will carry all before them. A crucial component will be
the actions taken and policies adopted by those authorities which regulate
commercial and cultural activity within a single market or financial-legal jurisdiction – that is, within the nation-state.

Notes

1 There is another dimension to this which I don't have space to go into here, and that is
   the challenge that comes from studies of production to a solely national focus for the
   analysis of television. Michael Curtin's (2004) work on media capitals, for instance,
   demonstrates the usefulness of a cultural geography of media production sites that
   focuses on individual cities (Hong Kong, Chicago, Bombay), and there are a number of
   scholars who have focused on geo-cultural regions as the appropriate sites for analysis
   (for instance, Sinclair 1999; Straubhaar 2007; and Iwabuchi 2002).

2 This argument intersects interestingly with the account presented in McMurria's (2007) history of the introduction of pay-TV in the United States, where he demonstrates how 'electronics manufacturers, advertisers, educators, law-makers, liberal democrats, cultural critics, and the high performing arts supported pay-TV to liberate a minority of "discerning" viewers from the "lowest common tastes" of a mass commercial broadcast culture' (2007: 52). It didn't turn out that way of course, but that is another story.

Chapter 6

Between the public and the private

Television drama and global partnerships in the neo-network era

Serra Tinic

In their embrace of neo-liberalism and globalization, governments around the world are increasingly reluctant to invest in sectors that have long been considered vital components of the cultural and political life of the nation-state. National public service broadcasting has been one such site of economic retrenchment. Established during an era of spectrum scarcity, public service broadcasting (PSB), in the Western European tradition, was based on the assumption that the airwaves were natural resources that should be managed to the overall benefit of society. Consequently, fostering a national cultural community through universal access to information and entertainment programming, protected from commercial motivations, became a common organizing principle for PSB mandates throughout the countries and colonies of Europe. That was more than 80 years ago. Today's new media environment of expanded channel capacity and multi-platform delivery has revitalized debates about the continued relevance and legitimacy of public investment in broadcasting in an age of spectrum surplus.

Pessimism about the future of PSB is not limited to state actors and multinational media corporations who advocate marketization. Media studies scholars, too, are questioning the fundamental principles of contemporary public service broadcasting. Given the parallels between academic debates and those of media professionals, executives and policy makers – as evidenced in the recent spirited exchange between Elizabeth Jacka (2003) and Nicholas Garnham (2003) in a special issue of *Television & New Media* – the time has come to complicate our assumptions about the public–private broadcasting divide, particularly in light of technological convergence and global media flows. Jacka aptly contests the customary academic depiction of PSB as the ultimate arbiter of a mediated Habermasian public sphere. Her critique contrasts the modernist tendency to associate PSB with rationalism, civil society and the paternalist state against the emergence of a new media ecology that encourages decentralized identity and community formations. Herein, the expansion of digital windows that facilitate do-it-yourself (DIY) cultural politics are seen to resolve the 'market failure' argument that has long served to justify the existence of PSB, leading Jacka to conclude: 'I must confess, I cannot see the future for publicly funded media; I am not sure it has one' (2003: 188).

Garnham refutes Jacka's bifurcation of the commercial and non-commercial media spheres, and asserts that public and private broadcasting not only coexist within national broadcasting structures but, moreover, many PSB networks now rely on advertising for a portion of their overall operating budgets. Consequently, the future of PSB need not continually be framed within either/or scenarios. However, most troubling for Garnham (2003) is how 'popular' programming is equated with commercial media in a manner that presupposes a liberating, radical democratic potential juxtaposed to a caricature of public broadcasting audiences as coerced by programming that is 'unpopular, elitist, and a killjoy' (2003: 199).

Democracy is a notoriously difficult concept to measure in terms of media content and audience reception, particularly within non-authoritarian media regimes. Consequently, this chapter continues the productive dialogue initiated by Jacka and Garnham but explores the contemporary moment and possible future of PSB within much narrower parameters. Rather than revisiting theoretical conceptualizations of the relationship between media structures and public sphere politics, the following sections examine the challenges facing PSB institutions to fulfil their mandate obligations while simultaneously restructuring their production and distribution strategies to meet the demands of a global, post-network media environment. In accord with Jacka's (2003: 188) assertion that public broadcasting must be considered through 'situated microanalyses', as opposed to generalized arguments about its 'natural superiority', I focus on the Canadian Broadcasting Corporation (CBC). As a PSB network that relies on both government funding and advertising revenue, the CBC epitomizes Garnham's depiction of the tensions between the commercial and non-commercial goals that characterize many PSB institutions around the world.

As I argue later, globalization and convergence may actually intensify, rather than resolve, the 'market failure' justification for PSB. Operating within a small-market nation that is situated next to the world's largest cultural superpower, the CBC has been at the forefront of developing global co-production partnerships with other public broadcasters to avoid 'niche marginalization' and maintain its capacity as a 'full portfolio' programming broadcaster (Bardoel and d'Haenens 2008: 344). Despite the breadth of academic analyses of PSB, few works examine the actual programmes that are expected to distinguish it from its private network counterparts. This is particularly true of 'popular' television drama. Consequently, I briefly compare two international co-productions to show how different institutional formations, public and commercial, can either restrict or augment the ways in which the same story can be told. The discussion concludes by examining the potential of such international co-productions, based on a shared public institutional ethos, to bolster the transnational profile of PSB as well as supplement the escalating need for national content across multiple media platforms.

Public service broadcasting at the crossroads

In most European countries, PSB organizations enjoyed a relatively stable existence until the late 1970s. Supported by government appropriations, licence fees or a combination of the two, few public networks had to compete directly with domestic commercial television broadcasters for revenue or audience share. With the expansion of cable and satellite distribution in the 1980s, PSB television networks quickly found themselves competing for an increasingly fragmented audience in order to legitimate their claim on government subsidies. A decade later, many European PSB institutions were effectively transformed into 'dual systems' as telecommunications regulators across the continent relaxed restrictions to allow public broadcasters to establish arm's-length commercial ventures to support programme production at their main networks (Seneviratne 2006). In a telling turn of events, private broadcasters who initially fought the monopoly status of PSB have now changed their course of attack to claim that, in a depressed advertising environment, government support of public television violates European Union competition and fair trade policies. Commercial networks advocate restricting PSB to niche programming – or, in other words, genres and narrative forms that hold no market value for commercial broadcasters (Coppens and Saeys 2006). Consequently, PSB in Europe finds itself in an untenable position, caught between mutually contradictory forces. In order to fulfil its obligation to provide universal access to a diverse array of programmes that speak to national communities, it must attract a large enough audience to justify its remit while simultaneously generating revenue to produce 'innovative' content. In the end, PSB programming must be popular, but not so popular that it impedes the interests of its private sector cohort. The problem is exacerbated as these national institutions struggle to maintain their mandates within the continental constraints of European Union treaty and trade provisions (Jakubowicz 2007).

This is, however, a very old story for PSB in Canada. Since 1953, when licensing fees were abolished, the CBC has relied on advertising revenue for 30 per cent of its budget. With the establishment of the first private national network (CTV) in 1961, the CBC has been in competition for audiences and advertisers for almost 50 years. The problem for the Canadian commercial–public PSB model is compounded by the expectations set forth in the Broadcasting Act that mandate the CBC to provide a full portfolio of programmes that are 'distinctively Canadian; contribute to a shared national consciousness and identity; and reflect the multicultural and multiracial nature of Canada'. This stands in marked contrast to the private television networks that are expected to meet minimal domestic content requirements and are allowed to fill their prime-time schedules with inexpensively acquired American programming. As a point of comparison, Canadian programmes account for 93 per cent of the CBC's prime-time viewing schedule as opposed to 20 per cent for its private network competitors (CBC 2007). Unlike their European counterparts, the Canadian private networks do not object to fair trade balances with the CBC. Indeed, Canadian commercial broadcasters benefit from public subsidies through cultural sovereignty policies that seek to provide a countervailing force against border spill-over from the American broadcast networks. Canadian private broadcasters receive between $270 million and $330 million in indirect government funding through tax incentives and simulcast regulations, wherein domestic advertising is inserted into imported American programming during the prime-time schedule (Nordicity Group 2006). Foreign ownership restrictions have also helped to consolidate vertically integrated media conglomerates within the private sector. Today, four corporations – Canwest Global, Bell Canada Enterprises, Quebecor and Rogers – operate as regional multimedia and telecommunications monopolies in designated territories across Canada. The private networks' primary objection to federal regulations has always been that they have to broadcast any Canadian entertainment content at all. With a population of approximately 31 million people, the potential 'market' for culturally specific television programming is not at all enticing for advertising-driven broadcasters. A cost comparison is important in this regard. The broadcast fee to purchase Canadian programming is C$200,000–250,000 per hour, with an anticipated return of C$65,000–90,000 in advertising revenue. The rights to simulcast American television content, however, cost C$100,000–125,000 per hour, with the expectation that the most popular programmes will generate C$350,000–450,000 in advertising revenue (CBC report, cited in Skinner 2008: 14). In the case of PSB in Canada, it is not difficult to argue that the 'market failure' argument persists, regardless of the number of new content delivery windows. In economic terms, there is little incentive to develop innovative programmes that speak to a culturally diverse population that will never be large enough to justify the cost–benefit ratio of production investment.

In Canada, government divestment from the cultural sector, rather than domestic fair trade complaints, has posed the greatest threat to PSB. The CBC's capacity to develop long-range programming strategies has suffered from uncertain, fluctuating annual parliamentary appropriations, ranging from C$780 million in 2002 to C$946 million in 2006 (CBC 2007). The CBC's already precarious foundation was further aggravated in the 1990s, when the government demanded its complete restructuring. In the interests of streamlining, in-house production was virtually eliminated and the national television network is now expected to commission the majority of its entertainment programming from independent production companies. Despite its drastic downsizing, the English main network sustained large national audiences in the areas that are considered the traditional purview of PSB: news and documentary programming. The continued investment in foreign news bureaux and investigative reporting has precluded the need to rely on international (particularly American) news feeds; therefore, the CBC continues to be viewed as the most authoritative news broadcaster in the country (Hoskins et al. 2001: 21–2). The network has also shown that it can achieve success in popular entertainment programming. Political sketch comedies, in particular, often rate well, drawing audiences away from imported programming on the private networks. The genre has in fact become one of the CBC's strongest offerings, given the commercial broadcasters' propensity to avoid controversial programming. Drama, the most expensive of genres, continues to be the weak link for the CBC, and for Canadian television in general.

In order to compete against the high production quality of American programming, the CBC reduced its overall level of dramatic production in the 1990s and focused its resources on a handful of dramatic series. It also began producing six-episode season runs as opposed to the North American standard of thirteen episodes. Politically and culturally, this strategy proved unsustainable, given the CBC's need to meet its remit as a full-portfolio public network. Therefore, in an effort to achieve a new annual goal of 250 hours of Canadian drama by 2009, the public broadcaster sought out new revenue sources and global production partnerships (CBC 2007). International joint ventures (IJVs) have long been the preferred production model for Canadian independent producers seeking to sell television drama to the domestic commercial networks and across global markets. With over 50 official co-production treaties, Canada has become the world leader in IJVs. However, in order to increase a production's international sales value, Canadian producers and their co-production partners often erase culturally specific markers and follow the grammar of Hollywood formulas and genres. These types of generic or 'industry' productions are commonly seen as the hallmarks of the culturally homogenizing impact of capital interests in a global media environment and, until recently, an unviable production model for PSB networks (Tinic 2005).

Since the rapid transformation of global media policies and regulations in the 1990s, however, PSB organizations worldwide now share the CBC's concern to maintain high-quality programme schedules with fewer and less reliable resources. Consequently, the IJV – once considered an inherently commercial production model – has become an attractive strategy for public broadcasters in need of content for both their main networks and emergent multi-platform windows. The case of perhaps the world's most venerable PSB organization, the British Broadcasting Corporation (BBC), provides a unique scenario in this regard. As Born and Prosser (2001) explain, when the BBC was restructured in 1996 into production and broadcast divisions, and BBC Worldwide was established as a commercial subsidiary to supplement the BBC licence fee, BBC producers had to compete with the independent production community to sell programming to their own network. They subsequently introduced international co-productions with other national public broadcasters and commercial partners in order to remain cost-effective in the bidding process. The changing landscape of British television created new opportunities for Canadian independent producers and, by extension, the CBC. In 1995, Canada did not even have an official co-production treaty with the United Kingdom. However, by 2001 the United Kingdom had replaced France as the country's largest co-production partner and contributed 57 per cent to Canada's treaty co-productions. That year, the total budget of Canada–UK co-productions was C\$302 million, with an equal investment by both countries (CFTPA 2002).

The move into the IJV sphere has raised fears in Britain of a diminished commitment to pursuing 'risky or innovative projects as well as those oriented to national minority audiences' (Born and Prosser 2001: 669). This is a legit-imate question, given the history of the aforementioned 'industry' co-pro-ductions that operate according to globally generic objectives. Yet risk taking and innovation need not be sacrificed if both co-production partners come to the table with a PSB remit based on similar mandate missions. In other words, a common institutional ethos, whether it be a PSB joint venture or a com-mercial co-production, may be the most important determinant of how a story can or will be told. The apprehension about national and minority audiences is far more complex. On the one hand, all IJVs must negotiate questions of cultural specificity and domestic audience markets. However, PSB co-productions may provide opportunities to speak to the ever-increasing complexity of multicultural communities as globalization processes complicate the 'nation' as a stable category of identification. A brief comparison of two Canadian IJVs epitomizes the relationship between institutional ethos and, in particular, the PSB capacity to push the boundaries of storytelling in a way that is not always possible within the more risk-averse commercial industry.

Sex Traffic and Human Trafficking: a tale of two co-productions

In 2003, the CBC and Canadian independent production company Big Motion Pictures entered a co-production agreement with Britain's Granada Media and Channel 4 to produce Sex Traffic (aired 2004) – the biggest-budget dramatic mini-series that either broadcaster had ever developed (Gillian 2004). Channel 4, described as an 'alternative public broadcaster', was established in 1981 with the mandate to provide innovative and experimental programming for minority audiences not typically catered to by the BBC or ITV. In fact, to discourage mass market programming, the new broadcaster was not supposed to strive for more than 10 per cent of the national audience (Hobson 2008). Channel 4 was also intended to help grow the independent production com-munity, and therefore served as a 'publisher' rather than producer of pro-gramming (Brown 2007). The broadcaster was initially financed through a combination of government support and a portion of ITV's commercial rev-enues. While Channel 4 continues to receive public funding, it was allowed to begin selling its own advertising in 1993. Consequently, there are several organizational similarities to the CBC, and therefore a co-production between the two was seen as an appropriate fit for the Canadian broadcaster.

Sex Traffic was based on a series of investigative news reports and books that exposed the plight of Eastern European women who were kidnapped and sold into the global sex trade after the fall of the Soviet Union. With an eye to the economic collapse of most of the region, the mini-series details how women are lured by promises of a better, more prosperous life in the West. The story is told predominantly through the eyes of two Moldovan sisters who are promised by a local man that jobs are waiting for them in London. When the women arrive at the designated location to begin the journey, their passports and other identification documents are confiscated and they are then smuggled and sold in nightclubs and brothels throughout Europe. *Sex Traffic* unsparingly depicts the brutality endured by these women. Violence, both actual and threatened, is constant and there is one particularly graphic, uncensored rape scene. The producers' commitment to realism and a docudrama style is especially risky, as the mini-series was broadcast one hour prior to the start of the prime-time schedule on the national CBC network.

There is no attempt to simplify the issues of a larger global crisis. The captors and criminal organizations are, not surprisingly, characterized as evil and brutal, but the central villain in *Sex Traffic* is explicitly global capitalism. As the story unfolds, the audience learn that the slavery network exists through the cooperation of a complex network of corrupt local police forces, UN peacekeepers in Bosnia and Sarajevo, and private security officials working with American multinational corporations and defence contractors. This narrative is not fabricated to intensify the suspense value of the topic, but rather alludes to factual material reported by Canadian and British journalists since the mid-1990s. Moreover, the people fighting sexual slavery in the mini-series are not law enforcement or intelligence agents but representatives of charitable organizations dealing with forced migration. The overall thematic is best summed up in a scene where a local officer assisting a charity worker (British actor John Simm) enters a slave brothel and says: 'Welcome to the free market.' There are no international celebrities in the cast of *Sex Traffic*. In keeping with the goal of authenticity, the two lead characters are portrayed by Romanian theatre actresses Anamaria Marinca and Maria Popistau, who are largely unknown outside their own country. Although one sister does eventually make it home, there is no happy ending to let the audience off the hook. Rather, the final scene shows, through the eyes of a local Moldovan police officer, the process beginning anew as another young girl follows a suspected trafficker to her fate: the global economy rolls on and the powerless become tradeable commodities. *Sex Traffic* received international acclamation and was described by one television critic as 'trenchant and powerful, frighteningly real and utterly convincing. It's not easy to watch, but it demands to be seen' (Strachan 2004: D6). The mini-series eventually won eight BAFTAs (UK), four Geminis (Canada), the Prix Italia and two Monte Carlo TV Festival awards. Equally important, the CBC and Channel 4 reinforced their profiles as quality international broadcasters and, more implicitly, accentuated the value of PSB as a compelling 'brand' of programming.

Human Trafficking, a co-venture between the Canadian production company Muse Entertainment and the US cable channel Lifetime Television, aired the year after *Sex Traffic* and was primarily targeted at American audiences. Although this mini-series is based on the same factual circumstances, the dominant discourses and genre, character and narrative considerations are radically different from those of its predecessor. *Human Trafficking* minimizes, and at times completely elides, the issue of global capitalism. There is certainly no reference to American corporate culpability, either ideologically or in practice. In fact, scenes throughout the drama prominently display Homeland Security insignias and badges. This is not astonishing, given that the US Department of Homeland Security served as an adviser to the production. And, whereas *Sex Traffic* might best be described as a high-concept social drama, *Human Trafficking* quickly evolves into a crime procedural. The intertwining storylines of the women who are sold into sexual slavery are at the forefront of the narrative, but the clear protagonist of the drama is American actress Mira Sorvino.

Sorvino plays a NYPD detective who investigates a series of local murders of young immigrant women and begins to suspect that they are part of a larger slavery network. She subsequently asks to join an Immigrations and Customs Enforcement (ICE) task force led by Donald Sutherland (whose Canadian citizenship adds Canadian content points to the production), which will allow her to work full-time on the investigation. The majority of the cast members in *Human Trafficking* are Canadian and American actors, including those who portray the kidnapped women from Eastern Europe. One exception is British actor Robert Carlyle (of *Full Monty* fame), who plays the Russian crime boss Sergei Karpovich, the apparent mastermind of the global sex-slave trade. The fact that the villain in this version is an identifiable individual provides the audience with a convenient foreign 'other' to blame for the torture endured by the women kidnapped into the network. Good prevails over evil when Sorvino goes under cover as a Russian mail-order bride and infiltrates a holding house for the women under Karpovich's control. Dramatic resolution is complete when Karpovich is killed in a shoot-out with ICE agents and Sorvino rescues all the women and provides them with documents that grant American residency to those who want to remain in the United States.

Whereas the Canada–United Kingdom co-production focuses completely on the victimization of Eastern European women, *Human Trafficking* adds a discordant storyline about a teenaged American girl kidnapped from a crowded market and sold into the sex-slave network while on vacation with her parents in the Philippines. The perceived need to continually domesticate the suffering is emphasized at the conclusion of the final episode, when Sorvino at a press conference – standing in front of yet another large Homeland Security banner – gives an impassioned speech in which she quotes the 13th

Amendment to the Constitution, which abolished slavery in the United States. This is not to say that *Human Trafficking* does not draw attention to and create broader dialogue about a global human tragedy. Rather, the narrative structure and use of star-status actors keeps the audience at a greater emotional distance from the issue. Although acts of brutality are implied, they are never explicit and the relatively positive ending provides audiences with a sense of respite that is not forthcoming in *Sex Traffic*. Indeed, according to a script adviser for Lifetime, the objective was 'to give a portrayal of the trafficking issue in a way that's palatable to American audiences' (interviewed in Aurthur 2005).

Comparing the two co-productions highlights the capacity of PSB programming to engage in-depth structural critique that is less possible within the constraints of commercially driven television. Advertisers are hesitant to support programmes that impede a 'happy buying mood', and they are certainly wary of any criticism of corporate capitalism. This stands in marked contrast to the comments of Slawko Klymkiw, the executive director of CBC network programming, who 'wanted to push boundaries' by airing *Sex Traffic*: 'As a public broadcaster, we ought to be taking chances. We ought to be provocative. It's just what we should do' (interviewed in MacDonald 2004: R10). Thus, to return to Garnham's argument, it should not be an either/or scenario between public and private models. Sustaining PSB alongside commercial media networks ensures that both types of story can circulate globally.

Projecting an alternative future for PSB

At the time of writing, the Canadian Radio-television and Telecommunications Commission (CRTC), which regulates all domestic media and communications networks, has proposed splitting the Canadian Television Fund (CTF) into private and public streams. The CTF is a production fund that supports domestic independent productions that fulfil Canadian content regulations aimed at ensuring cultural specificity in television programming. The fund is generated from cable and satellite companies that are legislated to contribute 5 per cent of their annual revenues to the CTF in exchange for their regional monopoly status. This market-oriented, entrepreneurial shift in CRTC policy is particularly evident in its assertion that applications to the private sector fund must 'incorporate a "hit factor" that takes into account the differing business models of conventional and specialty television' (CRTC 2008). It will be a significant blow to the CBC if the government accepts the CRTC's proposal. Most independent producers who fulfil the spirit of Canadian content regulations work with the CBC, and if the fund is split into two sectors the reduction in support will shrink the PSB window and force many within the independent production community to focus on mass-appeal programmes for private broadcasters who have little interest in domestic programming. Consequently, international co-productions with other PSB institutions will become even more important to the CBC.

The CRTC's recommendations should also be viewed in light of the regulator's anticipation of a digital, multi-platform future in which the proliferation of new delivery technologies is presumed to immediately translate into a diversity of niche programme options. These types of strategic policy assumptions exemplify what Born (2003: 775) refers to as 'projection: predictive, future-oriented discourses that are informed by the new kinds of abstractions and interpretations of past and present given by media analysts'; discourses that gain momentum in liberal-pluralist visions of a 'something for everyone' digital future. However, the proliferation of new technologies does not preclude the possibility that new oligarchies will develop in the new media environment. As the members of the Canadian Film and Television Production Industry (CFTPA 2002) argue, convergence is increasingly becoming a 'buzzword' that hides the tactics of vertically integrated companies to increase their global reach and push for actual deregulation of both foreign ownership and content regulations globally. This corresponds with media analysts' and some national regulators' (e.g. Britain's Ofcom) assumptions that digital switch-over and broadband distribution will aggravate the ability to enforce national content regulations, and may in fact lead to private network threats to dispense with their licences altogether (Jakubowicz 2006; Hoskins et al. 2001). From this perspective, PSB remains an important guarantor of culturally specific content as well as programming that does not conform to the dictates of commercial constraints or the 'walled gardens' of multi-media conglomerates (Steemers 2001: 74). Moreover, as cultural productions become increasingly commodified, global partnerships among PSB organizations provide a 'strength in numbers' approach to counter the increasing power of commercial media lobby groups in multilateral trade negotiations.

In the end, however, the future of PSB in a post-network era will be determined by content that remains universally accessible and speaks primarily to the unique demands of the diverse communities that reside within national borders, and secondarily to global audiences. Despite the predictions of globalization, the nation persists as the primary site of both policy and activism, and to that end PSB provides an important counterbalance to the commercial voices that promise to deluge the multi-platform media world. Indeed, the 'local' takes on a renewed importance as people search for 'secure moorings in a shifting world' (Harvey 1990: 301–4). PSB's most intangible yet valuable resource in a post-network era may be the enduring credibility and trust that remains the standard-bearer of most public networks. In this respect, international co-productions between PSBs are one example of the possibility of a 'virtuous circle of benign effects' where transnational storytelling may supplement rather than supplant the core national goals of public service broadcasting networks in an era of government withdrawal from the public sphere (Born and Prosser 2001: 686). So, contrary to Jacka's (2003) assertion, there is indeed a future for PSB in the new global media ecology – albeit a far different one than what was imagined 80 years ago.

Chapter 7

Approach with caution and proceed with care

Campaigning for the US presidency 'after' TV

Toby Miller

> The Internet is the new direct mail and talk radio of the 1980s, but instead of the Republicans leading the Democrats have control of this new medium.
>
> (JimVandeHei, founder of *The Politico*, quoted in Institute for Politics Democracy & the Internet 2007)

> This is ... the first campaign strongly shaped – even, at times, dominated – by the new media, from viral videos and blog reports that 'go mainstream' to profoundly successful online fundraising ... The rules have been changed forever – by technology ... This year's campaign, in fact, has been dubbed the 'YouTube Election' or 'The Facebook Election'.
>
> (Greg Mitchell, editor of *Editor & Publisher* 2008)

> 'I Got a Crush ... on Obama.'
>
> (YouTube, www.youtube.com/watch?v = wKsoXHYICqU)

After 15 years of predictions by business boosters and their cybertarian equivalents in academia, from management to media studies, we seem no closer to the collapse of television and the suzerainty of the internet. This is particularly true in the field of US electoral politics. Of course, hype in and of itself *is* evidence, as the first two fantastical epigrams above indicate. People believe these things, just as they believe in neoclassical economics and religion. Such beliefs have real, material implications, even if their origins lie in fictions. We have long been promised 'a golden era of politics' as the internet enters 'Americans' cultural imagination' (Cornfield 2006). Unless you regard the forms of democracy, policy making and programme management offered by George Bush Minor as 'golden', this may seem an overstatement. But perhaps the lowest rates of electoral participation in the First World are 'golden'.

As at July 2008, the US population's use of television, versus the internet and cell phones, to watch screen texts disclosed that TV was more popular than ever. People watched 127 hours of it a month, as opposed to spending 26 hours online and 2 hours with their cell phones. Video texts are mostly consumed on television and in real time: time shifting occupies just 5 per cent of spectators. People under the age of 24 spend fewer hours on the internet than older users, but watch more video. Those born between 1984 and 1990 – a desirable demographic both commercially and politically because their fundamental desires are not yet formed in terms of preferred brands – choose TV over the internet and the cell for both entertainment and information (Nielsen Media Research 2008b).

Yet faith in the internet as a transformative element in US politics that will transcend the unidirectional sway of television is widespread among activists and pundits, as these quotations illustrate:

> 2005 – The Year of the Digital Citizen.
>
> (*BBC News*, Twist 2006)

> 'We are ... returning to an era of participatory politics rather than broadcast politics.'
>
> (Jimmy Wales, founder of Wikipedia, quoted in *Mother Jones* 2007b)

> '[T]echnology is unleashing a capacity for speaking that ... was suppressed by economic constraint.'
>
> (Lawrence Lessig, founder of Creative Commons, quoted in *Mother Jones* 2007b)

> 'The future is now ... Everyone who reads these words is part of it.'
>
> (Brent Budowsky 2006)

> 'The Internet is the most important tool for redemocratizing the world since Gutenberg invented the printing press.'
>
> (Howard Dean, quoted in *Mother Jones* 2007b)

Internet salvation: harnessing an inherently democratic, interactive and communal medium, with the potential to instantaneously tap into the collective intellectual, political and financial resources of millions of fellow Americans to create a juggernaut for social change.

> 'Anybody with a little bit of effort, but not a lot of capital, can be heard by millions.'
>
> (Micah Sifry, cofounder of the Personal Democracy Forum, quoted in *Mother Jones* 2007b)

> 'The Internet provides us as a country and as individuals with unparalleled powers to turn information into ideas and ideas into action. It links us to each other, and to our neighbors here as well as around the world, enabling us to organize to solve problems, transform our economy, help foster security, better deliver public services, and build our democracy.'
>
> (*Personal Democracy Forum*, Rasiej et al. 2008)

These cybertarians invoke 'open-source politics', a new Eden where cynical machine politicos are displaced by open-hearted suburbanites, and centralized TV production gives way to universal amateur video. Party-political advertising is overwhelmed in this utopia by instantaneous flash mobs, which become the *leit motif* of the age (*Mother Jones* 2007a).

But the key elements to comprehending US politics are not cybertarianism or technology. They are as follows:

White men form the bloc that most frequently votes and is most conservative. They are responsible for Republican hegemony.

Electoral participation is abysmal by comparison with such vibrant democracies as India.

Disenfranchisement is huge and rising.

The cost of entry to elective office is gigantic and increasing.

The media have been freed of regulations requiring them to speak for the public good, under pressure from monopoly capital (for a useful account, see vanden Heuvel 2008).

So where do we stand in electoral media politics? Advertising expenditure is up at all levels of politics, from the presidency to Congress and the states, with TV dominant and the internet peripheral (*PQMedia Data* 2006; TNS Media Intelligence 2007). During the 2004 US presidential election, 78 per cent of the population followed the campaign on television, up from 70 per cent in 2000. Just 9 per cent routinely read political blogs, though the absolute numbers were very high on election day (Project for Excellence in Journalism 2005; Pew Research Center 2005; Gueorguieva 2007). Between the 2002 and 2006 mid-term elections, and across that 2004 campaign, TV expenditure on political advertising grew from US$995.5 million to US$1.7 billion – at a time of minimal inflation. That amounted to 80 per cent of the growth in broadcasters' revenue in 2003–4, for example (vanden Heuvel 2008: 34). The 2002 election saw US$947 million spent on TV election advertising; 2004 US$1.55 billion; and 2006 US$1.72 billion. The correlative numbers for the internet were US$5 million in 2002; US$29 million in 2004; and US$40 million in 2006 (Gueorguieva 2007). The vast majority of electronic electoral campaigning takes place on local TV – 95 per cent in 2007 (TNS Media Intelligence 2007; Bachman 2007).

The Obama campaign spent the vast majority of its energy and money on television. The US presidency cycles with the summer Olympics, broadcast by General Electric (GE) subsidiary NBC, but few candidates commit funds to commercials in prime time at this epic of capitalist excess, where the classic homologues of competition vie for screen time – athletic contests versus corporate hype. Obama, however, took a US$5 million package across the stations owned by GE: NBC (Anglo broadcast), CNBC (business-leech cable), MSNBC (news cable), USA (entertainment cable), Oxygen (women's cable), and Telemundo (Spanish broadcast) (Teinowitz 2008).

The lesson of new technology remains the same as ever: as per print, radio and television, each medium is quickly dominated by centralized and centralizing corporations, despite its multi-distributional potential. This centralism is obviously less powerful in the case of the internet than technologies that are more amenable to being sealed off. And the cost of producing electronic media of high quality has diminished, thanks to new technology. The cybertarian interpretation of this emphasizes the technical ease of entry for new players on new platforms, but the most influential change derives from the massive increase in political TV advertisements occasioned by this price reduction (Preston 2007). In terms of active participation through discussion of favourite texts, 79 per cent of the US population talk with neighbours, colleagues, families and friends about TV shows; 38 per cent exchange views about websites (Deloitte Touche Tohmatsu 2007).

There is now a history of notable electronic campaign successes and failures using new technologies: the first websites for candidates in 1996; emails from Jesse Ventura seeking the governorship of Minnesota in 1998; Howard Dean's blogs in 2003 and 2004; Bush Minor's house parties orchestrated through the internet in 2004; and the popularity of YouTube and MySpace in 2006. Howard Dean argues that YouTube 'basically turned the U.S. Senate over to the Democrats' (Gueorguieva 2007; Dean quoted in 'Politics 2.0' 2007). But 87 per cent of YouTube visitors are white, and just 0.2 per cent of visits involve posting videos; only 9 per cent of people read political blogs, and 75 per cent of them are men with average annual earnings of more than US $80,000 ('Politics 2.0' 2007). Well over half the people using YouTube in the United States are over 35, and MySpace is increasingly dominated by that group (Gueorguieva 2007). This doesn't look like a new age of politics to me.

After John Kerry's election defeat in 2004, many leading Democrats embraced blogs as a high-technology alternative to the Republicans' effective suburban organizing, hoping to use 'netroots' as opposed to congregations. Blogs were favoured because they were interactive, and inexpensive and quick by contrast with older media. This was the message from the party's 'blog evangelists' (Chaudhry 2006: 25). The results? In the 2006 mid-terms, 15 per cent of voters got their primary electoral information online, down from the 2004 campaign but twice the 2002 mid-terms, and just 25 per cent used the internet at all for political purposes. Those who did so generally visited not YouTube, not blogs, not MySpace but CNN.com and ABCNews.com – TV news sites. For more than 70 per cent of voters, television was their principal news source. It was the favoured medium for all genres, but its lead was greatest for election programmes (Rainie and Horrigan 2007). The Republican Party lost because of people's view of the war in Iraq as communicated on television, not because of the internet.

The evidence suggests that blogs are closed environments – few are read by anybody at all, and of those to do with politics, only a handful are popular. The reality is that class, race, money and age delineate blogs in terms of who

reads and cites them, with key male bloggers routinely hired as political con-
sultants. Many Congressional staffers and journalists are influenced by them,
but that does not amount to a new openness politically. Rather, it provides a
new tool for authors to tap into what public-opinion elites are expressing
(Chaudhry 2006: 28; Glaser 2007; Sroka 2006). Even true believers
acknowledge that 'the news' is elsewhere rather than embedded in new social
networks. So expressions such as 'MySpace made the news' (Gueorguieva
2007: 1) are common, offered in an unreflexive but telling way.

In 2008, YouTube set up You Choose, a sub-site of campaign videos, and
MySpace created The Impact Channel for profiles and requests for support
(Gueorguieva 2007). Of the two main parties' 16 candidates for nomination in
2008, 7 launched their campaigns online rather than in person. Ron Paul, a
nutty outlier ranting about the need to set the value of money via the gold
standard who eventually fell back into the ranks of fundamentalist anti-statism,
was an immediate hit with anti-Iraq war cybertarians who knew nothing
about politics. Using internet social networks, he raised an astonishing US$6
million in a single day early on, mostly from small contributors (*Economist*
2008). I don't wish to deride all these efforts. Who among us in cultural studies could fail to be pleased that, as at September 2008, Obama had half a
million friends on MySpace to McCain's 82,000? But let's be frank: people
who have seen candidate materials created for YouTube generally watched
them on television (Pew Research Center 2007). And website visits of candidates' campaigns in 2007 were negatively correlated with their electoral success in the primaries: Hillary Clinton was ahead of Obama, and the leaders on
the Republican side were Rudy Giuliani, Mitt Romney and Fred Thompson
(Bachman 2007). Where are they today?

As early as the northern spring, interest in the 2008 election was unprecedented (in the contemporary era). A third of the population followed media
coverage very closely; 40 per cent used the internet to do so, as opposed to 31
per cent at the same point in 2004, but just 6 per cent directly participated via
the internet, and 4 per cent via text messaging. Sixty per cent of online citizens saw the internet as a source of propaganda and misinformation, and only
a quarter felt connected to candidates through it (Smith 2008). We also know
that people involved in political debates in the United States who predominantly used cell phones rather than landlines for the purpose were more
affluent and more educated than those who didn't (Keeter 2008) – so enough
of being told how wonderfully inclusive and cross-class the cell world is!

I don't welcome these realities. TV continues to be intensely and inten-
sively reactionary. Content analysis shows that, at the conclusion of the primaries and prior to the conventions, the principal Anglo networks (ABC,
NBC and Fox) slanted their coverage massively in favour of McCain, albeit
with both candidates mostly criticized rather than celebrated or simply reported upon (Center for Media and Public Affairs 2008). And the cable news
networks – MSNBC, CNN and Fox News – dedicated much more airtime to

the August 2008 Republican Convention than the Democratic one (*Media Matters for America* 2008). During the conventions, key issues were essentially left uncovered by the media. The alibi for these events – that they enable voters to compare candidates based on their ability to make and implement policy – was simply left behind in a trail of gossip and personality. Iraq, Afghanistan and Russia were displaced by Biden, Clinton and Palin, and the economy disappeared from discourse (Sartor and Page 2008).

Why is this? The lapsed Australian plutocrat Rupert Murdoch is part of a long tradition of reactionaries who set up media outlets to further their cause. This heritage started with Alexander Hamilton and the Federalists, moved on through William Randolph Hearst and Sun Myung Moon, and culminated in the Dirty Digger's Fox News Channel. For all that Fox News is barely watched (1.5 million viewers out of a population of 300 million), it is a lightning rod for both bourgeois journalists and bloggers, ensuring that its influence – like that of the *New York Times* – transcends its limited direct appeal. Fox News matters not because its audience is the elite, as per the *Times*, but because its audience is powerless: the network largely appeals to white, uneducated people aged over 50. Their power is biennial, in that they vote more regularly than any other cohort in society, so their interests index where a vital psephological formation is heading. For good measure, Murdoch even purchased the paper Hamilton and his forces of darkness had started, the execrable *New York Post* (Shepard 2008a, 2008b). Fox News is a mouthpiece for the Republican Party, particularly via its dozens of pundits. In the words of Bush Minor's former press secretary, Scott McClellan: 'We at the White House were ... getting them talking points and making sure they knew where we were coming from' (quoted in Shepard 2008b).

The Right's assiduous cultivation of favourable outlets is twinned with a conspiracy theory about the evils of all other media. Instead of being dismissed by the mainstream, this illogicality has seen conventional journalists extend more and more positive coverage to reactionaries, especially during elections. Consider *American Thinker*, which argues that the US media 'have been one-sidedly Leftist' and are 'a tiny, unchecked power elite' who are single-handedly responsible for Democratic success and that only the new media can deliver power to conservatives (Lewis 2007).

When Bush Minor argued in 2004 that 'I'm not sure it's credible to quote leading news organizations', he was doing three things: appealing to his support base; denying endless scholarly proofs of the reactionary rather than progressive tilt of the bourgeois US media; and further frightening proprietors and editors (Bush Minor, quoted in Foser 2008). A case in point was when Sarah Palin was nominated as the Republican vice-presidential candidate by the McCain team. When questions were posed about her record, 'the story' quickly became the propriety of doing so, as the anti-media rhetoric of McCain effectively bought into decades of conspiracy theories by reactionaries.

Fox News and its fellow travellers maintain key links to the internet at an institutional level. So when *Insight*, part of Moon's media empire, claimed in 2007 that Obama was hiding his (of course non-existent) 'Muslim heritage', Fox News picked up the claim, and without any research repeated it over and over for an entire year, similar to the way it had tried to attack John Kerry's massively decorated war record in 2004 without a shred of evidence from eyewitnesses in support of Republican front organizations' claims that his medals were undeserved (quoted in Shepard 2008b).

The Democrats are far ahead of the Republicans in new-media terms. But is this an advantage? Even heavy users of the internet for political information regard it as significantly less reliable than television. They favour computers due to ease of access rather than credibility of content, and they do not see themselves as more likely to volunteer or vote in the election thanks to the internet. Young people are much more credulous and cybertarian than adult groups (Waggener Edstrom Worldwide 2008).

YouTube, Facebook and MySpace present both opportunities and problems for campaign managers. In 2006, MySpace garnered major media attention politically because it had a voter-registration drive, and YouTube for screening racist abuse from Republican Senator George Allen to a Democrat staffer and showing Republican Senator Conrad Burns snoozing in Congress – recorded and posted by Democratic staffers. Cheap exposure can lead to cheap *exposé*. There *is* less control over messages and their management, by contrast with what is achievable with the press corps. But is the outcome 'more natural, direct and honest' (Gueorguieva 2007)? New technology is already generating the hyper-discipline of TV, with semi-public moments subject to scrutiny after the fact, and pernicious re-editing distributed without even quasi-professional journalistic filters (Eggerton 2007).

YouTube encapsulates the asinine trivia of US electioneering. Each 2008 candidate had a channel. By mid-August, McCain's had been watched 9.5 million times, Obama's 52 million times. Three weeks later, the respective numbers were 14.5 million and 61.8 million. In February 2008, Will.i.am's 'Yes We Can' was launched. Within six months, it had been watched by 9 million viewers, at which point McCain's people released an advertisement that likened Barack Obama to Britney Spears and Paris Hilton. His celebrity standing was equated with theirs, his depth and seriousness as well. Within two weeks, it had been viewed 2 million times; Hilton had issued a spirited riposte in which she sardonically greeted 'the white-haired dude'; the Obama people had produced a counter-text via the 'Low Road Express' website; and other media had over-reported the controversy, even as they under-reported McCain's sordid business dealings, slavish devotion to US imperialism and corporate capital, and callous disregard for his first wife (*Economist* 2008).

By the time you read this chapter, you will know the identity of the US president as of 20 January 2009. Whoever that is, the post will be occupied by a bought politician. For the two party conventions of 2008, private sponsors contributed an estimated 80 per cent of costs, in return for guaranteed access to elected officials in the next administration. The parties' alibi is that these are local businesses seeking to assist their cities, but few donors were head-quartered in Minneapolis or Denver. The reality is that corporations were ensuring that whoever won in November, donor business interests had a central place in the West Wing in the new year (Campaign Finance Institute 2008). The message will be insistent from the voices that pay the most: law, finance and real estate (vanden Heuvel 2008: 33).

Internet or no internet, cell phone or no cell phone, cable or no cable, broadcast or no broadcast – the steadiest and most insistent drumbeat echoing in the January cold will be the political economy in its corporate mode. Whenever TV and internet campaigning merge in the United States, as will undoubtedly happen, this real political economy will still be in play, wielding its infernal magic for the umpteenth time. Media studies should devote less energy to trumpeting the internet over television, or vice versa. We must instead urge the media to take this everyday structural corruption to task. If he leads the way, I'll have a crush on Obama, too!

Chapter 8

Reinventing television

The work of the 'innovation' unit

Stuart Cunningham

Rumours of the death of television may be exaggerated, but there is no doubt that the head-in-the-sand option has long passed. Television audiences in aggregate have been slowly declining over some time. For example, in Australia, from a regular peak of more than three million per night in the 1990s, average prime-time audiences have fallen by several hundred thousand and there is no suggestion that this trend will abate in the future. Naturally, aggregate audiences remain comparatively very high compared with those for other media, but significant declines among young people are of particular concern to the longer-term future of the broadcast format. The 'death' of broadcasting is a staple of the IT and business press, and reaches its apogee in *Wired*'s (www.condenet.com/mags/wired) discourse and titles such as *Television After TV* (Spigel and Olsson 2004), *The Death of Broadcasting* (Given 1998) and 'Free-to-air TV Heading the Way of Vinyl Records, Says Media Expert' (Tabakoff 2008). It may even be implied in the title of this book.

Whatever the level of rhetorical investment, broadcast TV is widely regarded as a mature industry undergoing slow decline and being challenged fundamentally by viewer shifts to online and interactive engagement. Complicating this 'substitutionist' view – after all, as Brian Winston (1998) and most scholars of media and communications history attest, it is rare that media forms are definitively extinguished by the arrival of the new – this chapter explores the 'reinvention' of TV through: its interactions with new, internet and mobile media; experiments in the capacity of digital TV's interactivity; and specific units, often within public broadcasters, that are charged with innovation.

How is television reinventing itself in response to the major challenges to its long-term future? Can a mature industry make the necessary transition to a more fragmented market and a less hierarchical relationship to its 'user base'? As it examines the answers to these questions, this chapter also broadens the academic and disciplinary frame of reference for television studies to include innovation research.

'Hidden' innovation

Much innovation in the broad services sector of the economy – which includes media – has been 'hidden'. Services do not fit the standard definitions of R&D and innovation in the Oslo Manual (www.oecd.org/dataoecd/35/61/2367580.pdf), which is followed by most countries, and have been regarded until recently in standard economics as a merely residual category. There has been a belated recognition that advanced economies rely heavily on service industries not only for employment and aggregate GDP, but increasingly for sources of innovation and growth, overturning the received wisdom that they are economically parasitical, weak in export potential and lacking as productivity drivers. (Measures in many national and supranational innovation systems now, to some extent, are being developed to address this major gap.) It is also the case that, even as services innovation has received growing attention in both the academic literature and policy circles internationally, the burgeoning media, communications and entertainment industries have remained hidden (Crossick 2006; Cunningham 2004).

This chapter provides some insight into how television – still one of the largest components of these industries – innovates. Rather than approaching this from a 'top-down', systems-and-policy perspective (see Cunningham 2005), the chapter approaches the issue more inductively, through snapshots of actually existing organizational, production, delivery and engagement activity in three major public broadcasting organizations.

Media, culture and communications studies have had a well-established tradition of what might, from the current perspective, be regarded as innovation within film and television systems. This literature sought to bring out what was distinctive in the relations of production, output and vision of a 'creative ensemble' at a particular historical moment within a larger organization or industrial field, usually of mainstream entertainment. Most of this literature analysed the negotiation of difference, change or what we might now call innovation within the broader system. This so-called 'house style' focus had early predecessors in Hugh Fordin's (1975) study of the Freed Unit at MGM and David Pirie's (1973) *A Heritage of Horror* on the Hammer Studios in England. A crucial advance in the production house case study method was provided by Charles Barr's (1977) and John Ellis's (1975) work on Ealing Studios. Building on these studies, research into 'contexts of creativity' was continued by the Leicester Group (Murdock and Halloran 1979), among others, and full-blown production house case studies such as those on Euston Films (Alvarado and Stewart 1985) and MTM (Feuer et al. 1984) have been published. Approaches to the 'genius in the system' of creative innovation within television in the Australian context were developed by Moran (1982, 1985) and Cunningham (1988).

There is a small but growing innovation literature focused on the media and the broader creative industries as key, fast-growing parts of the service sector.

Consistent with the United Kingdom's growing policy interest in the 'creative economy', much of this has been generated out of one of its key policy research think-tanks, the National Endowment for Science, Technology and the Arts (NESTA). Studies of the business-to-business and employment links between the creative industries and firms in other sectors of the economy suggest that the creative industries may play a greater role in the United Kingdom's innovation system than has previously been recognized by policy makers (Higgs et al. 2008; Bakhshi et al. 2008). The importance of 'soft' innovation – constant improvement in services, processes, responsiveness, and functional as well as experiential design that affects potentially every member of society – comes to prominence (Stoneman 2007, 2008). Revealing the hidden innovation in advertising, independent broadcasting, games and product design sees these industries 'emerge as particularly innovative enterprises, in terms of technological and wider innovation' (Miles and Green 2008).

Why PSBs?

Why should public service broadcasting (PSB) be privileged in such a study? PSBs in most cases are governed by a charter or other form of statutory responsibility that includes a role as a 'market organizer' (Leadbeater and Oakley 1999) or a 'lead market' (Georghiou 2007). These are terms in the innovation literature to describe an agent in a market that sets itself the task of innovating or setting standards for, in this case, content production, procurement and delivery. Market organizers can also play this role by their sheer size as compared with other players in a market, although that is not regularly the case with PSBs, with the exception of the BBC and possibly Japan's NHK. As a 'demander' of innovative content and services, a PSB can play a role that is identified in the literature as public sector innovation.

PSBs also see themselves as providing essential R&D into their respective national broadcasting systems. PSBs typically straddle the boundary between the market and community or civic space. They have complex nation-building roles – delivering key information and news and current affairs unburdened by commercial interests, and thus performing a key informal educative function (and in so doing, maintaining a 'trust' relationship in a 'risk' society) – but also providing experimental domains for new technology and creative R&D, while connecting with a broad-based audience.

Bringing TV, PSBs and innovation together

The organizational studies/house style literature in media, cultural and communication studies highlighted the 'genius' in the system – how innovation occurred *within* the broadcasting system. The services innovation literature, and the place of television within it, allows us to focus more broadly on the contribution that such activity makes not only to a single information and communication system within society, but to wider systemic approaches to innovation.

The contemporary policy debates on broadening the focus on innovation suggest that there may be four areas within which innovation can meaningfully be examined. The dominant field is innovation based on science and technology, but in addition there are creative innovation, public sector innovation and social innovation. Public service broadcasters can play an important role in each of these dimensions. Science communication, as practised by PSBs, embeds an understanding of, and an appreciation for, scientific and technological advance in the citizenry, thus improving its capacity to absorb and adapt to innovation. PSBs play a major role in increasing the capacity of the independent creative production sector through their procurement and commissioning practices. This is also a major feature of public sector innovation, but we shall see others when the dynamism of a Channel 4 health promotion project is compared with government services. The chapter also profiles innovation in social engagement with children, teenagers and young adults.

ABC and the innovation unit

Australia has not experienced the degree of main market multi-channelling and audience fragmentation that many, if not most, major television systems worldwide have. ABC Director of Television Kim Dalton remains confident that 'there is no doubt that the bow of the ship is still the television in the corner of the living room' (quoted in Galvin 2008). Unlike its commercial competitors, the ABC can experiment and innovate with new technologies in a non- or pre-commercial environment. It is much more difficult for the commercial broadcasters to engage in risk and experimentation without a guaranteed revenue model for any new initiative. The traditional claim for major PSBs such as the ABC – that they play an overall R&D for the television system in a country – may have even greater credibility now, in the context of powerful technological, cultural and viewing changes, than it did a decade or more ago.

Technological change in broadcasting is critical to PSB innovation. One of the most obvious benefits of spectrum reform and digital delivery for the ABC is to be able to multi-channel to address the often non-commensurate, broad-ranging nature of its charter responsibilities. There is currently a very constrained multi-channel environment that will obtain in Australia for the near future, with only the two PSBs permitted to multi-channel. The ABC currently uses its second channel to replay the most popular programming and to address weak demographics for the ABC, such as young people.

The ABC's ideal multi-channel future is to add a dedicated non-commercial children's channel with at least 50 per cent Australian content, and an education channel providing English and other language tuition, curriculum material and a digital resource base for the newly developing national schools curriculum, with again at least 50 per cent Australian content to address teacher and student needs. This could be feasible from a technical and content supply perspective, but relies on the organization winning political support for increased funding, based on the now-refurbished PSB claim to be delivering qualitatively distinct elements into a fragmenting and globalizing information field (Scott 2008).

The ABC created an Innovation division in 2007 to drive 'strategic innovation and development in content creation, audience connection and new platform distribution in partnership with other divisions' (ABC Innovation intranet, accessed 1 April 2008). The innovation unit was created to act as a catalyst to help the organization 'move into the digital space'.[1] Its functions include managing purely online projects and portals, extending ABC content to new platforms and developing multi-platform opportunities. It is to develop and manage strategic projects for the ABC, including identifying key audience, industry and technology trends and capitalizing on the opportunities they present. It is also to develop R&D projects with other divisions that can be migrated outside of Innovation once established, and to provide specialist expertise and solutions to assist other divisions in developing new ways to connect with audiences.

The two sides to the innovation unit's role – managing the organization's online presence for usability and growth, and forward scanning and strategic development – are intimately linked. This is because the drive to repurpose and multi-platform all content (an efficiency drive) is also by its very nature an innovation drive. Digital technologies concentrated in the online space enable efficiency gains – the garnering of new audiences that may have been lost to the conventional broadcasting spheres – and drive cultural change within a large organization accustomed to coexisting in distributed and distinct silos.

It would be too much to claim that, within an organization employing well over 4,000 staff, the 15-person Innovation Strategic Development unit can materially effect dramatic cultural change. But it is the case that the flexibility and diversity of the Innovation unit – which is composed of producers, designers, developers, research, technical and creative directors – does offer a prototype of human resource management dedicated to innovation. It has a different culture from other divisions in the ABC: whereas content from the Television division must be perfect when it is launched, the Innovation division is trying to get things out in beta format and involve the public in the development process.

For example, the major initiative iView (www.abc.net.au/iview), launched in 2008, is a free internet TV service offering 'CatchUp', a short back-catalogue of popular programming, the latest news and current affairs, a children's fantasy channel, a selection of popular documentaries, an arts channel, and a channel through which rental or purchase of downloads can take place. ABC iView was developed in 'closed beta' format, using 5,000 people to test its capacity and usability and provide detailed feedback. About 3,000 people trialled the service, providing comments on a message board and engaging in online discussion. This is a software or games development model applied to the broadcasting environment.

The Innovation unit extends this IT/software model of R&D to the creation of prototypes. ABC Earth is an ABC content layer within the Google Earth application. It contains contemporary and historical ABC news content with up to 50 years' back catalogue of selected materials that have been geo-tagged. The purpose is to achieve proof of concept. The full rollout of such an application is beyond the resources – and possibly the role – of the ABC Innovation unit, but it is launched with a view to attracting interest in taking it further: 'We would be happy if other broadcasters and media companies created their own Google Earth layers and momentum was created behind the idea of using location based content in the ubiquitous Google environment.' While there are always resource constraints, real experimentation can be done on minimal budgets. A small downloadable 'widget' that sits on the desktop and brings together the best of the ABC's podcasts according to a user-pre-ference-driven menu (ABC Now – www.abc.net.au/now) is an example.

Another aspect of the Innovation unit's role is to partner with third parties around both the ABC's organizational cultural change and its innovation in the emergent digital media industry in Australia. A partnership with Deloitte to embed more formal processes for organizational innovation within a large organization has as its focus the Japanese-style releasing of the innovation ideas of all staff and, through a judging and selection process, the resourcing of innovation prototypes within the organization. The more externally focused 'AIMIA Innovatives' is a partnership with AIMIA, Intel, Deloitte and the ABC to provide multidisciplinary assistance in developing the fledgling digital media industry.

The ABC has positioned itself to take advantage of a policy and industry environment in which the choice to innovate is no longer optional. However, given its dominant PSB status, it has been less disposed to address the question of user-generated content than has a PSB-like Channel 4, which has reason to differentiate itself more radically from its 'big brother'.

Channel 4: public service beyond broadcasting

Channel 4, by virtue of its structure as, fundamentally, a commissioning and publishing entity, has assisted the creation of a highly successful independent sector currently worth about £1 billion. About 30 per cent of Channel 4's production capacity is sourced outside London's M25 orbital motorway. Again, because it is mainly a commissioner, broker and deal-maker, Channel 4 has always had porous boundaries and extensive partnerships. This extends to long-term relationships with regional players such as local universities. But I concentrate in this snapshot on the positioning of Channel 4 as a public service provider leading in social innovation.[2]

In the context of the British policy framework of creating public value (a demand-oriented approach to public service provision that focuses on measurable improvements in the lives of citizens) and in the timeframe of the possible contestability of the funding available through the licence fee in Britain, Channel 4 has innovated by developing a philosophy of public service media 'beyond broadcasting'. Channel 4 is using the interactive potential of digital media to refocus on public service.

Adam Gee describes his responsibilities as commissioner for factual cross-platform programming as a sort of 'de facto' R&D role – de facto because, as a relatively smaller broadcasting organization (about 800 employees compared with ITV's 5,000 and the BBC's 23,000 employees), Channel 4 has no formal R&D or innovation department.

An example of public service media 'beyond broadcasting' is the *Embarrassing Bodies* project (www.channel4.com/bodies, accessed 5 August 2008). In this project, Channel 4 addressed a series of public health issues to its audience base 'better than any government health service could'. The programming and website addressed an audience centred on its prime-time features viewers, but extending also to the teenagers and young adults who are a core demographic strength of the channel, with a level of 'risky' explicit nudity and direct information about self-examination of 'embarrassing' body parts rarely seen on public-service TV – or indeed on the web. The content, Gee says, was 'honest, unflinching, open and non-judgemental'. It also was prepared to risk engaging users coming from a prurient or tabloid perspective with a view to drawing them in to engage with the site's core preventive healthcare messages, addressing teenagers and young adults in particular on their own terms.

Embarrassing Bodies led with television content but springboarded from there to highly integrated online content, centred on specially commissioned broadband and mobile video and interactive components to complement the TV series. Early in 2008, *Embarrassing Bodies* went out as a 4 x 1-hour stripped programme screened at 10.00 p.m. and garnered a cumulative audience of 12–13 million. Online, the content over the launch week produced 3.5 million page views, 500,000 views of the self-check videos, 12,000 downloads to mobiles and 3,500 pre-moderated comments (as in-line comments adjacent to the editorial).

In its launch phase, *Embarrassing Bodies* was producing four times the online engagement rates being generated by the most popular Channel 4 entertainment programmes. The market research feedback suggested that the initiative had produced marked behavioural response and had made a significant impact in comparison to government health sites. The contrast with the NHS (National Health Service) Choices website (www.nhs.uk/Pages/homepage. aspx, accessed 7 August 2008) is stark. While both sites deal extensively with sensitive health issues using video clips and user forums, the NHS content is traditional talking heads and diagrams, and has little in the way of user-generated content. On the other hand, *Embarrassing Bodies* presents the content explicitly and with less formality, a richer mix of media and a more engaging creative approach. Adam Gee regards this is a good example of actually *defining* as well as realizing public value, and contrasts it with the 'difficulty' the BBC has talking to teens due to its position as a voice of authority – Channel 4 has a 'definite advantage' in that respect, being perceived as more rebellious and bold.

Another example is the Big Art Project (www.bigartmob.com, accessed 6 August 2008). This is an example of a huge extension of public service *into* the community. User-generated content, despite its seeming ubiquity, is in fact very hard to generate unless a supply-side organization can identify a public task that people consider worthwhile. The Big Art Mob project was designed to encourage widespread involvement by young people and art enthusiasts in mapping public art across the United Kingdom. Strategically neglecting to define what public art was or wasn't (beyond the narrow legal definition), Channel 4 set up a state-of-the-art cross-platform digital infrastructure (mobile with a very stripped-down and functional WAP interface, TV, web, together with real-life engagement), enabling virtually instant publication via mobile photography and uploading. Channel 4 had 4,000 pieces of user-generated content mapping the shape of public art across the United Kingdom within the first year of operation, with no media push behind it – just word of mouth. It has now been taken up and added to beyond the United Kingdom, in Europe, North America and Australia. All of this preceded major broadcast television coverage. The project has been nominated for three BAFTA TV awards before it has been officially broadcast, as well as winning an RTS (Royal Television Society) Award. It is a case of online, user-generated content in full flower before broadcast, and points the way towards online-led rather than broadcast-led projects.

A lot of the content and editorialization around the Big Art Mob project was moderated by the online community itself, and thus represents a departure for broadcasters for whom editorial control – and therefore moderation of user content – is mandatory. Engaging with user-generated content is not just about fashions: 'Just as we acted as a catalyst for growth of the independent production sphere in the last 25 years so we will want to repeat that in the digital sphere.'

Children's BBC (CBBC): building audiences for the future

The BBC was extensively reviewed recently. With the establishment of a trust to replace the BBC board, the BBC's charter was expanded to have it support 'sustained citizenship and civil society' and help in 'building digital Britain'.

With this charter-driven impetus, the BBC is called on to play a lead role in public sector innovation, demanding as well as providing leading-edge digital content and services. It is also charged with providing digital platforms that broaden a broadcaster's role from supplying content to enabling interoperability and connectivity for communities and government services. The BBC has a formal R&D unit, as would be expected of the world's leading PSB. However, it focuses strongly on technological change (www.bbc.co.uk/rd/milestones/index.shtml, accessed 8 August 2008). Instead of profiling this unit, I turn to what the BBC is doing about building audiences for the future.

CBBC (BBC children's interactive and on demand) has developed rapidly over a four-year period into a unit within the BBC which is distinctively pro-social in its focus on non-commercial address to children, innovative in the extent to which it brings broadcasting and online interaction together, and markedly popular among 0–12 year olds.[3] If children have grown up with the experience of the most engaging, tailored online and broadcast experiences, such innovation can help to secure a future for free-to-air broadcasting.

In a crowded market space of 26 channels for the 6- to 12-year-old age group, CBBC's channel share is 9 per cent. Because the ban on junk food advertising in 2004 decimated the potential advertising revenue for local UK content on many of these channels, Ofcom, exceptionally, found that there was market failure in children's content because of the lack of locally sourced content. CBBC has been left to lead the development of UK content in the digital television space in the United Kingdom.

There are different ways of progressing towards integration of linear and interactive experiences for children. CBBC has shifted from approaching the relationship between broadcast and interactive online as 'programme enhancement', to fuller integration between linear and interactive content and delivery. Previously, only about 20 per cent of programmes received online enhancement. There is 'reverse engineering' or 'programme enhancement' (where a linear television show is given an interactive layer) to what Marc Goodchild calls the '360 degree treatment' (a symbiosis, when a TV programme can't exist without its online partner and online can't exist without the TV show). An example of the 360 degree treatment is *Mi High*, a children's spy show that was second in the UK children's top programme list in April 2008. As Goodchild says: 'The show is screened each week, but there are narrative strands left hanging, so you go online and get stuck into a very immersive experience, continuing the narrative online. You are now the character – you are in the show.'

Conclusion

The social sciences literature on innovation places increasing importance on service industries rather than only on manufacturing, agriculture and mining. It is the contention of this chapter that entertainment and information services – in which television remains the major part – are critical to the way the population at large experiences and interacts with innovative practice. There is a tradition in our discipline fields of media, culture and communication studies that attends to the dynamics of aesthetic and organizational innovation, but it needs to be refreshed through engagement with contemporary social sciences approaches. The increasing focus in this literature on public sector innovation will reveal rich evidence of the reinvention of television within public service broadcasters, whose disposition, either formally or de facto, is to innovate in their organizational, technological and social dynamics.

Notes

1 Quotes and some background material in this section are drawn from an interview with Abigail E. Thomas, ABC Innovation, 19 June 2008, ABC Sydney.
2 Quotes and some background material in this section are drawn from an interview with Adam Gee, New Media Commissioner – Factual, in an interview at Channel 4, London, 19 May 2008.
3 Quotes and some background material in this section are drawn from an interview with Marc Goodchild, Manager, CBBC, 23 May 2008, BBC London.

Part Three

Television and social change

Introduction

> *Fry:* Trust me on this. While other people were out living their lives, I wasted mine watching TV, because deep down I knew it might one day help me save the world.
>
> (TV series *Futurama*)

Despite years of highly nuanced and rational academic accounts of what television can and cannot do, the contradictory idea of television as a provocateur both of change and of a complacent acceptance of the status quo is still prevalent, and sometimes even funny. The chapters in this Part investigate television's performance of both these functions as they examine the continuing and important role that television plays in organizing, generating and communicating change in a variety of political contexts. There is a particular concentration in this Part on the Asian markets. Not only is China now the largest television market in the world, but the partnership between the commercialization of global television and significant structural and social change across much of South and East Asia has been of profound significance. In this region, the social order is still unfolding – sometimes in response to drastic political or environmental shifts – and television is often implicated in the process through which new social formations have emerged – or indeed through which the state has intervened.

The most trenchant account of this latter iteration of the process comes from Sun and Zhao's chapter on the social contexts within which the marketization of the Chinese media has occurred. The provocation for their discussion is the common perception that China's gradual entry into global media markets has carried with it significant and liberalizing social and political changes. Sun and Zhao's powerful piece categorically refutes suggestions that the marketization of the Chinese media industries might be read as the beginnings of a form of democratization; they demonstrate that, at least so far, market change has not necessarily generated an equivalently liberalizing agenda of social change. The new factual yet entertaining formats that dominate the Chinese market, as well as those elsewhere, may proffer legal and technical guidance to audiences as means of arming the new citizenry in the new marketplace. However, Sun and Zhao argue that what remain to be effectively addressed are the fundamental mechanisms masking the ideological and political structures that protect long-standing social inequality.

Moving on to the smaller Chinese-language markets in the region, Jinna Tay pays attention to the rise of the regional Chinese popular market and the trend towards various forms of deregulation in Singapore, Hong Kong and Taiwan. China's indirect influence in the region is a mental and economic hurdle that must be addressed by these markets in the long term, necessitating industrial change. Furthermore, the productive aspects of content development and distribution have become key strategic issues, as well as factors contributing to the possible futures of these national/regional media and television industries. While they operate within a highly competitive international market, the underlying platforms upon which these industries are based have at times been strenuously regulated by their national governments. The nature of the regulatory, or deregulatory, control works to define – or indeed limit – the context within which any industrial or cultural development can occur.

Zala Volcic's analysis of the role of television in the Balkan region provides us with a most explicit demonstration of television's imbrication into a programme of social and political change aimed at determining the character of newly formed nation-states. As she describes it, television has been put to work in the service of what Morley calls 'born again nationalism' (2004: 317) as it produces highly politicized television that nonetheless sets out primarily to entertain. Volcic's analysis of this phenomenon, which she labels 'commercial nationalism', refers to a unique blend of emergent popular culture that is tightly articulated to an invented nationalism. Here she describes how television constructs its nationalist myths and discourses virtually out of thin air, as the neophyte nation-states embed historical discourses of national identity within new forms of commercial television programming. Given the content of many of these discourses, the regressive potential of this development for the nation-states in the region is significant. It is a strong reminder that, while many of the chapters in this book describe the resilience and persistence of the national within what many would call a post-national media environment, it is important to remember that the social and political potential of nationalism is not necessarily benign.

While television is shown to be still deeply implicated at the national level in these developing nation-states, it is useful to move towards one of the more mature (inter)national industries to examine how television there relates to its national context. Stephanie Donald uses the BBC production of *Robin Hood* as a text through which the processing of versions of nationalism and power may be analysed and critiqued as reflecting significant changes in the social construction of a British national identity. Like Volcic, Donald demonstrates how television works as a dissonant object, promoting both disjuncture and historical continuity, simultaneously and synchronically. Her argument is that television texts and public memory often move anachronistically – that television at times is a reference point *for* national reflexivity, rather than *the* conversation where such reflexivity occurs. So the text is a site for limited polyphonic convergence, where social change may be reflected, but not in ways that are necessarily coherent. Television now addresses its audiences in a more sophisticated manner and across a wider variety of genres, subjects, formats and media platforms than ever before. Both Donald's chapter and Sun and Zhao's remind us of the crucial issue of the audience's agency in that context, and the importance of the audience's public memory, their level of consumer 'savvy', and their individual capacity to participate and respond within particular political and spatial locations.

Chapter 9

Television culture with 'Chinese characteristics'

The politics of compassion and education

Wanning Sun and Yuezhi Zhao

On 12 May 2008, an earthquake measuring 8 on the Richter scale hit Wenchuan and its neighbouring towns in Sichuan province, killing upwards of 70,000 people and leaving millions homeless. For two weeks after the quake, China Central Television (CCTV) covered the rescue and relief efforts live, 24 hours a day. Dramas of survival were emotionally powerful and morally uplifting, and viewers were moved to tears by countless examples of selflessness and heroism. A nation of television viewers, including survivors of the earthquake, was overwhelmed by the unconditional support shown by both individual citizens and the central government. One week after the earthquake, on 18 May, the network hosted an evening-long television event titled *Dedication of Love: Raising Funds for Victims of the Earthquake*. Musical performances were interspersed with a seemingly endless procession of celebrities, most of them household names, filing past the camera and, with both hands, slipping an envelope containing money through a slot in the large donation box onstage. To the tune of songs such as 'We are All Brothers and Sisters' and 'Let Love Fill the World', the programme's hosts waxed lyrical: 'Let the spring breeze of harmony sweep across the entire nation, for it's our Party and socialism that see us through these difficult times.'

After viewing such a spectacle, one could be forgiven for thinking that, thanks to three decades of economic reform and market liberalization, China enjoys unprecedented harmony despite stratified socio–economic interests and rural–urban inequalities. Viewers saw images of grateful rural folk being saved by brave soldiers and generously helped by city residents. Nobody was encouraged to remember that, not long before the earthquake, the same people – mostly from disenfranchised rural communities – were battling with exorbitant agricultural taxes, inadequate welfare, sub-standard infrastructure and schools, mounting educational costs, and a lack of affordable public medical care. The names of the earthquake-affected counties, such as Wenchuan and Mianyang, previously imagined as little more than poverty-stricken supply zones for cheap labour to large urban centres, were now a metaphor for national solidarity.

The profound impact of these television events seems on the surface para-doxical: while viewers clearly knew they were being fed 'propaganda', as this is usually understood in the West, nevertheless they were palpably moved by it and could not get enough of it. But to suggest that socialist-style propaganda is still the only game in town after three decades of economic reform would be simplistic. In fact, a reconfigured regime of state control has incorporated more subtle techniques of discursive domination rather than blunt censorship, and the highly fluid dynamics of domestic and transnational market forces, the profit imperatives of private investors, the agency of media producers and an active television audience have interacted to create a highly dynamic and multi-faceted popular television culture in reform-era China. Within this 'polysemic and hybrid' Chinese discursive universe, official propaganda, middle-class social reformist sensibilities and popular concerns for hot social issues all jostle to be heard (Zhao 2008a: 216; Zhao and Guo 2005: 534). Furthermore, to suggest that China is still a nation of political subjects easily duped by state propaganda is equally misleading. As one seasoned television viewer put it: 'We know that TV only shows us what the government wants us to see, but that doesn't mean it's not worth watching. After all, I can always go to the internet if I want to get a different perspective.'[1]

To appreciate the 'polysemic' and 'hybrid' nature of Chinese television, one only has to turn to a well-established but still growing body of literature documenting the development of Chinese television, especially in regard to funding, ownership, censorship, regulation and institutional restructuring (Zhao 1998, 2008a, 2008b; Zhao and Guo 2005). The peculiar status of being government owned but operating as a business gives Chinese television at all levels – national, provincial and local – a distinctive, complex and often para-doxical outlook. This paradox can be seen through the prism of, for instance, format innovation and industries (Keane 2002a, 2002b); advertising and com-mercial culture (Wang 2008); the cultural politics of storytelling, particularly in television drama, China's most popular television genre (Keane 2001, 2005; Zhu 2008; Zhu et al. 2008; Sun 2007); and televisual texts as public culture (Rofel 2007; Lu 2000; Sun 2008, 2009a), as well as the politics of television spectatorship, particularly that of subaltern viewers (Sun 2009a, 2009b).

What is still largely missing from these works is an analysis of how television as a visual technology of storytelling and subject making articulates with the broad political economy of China's ongoing social transformation during the era of a worldwide 'neoliberal revolution' (Robison 2006: vii). To be sure, China is not an 'openly committed neoliberal capitalist social formation' (Zhao 2008b: 26). As a matter of fact, the Chinese state has continued to proclaim its commitment to socialism throughout the reform era. However, to the extent that China's reform programme has led to the 'construction of a particular kind of market economy that increasingly incorporated neoliberal elements interdigitated with authoritarian centralized control' (Harvey 2005: 120), it is easy to speak of 'neoliberalism with Chinese characteristics' (Harvey

2005) or the materialization of a particular form of neoliberalism in China (Breslin 2006; see also Wang 2003). Accordingly, the political economy and cultural politics of Chinese media transformation have been defined by an ambiguous and paradoxical process that has witnessed the progressive applications of the neoliberal strategies of market rationalization on the one hand, and the continuing and indeed intensified (re)articulation of China's socialist legacies on the other (Zhao 2008a, 2008b).

Neoliberal governance champions the logic of 'depoliticized politics' (Wang 2006) and depends on 'market knowledge and calculations for a politics of subjection and subject-making' (Ong 2006: 13). As the most far-reaching popular medium in reform-era China, television has a crucial role to play in translating neoliberalism into a specific set of moral-economic values and in producing knowledge that helps neoliberal citizen-subjects to survive market turbulences and cope with the destructive social impacts of an increasingly entrenched neoliberal economic order. This chapter addresses the cultural politics of neoliberal subject making in reform-era China by exploring a dual process that has become an imperative for Chinese television. In the first part, we explore an intriguing process by which television both exploits a socialist ethos of altruism and appropriates a socialist style of communication – a style that is familiar, even endearing, to many Chinese viewers – to manufacture 'cross-class love' in this era of accelerated class polarization and intensified social conflicts in a neoliberal market economy. This is followed by an analysis of a parallel process by which television, a technology of the self, assists both the state and the market in the ongoing business of turning its national viewers into functioning neoliberal subjects. This two-pronged phenomenon, we argue, is a defining feature of the cultural politics of China's ongoing transformation, and as such is crucial to our understanding of the social semiotics of power on post-Mao television.

The manufacture of cross-class love in a class-divided society

Since 1978, China has gone through a tumultuous period of social and ideological change. Starting with the replacement of the Maoist faction with pragmatic leaders in 1978, the first phase (1978–89) was largely a period of 'socialist self-adjustment' (Lin 2006: 271), in which the principal aim was the renovation of a system that had stagnated politically and economically, and was effectively on the brink of crisis. However, this initial period of 'socialist self-adjustment' itself led to the crisis of 1989. The political repression of 1989 set the context for more than a decade (1989–2003) of radical economic liberalization – the second phase of economic reform. Deng Xiaoping's ideological pragmatism resulted in unparalleled economic growth and a burgeoning consumer culture, as well as drastic economic stratification and widespread social inequality. So when Hu Jintao and Wen Jiabao came to power late in

2002, they were confronted with the task of repairing the social and ecological damage wrought by the previous 'long decade' of unchecked economic growth. The new leadership ushered in a third phase of restructuring (2003 to date), adopting a series of adjustment measures to build a 'people-oriented' and harmonious society characterized by 'coordinated and sustainable development' (Lin 2006: 276). This is also a period that saw the escalation of social conflicts, the intensification of elite and popular debates in the mass media and especially on the internet on the future directions of China's reform process, and the leadership's elevated rearticulation of its commitment to socialism in theoretical and ideological fields (Zhao 2008a). Because the leadership has vowed to deepen market-oriented reform while remaining committed to socialism, these developments have led to the further entrenchment of an ambiguous and seemingly contradictory coexistence of 'neoliberal strategies, socialist legacies' in the political economy and cultural politics of Chinese development (Zhao 2008b: 23).

With neither external colonies to exploit nor favourable international trade terms from which to benefit, China achieves its own industrialization and 'primitive accumulation' by the ruthless extraction of its domestic agricultural surplus and the exploitation of its vast rural population. Since its implementation in the late 1950s, China's long-standing and deeply ingrained household registration (*hukou*) system has effectively differentiated the nation along urban–rural lines, with up to 70 per cent of the population having rural *hukou*. While recent reforms in the *hukou* system have made it possible for 'ruralites' to work in the city and provide cheap labour for the country's rapidly expanding manufacturing and service sectors, the system remains discriminatory, since rural migrants – despite their indispensable economic role in the city – are still not entitled to urban privileges, including employment (especially in the public sector), public education, public health cover, subsidized housing and a wide range of other state-provided benefits (Wang 2005; Solinger 1999; Jacka 2006; Zhang 2002). This de facto class-based apartheid is particularly acute culturally, since the market has not helped to create an alternative cultural and media system outside official and urban-oriented cultures (Zhao 2008a). In addition, since the 'new normative figure of citizenship is the person endowed with high cultural capital and the power to consume', this is a 'norm from which peasants and workers are mostly excluded ... because their access [to] education and urban residence is blocked by structural inequalities' (Anagnost 2008: 499). Of course, socio-economic stratification is played out not only along the rural–urban divide, but also between the emerging economic elites and the urban poor. The richest 10 per cent of the urban population own 45 per cent of the assets in urban China, compared with 1.4 per cent owned by the poorest 10 per cent (Zang 2008). Public anger at the new rich in China is thus understandable, and popular anxiety over class polarization is particularly acute in a society that not only has strong egalitarian legacies but also continues to proclaim its allegiance to socialism.

How, then, do we read spectacles of socialist fantasy, such as the one that begins this chapter, against the backdrop of an entrenched market economy, widespread possessive individualism and consumer culture, and the dramatically reconfigured post-Mao social landscape of class polarization and social stratification? Here it is useful to note that this fundraising television event began with a chorus singing 'Aide Fengxian' (Dedication of Love). Most television viewers in China over the age of 35 could not have failed to recognize the ideological import of this intertextual reference. In 1989, Wei Wei, then a young and attractive but not yet famous singer, had sung 'Dedication of Love' for the Spring Festival Gala on national television, to accompany a story about a migrant woman from Anhui province who went to Beijing to become a live-in domestic worker. Two years later, this rural migrant was diagnosed with a spinal disease and her employer threw herself into caring for her. The caregiver became the recipient of care. This admirable deed moved many people around her, and they dug deep into their pockets. With their donations, the migrant woman was able to pay for a major operation, after which she recovered and was able to live an independent life again.

The song that launched Wei Wei's singing career in 1989 was unforgettable, in part because of what happened during the song itself: the rural migrant at the centre of the story was ushered into the television studio to embrace her former employer, reality TV style. To thunderous applause from tearful spectators, the appearance of this rural woman brought the evening's performance to an emotional crescendo, making it one of the most memorable moments in the history of CCTV. Nineteen years later, Wei Wei was back in CCTV's studio for the earthquake memorial, singing the very song that had made her famous, at an event that has also been dubbed 'Dedication of Love'.

The take-home message for audiences of the post-quake spectacle is clear: the CCP cannot be blamed for adversities such as natural disasters, disease and poverty, and should not be expected to solve all these problems, but it should certainly be credited with delivering love and compassion. In addition to showcasing the superiority of socialism and extolling collectivist virtues such as selflessness, personal sacrifice and allegiance to the Party, these 'indoctritainments' are also charged with the discursive task of generating cross-class love, a scarce commodity in post-Mao Chinese society. In these moral configurations, love and compassion are presented as the only solution to what are basically social and political issues. As Wei Wei sang: 'As long as everyone gives a bit of love, we'll have a beautiful world.' The production of cross-class love, embodied by this television event and others like it, represents the enduring potency of, and a renewed appreciation for, depoliticized socialist values that have been emptied of their original class content. In the year of the Beijing Olympics, with the Chinese leadership feeling more than ever the palpable threat to its legitimacy from mounting class-based discontent, the call for compassion that began on the cusp of the second and third phases of economic reform has now become a deafening roar.

The discursive project of producing love is not limited to the sort of sporadic television spectacles mentioned so far. It also emerges in the quotidian space of television narratives, and often in news and current affairs. In fact, to consume Chinese news media regularly in post-Mao China, whether through state television or commercial newspapers, means being constantly moved to tears by the helplessness of 'the victim' and the generosity of 'the helper'. Over the past decade or so, this species of journalism has increasingly been practised as a way of raising money for individuals in need. Day in and day out, urban readers/viewers/listeners are bombarded with heartrending images and sad stories, and are urged to 'donate love' (*xian ai xin* – literally 'give your loving heart') by sending money to the deserving, whether it be a migrant worker who needs an astronomical sum for her child's medical procedure, or the family of a peasant who commits suicide because he cannot find money to pay for his son's university fees.

The production of the neoliberal subject in a nominal socialist polity

Notwithstanding the phenomenal impact of Dedication of Love-style televisual spectacles, they alone cannot effectively address fundamental inequalities. What is also needed, at a minimum, is a discursive mechanism that provides quotidian guidance in a time of rapid social transformation. Here we suggest that, in order to understand television as a technology of social engineering, we need to go beyond television dramas and entertainment-oriented media formats and focus on an emerging genre on Chinese television that refracts social transformation in much less spectacular yet equally profound ways. We are referring to a constellation of television programmes that can collectively be described as '*ji shi*'. Translated literally, *ji shi* documents, reports or truthfully records. It implies that the people and events in these programmes are real and factual, and that the stories – like those in current affairs and investigative reports – are 'true'. Three examples will suffice to illustrate this genre.

The first comes from a television show called *Chuanqi Gushi* (Legends and Stories), a regular spot on the nationally accessible Jiangxi provincial satellite television in south-east China. The show is well known to audiences nationally for its riveting narrative and the personal touch of its host. On 11 May 2008 this show screened a story entitled 'Mother Under Contract', about an elderly rural woman and her two sons and two daughters. The woman lived with her unmarried younger son, who had been depriving her of food in the hope of starving her to death. She fainted a few times from hunger, but each time was rescued by concerned neighbours. The village chief intervened and called in all four siblings. After protracted negotiations, three of them agreed that the older son be made 50 per cent responsible for caring for their mother, while each of the married daughters would be 25 per cent responsible. The younger son refused to be involved. The programme concluded with this comment from the host: 'One can write a contract in relation to land or a business, but can one write a contract in relation to one's mother? People's behaviour needs to be regulated by morality, not by negotiation.'

The second example is from Jiangsu Satellite TV, a nationally accessible channel from Jiangsu province on China's eastern seaboard. On 21 July 2008, *Renjian* (Human World) ran a story titled 'Odd Bed-fellows Elope'. Despite protests from his five children, a chronically ill 90-year-old widower decided to marry his rural maid (*baomu*), 46 years his junior. He prepared a new will bequeathing all his assets to his new wife, which left his children without an inheritance. When his children learnt of this decision, they were enraged. Wilfully ignoring their father's intentions, and without troubling to wait for the old man's death, they sold one of his properties, a flat that was intended for his new wife. A lawsuit ensued, and conflict escalated between the couple and his children, with the latter repeatedly abusing their new step-mother, calling her a 'gold digger'. Fearing for their own safety and desperately seeking a quieter life, this odd couple went into hiding.

What are the socio-economic factors that account for the couple's respective motives for marrying each other? How are gender, class and rural–urban inequality played out in their marriage? The programme attempted no answers to these questions. Instead, it brought in independent legal professionals to shed light on the murky legal and ethical issues involved. The programme ended with the host giving this advice to the children: 'Marriage is protected by law, and you have no choice but to respect your father's legal rights.'

The third example comes from the Law Channel (CCTV 12). On 5 March 2008 its flagship programme, *Falu Jiangtan* (Law Forum), ran a story titled 'Crime and Punishment: A Fatal Abortion'. A doctor in a county hospital in Liaoning province performed an ultrasound scan on a pregnant woman and, succumbing to bribes, revealed the gender of the foetus to his patient. On being told that she was having a girl, the woman's family arranged for a village doctor to perform an illegal abortion, only to realize afterwards that it was a boy. Enraged and bitterly regretful, the woman's family sued the village doctor. An investigation followed, as a result of which the county doctor lost his licence to practise and the village doctor was sentenced to 10 years' imprisonment. As is often the case, this personal tragedy ended with legal and medical professionals reminding audiences of the need to know the law.

Televisual narratives such as these form the staple diet of most 'serious' non-entertainment channels on Chinese television. Combining on-location, reality TV style footage with current affairs style interviews, these stories may differ in details, but they often have some important things in common. First, they belong to an emerging television genre that turns private experiences into public narratives. They are human-interest stories of ordinary people making everyday decisions, of adjusting ethical and moral positions in a dramatically transformed social order. Second, the tragedies and dilemmas of individuals are presented as needing either a moral solution, as in the first example, or a technical solution – be it legal, medical or economic – as in the second and third examples. These stories provide the moral compass and the practical knowledge (legal, economic, scientific) that modern citizens need in order to survive the market environment. Routinely carrying statements from academics, professionals and policy makers that advise citizens of their rights and responsibilities, these stories present moral improvement, science, the law, medicine and education as logical solutions for the problems of contemporary Chinese society. It is also worth noting that these programmes are popular with viewers from disenfranchised social groups. Some migrant domestic workers explained that, while they enjoyed watching entertainment shows such as television dramas, they preferred programmes such as law and order, economics and science documentaries – programmes that 'taught them something'. Many migrant workers found these programmes useful, as they said they could acquire valuable information about how the law worked, while also improving their understanding of their rights as citizens. They also liked the fact that these shows often packaged this information in a 'good story'.[2]

The third and most significant common feature among these narratives is that they present human tragedies as either incidental or inevitable, all the while failing to acknowledge the social and political causes of individuals' suffering, which include lack of social welfare (especially for senior citizens), adequate healthcare (particularly in rural areas), and policies and practices that contribute to systemic gender discrimination. These are social issues for which both the causes and solutions must be seen as political and ideological – not, as neoliberalism would have us believe, as merely technical and scientific. Thus, while we agree that Chinese television documentaries may go some way towards meeting the challenge of *jie huo* (addressing the public's sense of bewilderment) in a confusing and fast-transforming society (Chu 2008), we do not see this trend as inherently democratic, despite its tendency to focus on 'ordinary people'. The *ji shi* genre – including discourses of compassion (Sun 2009a), CCTV's *Focus Interviews* (*Jiaodian Fangtan*) style of investigative journalism that functions as 'watchdogs on party leashes' (Zhao 2000, 2004) or CCTV's *Oriental Horizon* (*Dongfang Shikong*) style of television news magazines that offer 'morality discourse in the marketplace' (Xu 2000) – is at once socially conservative and progressive, simultaneously supporting and contradicting the dominant social forces. Neither spectacles of love nor narratives of personal challenge set out to lay bare and dispute the underlying social causes that make human compassion so rare and individual dilemmas so ubiquitous in the first place.

Conclusion

Given the deepening of structural inequalities in post-reform China, how to channel the desires and disappointments of the largest cohort of viewers in the history of television is the supreme challenge for CCTV's ever-expanding suite of channels and, to a lesser extent, for some of the ambitious provincial satellite networks aiming to secure a national audience. Consequently, a discursive regime has been put in place to provide both timely moral anchoring for the nation and practical and continuous orientation for individual citizens' self-development projects. The implicit assumption of this regime is that social conflicts will be resolved if two conditions are met. First, citizens from privileged echelons must develop a capacity for compassion; and second, everyone – particularly those from the marginal spaces – must equip themselves with the knowledge and outlook that are commensurate with their status as modern citizens.

If the neoliberal market economy has led to unchecked capitalism and social discontent, attempts to ameliorate this seem to adopt strategies that are no less neoliberal. Such strategies 'recast governing activities as technical rather than political and ideological' (Ong 2006: 3), while also cultivating 'self-governing' and 'self-engineering' subjects (ibid.: 2006: 6) who can cope with the downside of economic liberalization alone or by helping each other, but in either case without becoming an economic burden on the state. The Chinese central leadership and its political think-tanks often evoke a clichéd phrase, 'socialism with Chinese characteristics', to rationalize many contradictions in the nation's economic reforms. It is in the juncture between neoliberal strategies and socialist legacies that we can start to appreciate the 'Chinese characteristics' of China's television culture. Whereas, in Mao's era, dramas of phantom-like, class-based hatred were staged ritualistically in an effort to forge a proletarian consciousness, in the post-Mao era, a theatre of equally phantom-like cross-class love needs to be regularly performed, with the aim of dissolving, like sophisticated camera work, a background of social tension that is still essentially class based. In this historical phase marked by the contradiction between socialist legacies and neoliberal strategies, nowhere else are the ambiguities and paradoxes more vividly captured than in the television programmes that offer sublime moments of high morality on special occasions, and mundane and practical guidance on a daily basis.

Notes

1 This viewer, based in Anhui Province, China, spoke to Wanning Sun on 22 May 2008 by telephone.
2 Wanning Sun's fieldwork interviews with rural workers took place in 2005–6 in Beijing.

Chapter 10

Television in Chinese geo-linguistic markets

Deregulation, reregulation and market forces in the post-broadcast era

Jinna Tay

Introduction

As part of a larger comparative study on television in the post-broadcast era, this chapter takes a series of comparative snapshots of current developments in the Chinese geo-linguistic market: in China, Hong Kong, Singapore and Taiwan. In particular, it focuses on the progress towards market liberalization and on television's role as a nationalizing medium within the more general process of modernization in the region. The development of each of these markets has its specific nuances and national characteristics. The key trend is towards marketization, one of the outcomes of what is often described as a liberalization of the industry. But how this occurs, in what shape or form, and the effects on the culture of the nation-state as well as their television industries, differ in each of these locations.

The often-quoted work of Joseph Straubhaar on cultural proximity (1991) as an explanation for the success of imports and flows of media products across national borders has resulted in the understanding that audiences first prefer their own local national content, and then regional content that lends itself to cultural familiarity (Sinclair 1999). However, cultural proximity is also widely used as a means of capturing a general sense of cultural approximation rather than explaining the specifics of the regional cultural exchange. Hence, Iwabuchi (2002: 135) cautions against over-deterministic readings based on a presumed commonality while suggesting instead that we need to further interrogate precisely *how* the relations are proximate. This chapter is, to some extent, a response to that suggestion.

The chapter builds on the common cultural links between the four geo-linguistic Chinese markets in question here. They share a historical past, language (written and spoken Mandarin, variations of dialects), ethnicity (Han), and cultural practices linked to religions and rituals such as Chinese Lunar New Year/Spring Festival, Mooncake Festival and Qingming Day (equivalent to All Saints' Day). These shared social and cultural attributes have a material and ritual aspect that lends itself to regional circulation, participating in a wider received notion of the history and performance of Chinese-ness. Shared knowledge of common mythologies and parables further allows television historical dramas, novels and supernatural tales to recapture characters such as Nezha or the Monkey King and to retell the tales of the Eight Immortals for audiences young and old. These loosely structured socio-cultural links help create something of a shared present, which has recently been intensified, due to the economic opening up of the PRC, the return of Hong Kong to the PRC, Taiwan and the PRC's move to a more conciliatory position of sorts, and thus a possible indication of a tighter regional collaboration based on growing economic proximity and shared cultural tastes.

Pop culture China

Watching television in Asia now, one is spoilt for choice. From pay TV to free-to-air (analogue or digital HD) TV, audiences can choose from glocal or imported, fact or fiction, education or entertainment, live variety or scripted dramas, music, news, documentaries, sports, fashion, lifestyle – the list goes on. Pay TV offers a wide selection of languages: English, German, French, Hindi, Chinese, Japanese and Korean. And this does not include internet television. This multitude of choices emphasizes the scale of the changes that have occurred in Chinese television over the past two decades. These changes can be considered as more or less a reflection of the national interests and ongoing economic development of the state concerned. The television systems in three of these four locations began as a state apparatus directed to inform, educate and control the population (Lau et al. 2008), and to pursue the purposes of nation building (*New Straits Times* 2000). Television arrived at around the same time in each locale: Singapore in 1963, Hong Kong in 1963, Taiwan in 1962 and the PRC in 1958. However, the more recent story of each industry's deregulation and marketization has unfolded quite differently, as each history has been played out to the tune of its national political dramas. At the same time, they have also participated in the development of a Chinese popular culture that is not contained within national boundaries. China may be the most powerful and sizeable participant in this popular culture, but it is not necessarily leading the way in terms of content, style or influence.

Historically, Hong Kong has the most developed television market and system, due to its initial free-market operation in the British colony. Television serials from TVB have long had a regional presence on free-to-air television, its Cantonese dramas sometimes dubbed into Mandarin and played across such countries as Malaysia, Singapore, Taiwan and China (Curtin 2007), or accessed via pirated videos in the 1980s, then VCDs and now legitimate DVDs. While Hong Kong films have had their highs and lows (Curtin 2007), Hong Kong television serials have always enjoyed a popular reception in the region. Even now they are played in prime-time slots across homes in Singapore, Taiwan and the PRC. Today, however, there is a much broader market of cultural production and exchange that involves the whole East Asian region.

I argue that the sheer size and momentum of this regional exchange in media production and consumption – which involves the trade in media texts and celebrities as well as co-productions and collaborative financing arrangements – is a new phenomenon (also noted by Fu and Wildman 2008), even if it may have become entwined within the popular journalistic hyperbole of the 'Asian Century'. The evidence for such exchange occurs across the entire entertainment sector. Jay Chou, Rain and boy band F4 have sold out concerts even in places where Chinese is not a dominant language, such as the Philippines, Indonesia and Malaysia (http://male.thedailymodel.com/jay-chou). Other regional celebrities who preceded this crop, such as Andy Lau (Fung 2003), Faye Wong (Fung and Curtin 2002), Jackie Chan, Tony Leung and Chow Yuenfatt, have gone on to become international names. Popular phrases such as the J-Wave and the K-Wave have been used internationally to reference the Chinese-language market's popular uptake of television and film texts from Japan and Korea respectively; C-pop and M-pop have become standard shorthand terms for Cantonese or Mandarin popular music in the popular music press. Other interesting formations include the successful reality television formats adapted from the West which Keane et al. (2007) have examined. In a bilingual country like Singapore, the incremental play of Mandarin songs in new bilingual radio stations, a bilingual newspaper (*Wo Bao*) and the acceptance of Chinese music stars by a largely English-speaking public demonstrate the growing strength and popularity of a 'cultural China'.

Given the strength of this popular cultural industry, it is possible to think of the growth of Chinese popular culture in Asia in parallel to the recognition of the phenomenon of Bollywood. This phenomenon has led Singaporean cultural studies academic Chua Beng Huat (2001) to coin the phrase 'Pop Culture China', not only as an acknowledgement of this moment of arrival, but also as a description of the complex and linguistically diverse cultural traffic in the main economic corridors of the PRC, Taiwan, Hong Kong and Singapore (ibid. 2001: 115). Chua argues that, notwithstanding the cultural presumption of a sameness resulting from Chinese ethnicity and identity, there is still much academic work to be done to excavate the differences and to understand the uniqueness of the characteristics of these regional flows. Chua's model of a pop culture China is a geographically multi-noded and decentred site in which Mandarin does not occupy a privileged official spot, due to the mixed multilingual exchanges and accents noted across films, music, scripts and actors. Chua argues that while the notion of a shared past works to impose 'ideological motivations ... [and] ... intellectual or self-serving, commercial interests', 'such a configuration of cultural unity quickly rubs up against the reality of difference that crisscrosses this dispersed and diverse population' (ibid. 2001: 121). I argue that Chua's argument is a means of denying and resisting the strong calls for a superficial cultural and ethnic unity that is prosecuted through a geographically centred China. It is important to note the complex role played by the PRC within this context: it is both a cultural and

economic threat to the greater Chinese market, while also providing the cultural, economic and political bedrock on which that market depends.

Before we begin to explore the path towards media marketization, it is
helpful to point out that, as I am using it here, marketization refers to the
process and/or policy of exposing industries, services and so on to market
forces, especially in the situation of the conversion of a national economy
from a planned to a market economy (*Oxford English Dictionary Online*). This is
a process whereby the state relegates control to commercial interests and/or
allows such enterprises as, for example, Chinese Central Television (CCTV),
the Singapore Broadcasting Corporation (SBC) or Taiwan Television (TTV)
to open themselves up to market forces, profitability and costs imperatives.
The process has played out very differently in each of our locations. How
marketization takes place in these Chinese nations, and how they are shaped
via regulatory frameworks, become the points through which each media
system is differentiated here.

Deregulation

A number of outcomes and scenarios have occurred across the four nations as
a response to, or a direct result of, the process of deregulating the national
media. In Singapore and China, the media have worked – and in many cases
still do – as a substantive organ of the state, focused on the achievement of
government-directed national goals. Accusations of propaganda, censorship
and self-censorship are de rigueur among critics of these media. In Singapore,
the media are prohibited from reporting on topics termed 'out of bounds' –
subjects related to the religious, sexual, racial and political realms, which are
deemed to threaten national cohesion. These same areas tend to be sensitive
zones in China as well. However, a media worker in Singapore, who wants to
remain anonymous, has admitted that there are also individuals to whom they
are told not to provide airtime (Personal interview 2007). Loosening the
structures that may allow changes in ownership and media practices poses a
huge threat to the operations and stability of the incumbent governments in
both states, so the process is subject to close scrutiny and control. (The chapters in this book by Fung, and by Sun and Zhao go into this aspect of the
Chinese media in more detail.)

It is clear that the move to deregulate in Singapore and the PRC does not
mean that the press and the media can therefore function as a Western-style
fourth estate. However, it may mean that, as the media serve two masters (the
profit motivation and state imperatives) instead of one, the totalizing effect of
the state might be reduced through either more objective or more commercial
voices (Lau et al. 2008). Furthermore, since the expansion of the media marketplace has to take into account popular audience response, ratings and taste
formations, this could arguably lead to incremental shifts in the make-up of
the media.

The deregulation process in China was undertaken through the State Administration of Radio, Film and Television (SARFT), which was established in the 1980s as part of the 'Four levels of development and management of radio and television services' (Museum of Broadcasting Communications 2008). While a significant outcome of this policy enabled the central state broadcaster CCTV to compete for and draw on advertising dollars, the most immediate impact was felt in the expansion of mainstream television entertainment; substantial innovation in Chinese-produced entertainment programming occurred through the provincial television stations Hunan TV, Shanghai Media Group, Guangdong TV and Beijing TV. These developments were both assisted and constrained by the regulatory provisions developed in order to allow foreign media entry into the Chinese market through co-productions, investments, co-ownerships and direct productions. Developments on both these fronts – international investment and local entertainment productions – ushered in a new era for Chinese audiences, even though direct foreign media ownership was still not allowed.

In comparison, and at first glance, Singapore's deregulation strategies appear to be thoroughly commercial. The state broadcaster, Singapore Broadcasting Corporation, privatized in 1994 to become the Television Corporation of Singapore, and a further corporate restructuring in 1999 led to its present title of Mediacorp Singapore. Mediacorp Singapore, however, is wholly owned by Temasek Holdings (the investment arm of the government) and it holds a monopoly on free-to-air television in Singapore. Similarly, while the cable television provider Starhub Limited, which emerged out of the deregulation process in 2000, has a mixture of foreign and local ownership, the dominant shareholders are from Mediacorp and STT Telecommunications – again, government-owned companies. Thus, it is apparent that in Singapore, despite a degree of privatization in its deregulation of the media industries, the state presence is still guiding media operations. Nonetheless, the emergence of independent commercial media production companies in recent years does provide us with examples of grass-roots growth that has been enabled by this new media regulatory environment; this will be discussed further below.

Reregulation

In Taiwan, cable television developed in the late 1980s as a response to the bad reception of terrestrial services in mountainous regions. Many were pirate stations and at one point there were more than 20 cable operators in each city, providing largely the same content. By the late 1990s, a range of issues had plagued the industry, from loss of advertising revenues to management of media companies and cross-media ownership laws. In addition, controversy focused on consumer dissatisfaction with television content: tabloidization, sensationalism and politically partisan news services. The scale of the system is vast: Taiwan has one of the largest fleets of satellite news-gathering vehicles in the world; news is offered through nine different local cable news channels, on top of the three free-to-air channels. There are 66 cable television systems offering 130 channels on cable for less than US$15 a month. Nonetheless, as ratings for the terrestrial system declined and cable uptake increased, the Government Information Office (GIO) decided to address public concern about the quality of Taiwanese television by reregulating and adjusting this marketplace. The NCC (National Communications Commission) was formed in 2006 and took on the task of regulating the telecommunications, broadcasting and information sector (Government Information Office 2007).

In 1998, Private Television Services (PTS) had been established as an independent, not-for-profit station whose aim was to 'serve the interests of the public, raise the standards of Taiwan's broadcast culture, safeguard the public's freedom of expression and access to knowledge, and enhance national education and culture' (Press Reference: Taiwan). Gary Rawnsley's (2005) study argues that the eventual setting up of PTS was a triumph for the burgeoning civil society of Taiwan, as it provided a space free from political interference or commercial competition and an institutional structure which could attempt to 'influence government, scrutinize and challenge its decisions and demonstrate the authority of democratic culture, and thus facilitate the consolidation of democracy' (ibid. 2005: 25). However, it didn't stop there.

In order to rein in Taiwan's highly politicized media culture, the Terrestrial TV Share Release Act was passed in January 2006, whereby government and political parties had to relinquish their shares in the television companies. This meant that the three oldest television stations, Chinese Television System (CTS), Taiwan Television Enterprise (TTV) and China Television Company (CTV), had to undergo ownership transfers in the hope that structural and ownership makeovers would encourage more politically objective programming. Six months later, CTS was merged with PTS to form the Taiwan Broadcasting System (TBS), an umbrella media organization housing a further eight television channels (five stations), with the aim of showcasing and providing educational, cultural and ethnic diversity. Two of the five stations – Hakka TV and Taiwan Indigenous TV – are niche channels, in the Hakka and Minan languages respectively (www.tbs.org.tw/index_e.htm).

However, the issue of funding these alternatives remains a continuing problem. CTS receives no subsidies, as it is a commercial television station; PTS receives annual funding of up to approximately US$28 million from the Government Information Office; and Hakka TV and Indigenous TV received up to approximately US$12 million from the Council of Hakka Affairs and Indigenous People's Commission (Shan 2008). However, with CTS advertising revenues and ratings falling, policy makers are arguing that TBS cannot foot this bill and the NCC has been examining alternative means of generating income through subscription systems such as those used by the BBC or Japan's NHK. In 2006, a further US$140 million was granted by the Taiwanese legislature towards building the TBS digital terrestrial broadcasting platform.

The marketization of the Taiwanese media environment has led to a policy of complex reregulation, a package of tools intended to stall the politically partisan nature of programming in the Taiwanese media sphere as well as the downwards spiral in the quality of entertainment and news programming, while supporting the role of public television as a means of enhancing cultural diversity outcomes.

Competition and collaboration

As we have seen, the process of marketization in Singapore and the PRC has remained one in which the presence of the state is substantial. It is important to recognize, however, that even within systems that are largely directed by the state, the process of marketization has resulted in a massive expansion of commercial activity. Competition is a cornerstone in the Singapore economic marketplace; as a term, it is embedded in the operational mantra of governmental practices (MTI 2008) – such as Media 21, a blueprint to develop the media industries by encouraging expansion and further growth in skills and know-how. Competition is seen as a means of growing the content and cultural industries in Singapore, which are in turn regarded as integral to the development of the nation-state. The Media Development Authority of Singapore (MDA) has a two-pronged strategy to develop the media industries in Singapore. The first is to attract financing and investment; the second is the creation of locally produced content that can travel beyond the local market (Heng 2007). The external focus is essential for Singapore; as a small market, it needs to sell beyond its territory, but it also needs to source funds and expertise from outside.

The 2007 Asian Television Forum, the annual media buying and selling conference, was held in Singapore. A central theme was content creation, financing and the economics of new media. While many attended the sessions on new media, it was clear that there were no conclusive success stories. However, significant local co-production deals were generated through this event. An example is Upside Down Entertainment's S$18 million investment deal to produce the regional medical drama *Asian Crisis Centre*, to be filmed in Singapore, India and Korea. Gin Kai, one of the owners of Upside Down Entertainment, stated that while they have been expanding slowly and their economic fortunes have been unsteady for a while, the last two years have been progressively better for the independent producers in Singapore, due to the opening up of the international media market. Instead of selling their product to only one broadcaster (at the buyer's price), the entry of global cable channels such as HBO and Discovery Asia, interested in buying local content and in developing regional collaboration, allows the local media producers to pitch and form co-production deals. The MDA also maintains that it plays an important role in fostering and promoting local producers. From seed funding deals with the Economic Development Board of Singapore (EDB), to online and regional promotion through its trade offices, Heng argues that the MDA utilizes both policy tools and more hands-on initiatives to help these local producers achieve their commercial aims, and consequently the larger national goal of increasing local content and creativity (Heng 2007).

In a smaller market like Singapore, where a direct path of expansion isn't so obvious, governmental deregulatory practices nevertheless involve the state in determining growth areas, and then developing them by working with the players in that industry to achieve common goals. While China is clearly the emerging power in the region, both Heng and Gin note that Singapore media has also played in the global field, and many of its collaborations are with North America and Europe rather than within Asia. This is partly because English is Singapore's national language of business. For a nation that is proficient in English, in a region that is highly diverse and operates mainly in local tongues, the language becomes a useful passport for those who wish to use Singapore as their gateway to Asia.

Media bartering: Hong Kong and the PRC

The most distinctive aspect of Hong Kong's media is that, while it is privately owned, it has shifted from a highly deregulated market under British rule to a state-directed regime under the Chinese Special Administrative Region (SAR). Ironically, it now has to deregulate again as it becomes part of the media system of larger China (Lau et al. 2008). The recent Closer Economic Partnership Agreement (CEPA) between Hong Kong and Mainland China has taken on a direct role in framing the media environment for the Hong Kong television industries as well as determining what economic rewards it will actually bring.

In Hong Kong, the impact of the Hong Kong and PRC co-signed CEPA in January 2004 was an important step for Hong Kong–Mainland relations in terms of the regulation and trade in films and audio-visual content. The larger PRC market is an important one for Hong Kong, not just because it is tied legislatively to the PRC, but because it offers much-needed opportunities for expansion. Under the CEPA agreement, the Hong Kong television and film industries could bypass Chinese import quotas; some 374 forms of products from Hong Kong are given clearance to enter the PRC on zero import tariff. Importantly, it opens up the vast Chinese media market to Hong Kong producers. A subsequent CEPA II further specified that television co-productions between Hong Kong and the PRC would be broadcast and distributed as PRC-produced television programmes. In addition to the expansion of Hong Kong media companies into the PRC market, the CEPA reinforced Hong Kong's status as a media hub by allowing international media firms such as Columbia Pictures (which had offices in Hong Kong) rights to operate in the PRC. This is an important role for Hong Kong; its economic success in the region is based on its operation as a connection and access point for the region to the PRC (Curtin 2003), and vice versa.

For the domestic television stalwarts in Hong Kong – TVB and ATV – the CEPA offers legalized access into the southern PRC markets where the overflow of their television signals is received by Chinese audiences. Previously, the southern stations could recapture the signals and utilize the programming to sell advertising airtime illegally. This was an ongoing problem that the Hong Kong broadcasters had no means of rectifying. The CEPA, however, has enabled ATV to negotiate landing rights in Guangdong, where ATV Home and ATV World are sold, while collaborating with the Guangdong television station in programme productions, advertising and sales. TVB also received programming licensing rights to free-to-air channels and some cable stations in the PRC, which allowed it to barter and sell airtime to local and foreign advertisers (TVBI). These regulatory changes have enabled Hong Kong television stations to remain as the connective nodes to the PRC.

Detractors of the CEPA have claimed that the net economic benefits are still uncertain, with some claiming that it has more political implications than economic ones (Tsang et al. n.d.). Also, strict moral guidelines dictate the genres and content of audio-visual products. Recent hit films such as *Infernal Affairs* and *Blood Brothers* demonstrate that, although themes such as gangsters, ghosts or immoral conduct are popular staples of Hong Kong fare, SARFT considers these an unhealthy influence on the population. The importance of CEPA cannot be denied, even if it has more of a political than an economic impact; nonetheless, it demonstrates how a reregulated market like Hong Kong has had to reconfigure its media production and business priorities in light of new regulatory moves from the PRC.

Conclusion

A liberalized market has become an important marker of the maturity and capacity of the media industries in these locations. Their progress towards this end is being played out in the context of an emerging China. While China's force in the media industry is still a nascent one, it nonetheless exerts an influence and remains a long-term factor in the consideration of the strategies of these national media markets if they are to have relevance in the future. Of the three markets discussed, the one that must pay the most attention to Chinese media policy now is also the one that is geographically closest to it: Hong Kong.

This discussion has set out to illustrate some of the ways in which state media regulators and the industry have had to negotiate their relationship in order to stay in the regional media market, thus invoking the proverbial 'balanced market', and how that balance means different things in different contexts. In particular, the three case studies demonstrate three different forms of relationship: a top-down instrumental approach (Taiwan); a collaborative approach (Singapore); and a bartering relational one (Hong Kong). It is easy to regard the terms 'deregulation' and 'marketization' as referencing a relatively homogeneous set of processes, as if they are wholly instrumental processes that are inflicted on the industries or triggered by them. This study has sought to demonstrate that not only are the processes of deregulation and marketization contingent upon multilateral relationships, but also they are actively shaped by the intersecting and conjectural ways in which the participants become enmeshed. In Taiwan, the vastness and unruliness of the industry players persuaded the regulators to impose fines and open up new channels of information to achieve their goals; in Singapore, the nationalized goals have become the foundational base to encourage a burgeoning industry towards content creation; and in Hong Kong negotiation and bartering have been ways to situate their cultural products in the PRC market. Not only has marketization produced very different outcomes in these instances – for the audience, for the industry and for the nation-state – but also the processes themselves are constitutively and substantially different.

Chapter 11

Television in the Balkans

The rise of commercial nationalism

Zala Volcic

Introduction

Two recent television events epitomize the emerging and unique blend of nationalism and pop culture that characterizes the post-political form of what I want to call 'commercial nationalism' in Balkan broadcasting. The first is the ratings success of the 2007–8 trial of Serbian Radical Party leader Vojislav Seselj, accused of inciting the ethnic tensions that led to atrocities carried out by Serb paramilitaries in Bosnia and Croatia. Far from encouraging Serbs to reflect on their role in the wars of the 1990s, the trial was an entertainment spectacle, thanks in part to the antics of Seselj who, in defending himself, mocked the court and the entire judicial process, earning for the programme the nickname of 'Big Brother in the Hague'. Seselj successfully turned the Hague trial into a campaign spectacle for the Serbian Radical Party (Zarkovic 2008). Some of the television highlights included scenes in which Seselj told judges to remove their robes because they reminded him of medieval inquisitors, and mocked his court-appointed lawyer: 'You falsely presented this man with a bird's nest on the top of his head as my defense lawyer. He will never be my defense lawyer. You brought actors here to act as my defense lawyers but they will never be my defense lawyers. They are your spies' (*Mladina* 2008).

The second incident is the success of Serbia's entrant to the Eurovision Song Contest. The victory of the song 'Molitva' (Prayer), performed by Marija Serifovic, won Serbia the right to host the popular international contest in 2008. The result was greeted as a victory for pop-culture diplomacy at a time when Serbia continued to receive a bad press both for its behaviour in the 1990s and for its subsequent refusal to confront its actions. During the same period that Serbian television was effectively ridiculing the justice being meted out for the wars of the 1990s, the Eurovision victory served as a means of improving the nation's image – even in the eyes of its former enemies. Croatian radio journalist Kruno Vidic acknowledged the diplomatic clout of the Eurovision victory: 'Popular culture is the best kind of diplomacy. Light notes are what we all understand. It is a bridge that helps people leave politics behind' (Jovanovic 2008).

These two events help to trace the outlines of a new form of post-socialist nationalism – what I am describing as commercial nationalism – in Balkan broadcasting. They highlight the ways in which new commercial imperatives contribute to a twofold process whereby politics is transposed into the realm of entertainment and entertainment comes to function politically.

Although the Balkans are composed of different nation-states, these share both a regional history and a more immediate transition to capitalism which makes it possible to trace some connections between emergent forms of cultural nationalism in the region. Thus, notwithstanding the different ways in which cultures connect and overlap in the Balkan region, national culture is still used as a pre-eminent frame of reference. The point is to hold these two concepts of cultural regionalism and local nationalism together – that is to say, the apparently paradoxical way in which certain forms of nationalism are emerging might be described as specific to the region. The recent influx of private capital into the media sector coincided with both the 'Balkanization' of broadcasting and a resurgent emphasis on national and regional identity. On the one hand, in the wake of the fall of socialism and the end of the Yugoslav wars, Balkan television has been quick to respond to the trend towards globalization by opening up to foreign investment. Private media investors have expanded rapidly in all the Balkan countries, with the American company Central European Media Enterprises leading the way. On the other hand, and at the same time, there has been a consistent tendency towards nationalistic programming. This paradoxical trend of globally funded nationalism can be discerned both in the content of the television programmes and in the industrial structures that produce a hybrid form of national-commercial broadcasting.

In the Balkans, national identities retain an important ideological function – even when the nation-states concerned are relatively recent inventions. Towards the end of the 1980s and the early 1990s, when the nationalisms of all the republics of the former Yugoslavia escalated, each community reactivated or recreated national television systems in order to reinforce and reinvent a discourse of national identity and difference (Thompson 1994). All seven former Yugoslav nation-states – Slovenia, Croatia, Bosnia-Herzegovina, Serbia, Kosovo, Montenegro and Macedonia – have gone, or continue to go through the process of transition from a centralized, socialist, state-run economy to a privatized, market-driven economy. Politically, these new nation-states are also involved in the project of national identity building, since few of the republics had the historical experience of being an independent nation-state. As a result, Balkan television has taken to 'commercial nationalism' to help prosecute the not yet fully accomplished goal of nation building. This goal is a familiar one, but it is important to understand its historical specificity in the post-socialist, post-war era of neoliberalism. The tools and strategies chosen for the task of nation building are shaped, I would argue, by the fact that the region is also going through 'neoliberal' restructuring that involves the 'privatization of government enterprises and public responsibilities; and large cutbacks in social programs' (Kotz 2003: 15).

The aim of this chapter is to develop the notion of commercial nationalism as a recent formation in the Balkans in order to shed light on a phenomenon that has broader relevance to other resurgent forms of nationalism in the global media environment. To do so, the chapter draws on several case studies, as well as on interviews with media professionals from the Balkans.

Some historical and political contexts

After the former Yugoslavia collapsed in 1991, the period of the 1990s wars was characterized by the dismantling of a sense of pan-Slavic unity and the emergence of a strongly nationalist and populist TV culture. The majority of mainstream broadcasters in all parts of the former Yugoslavia turned to national(istic) tradition, history and myths.

Since that time, the Balkan region has been playing a failed game of follow-the-leader with Western Europe when it comes to broadcasting policy. The dual goal has been to adjust to post-communist marketplace freedom as well as to win acceptance into the European Union. The key stages in Balkan broadcasting transformation thus follow a familiar Western European pattern, although lagging by several years and quite a bit more chaotic and free-wheeling. The progression goes as follows: first, the destruction of the state monopoly on broadcasting by throwing open the broadcast frequencies to private capital; second, the largely unsuccessful transformation of state networks into independent public service broadcasters, which remain subject to the heavy-handed political pressure of state authorities; and finally, the emergence and proliferation of commercial channels and platforms, often unlicensed and illegal.

All the Balkan countries have brought their broadcasting regulations broadly into line with Western European standards. Broadcasting is now organized according to a 'dual' system comprising a commercial sector and a public service sector supported by a hybrid of state and commercial funding. There are two main trends that contribute to the emergent forms of commercial nationalism. First, as many point out, 'public' television has lost audience share, is poorly funded and is subjected to political pressures (Splichal 2006; Trpevska 2003). Second, the regional commercial media landscape is highly fragmented. Rather than the highly concentrated media markets that have emerged in more established capitalist democracies, the Balkan media scene is saturated with relatively small private, commercial stations. Many stations are run for political interests or prestige, rather than for profit, by local business-people and power brokers. For example, in the republic of Macedonia, the substantial broadcasting reforms in this country of only 2 million are still under way, in part to address the problem of media saturation. The broadcasting market is clearly overcrowded, with 52 television broadcasters and 62 radio stations.[1] This multiplication of broadcasters may represent a transitional stage between centralized control and emerging forms of media oligopoly. That is to say, it is unlikely that so many broadcasters will be able to coexist profitably, and it would not be surprising if the more successful ended up buying out rivals or merging with them. In this context, Serbia's Pink TV is becoming one of the strongest regional players – it gained in popularity as a nationalistic, entertainment-oriented station during the wars, and managed to parlay its particular style of broadcasting into regional market success in the post-war period.

'Paint Your Life Pink'

Shortly after the start of the wars in the former Yugoslavia, a commercial broadcaster that would come to define this version of apolitical but nationalistic commercial broadcasting got its start. Pink TV, with its ironic reference to the replacement of 'red' ideology by a more market-friendly colour, started operation during the reign of Milosevic, in 1994. The station's official motto, 'Paint Your Life Pink', was perhaps best explained by the unofficial version circulated internally: 'no news, no sports, just entertainment' (OSI 2005). Given its stated agenda, the station proved to be a perfect 'bread-and-circuses' complement to Milosevic's disastrous nationalistic agenda. During the period of his political dominance, and the wars he helped to foment in Croatia, Bosnia and Kosovo, the kitschy aesthetics of Pink TV, which consisted primarily of local celebrity talk shows and pop music, became successful and heavily embedded in the largely unreflective and apolitical milieu of Serbian popular culture.

Pink TV, which was 'owned by people close to the Serb regime' (Norton-Taylor 1999), thrived during the period of wars, violence, poverty, xenophobia and hyperinflation of the 1990s. Intriguingly, it did not disappear with the Milosevic regime; it not only endured, but expanded to become one of the region's most popular entertainment broadcasters, despite its one-time association with Serbian nationalism.

Pink TV's owner, Zeljko Mitrovic, started creating his media empire in the late 1980s and was supportive of Milosevic's regime – not surprisingly, given the need for any enterprise that sought success in those years to get along with the political leadership. Even though Pink TV studiously avoided news and serious political coverage, its ideological significance should not be underestimated. It helped to legitimate, normalize and institutionalize Serbian mainstream nationalistic culture – a culture in which paramilitary war criminals and gangsters were widely celebrated as role models (Tarlac 2003; Kronja 2001). This was a culture created and enjoyed by the new, often criminal, elite that benefited from and exacerbated the 1990s wars.

Pink TV's veiled wartime propaganda machine showed mostly cheap entertainment programming and (nationalistic) turbo-folk music video spots.

Indeed, it is impossible to tell the story of Pink TV without reference to the genre that it helped to popularize. Turbo-folk music is a hybrid of Balkan folk, Middle Eastern beats, Turkish and Greek pop music, and contemporary electro-pop-dance music. As Kronja (2001) argues, it has been associated with Serbian nationalism in its more militant forms, using aesthetically kitschy, provocatively dressed female performers pumped full of silicon, singing about death, love, passion and blood sacrifice for the Serbian nation. Turbo-folk was used as a motivational tool for regular and paramilitary soldiers in the battle-fields of Croatia and Bosnia (Kronja 2001). In this regard, Pink TV helped give expression to a post-socialist version of Serbian nationalism.

After the fall of Milosevic in 2000, Pink TV tried to distance itself from the 'traumatic' past and its association with cheap programming. In 2003, it began to produce news programming, with the goal of creating a more 'prestigious' brand that could compete with other popular news shows. In the Balkan region – in contrast to, say, the United States – the evening news remains the most popular programme, with the highest ratings. In 2002, the evening news had an average audience share of around 40 per cent in Croatia (*HRT Report* 2003). One of the legacies of state broadcasting is that news programmes still occupy a central place in Balkan television production and lie at the heart of national TV viewing.[2]

Appadurai (2006) has suggested that global news channels offer some sense of immediacy and simultaneity by connecting us in a global world. Yet, at the local level, news programming resists globalization – in fact, it usually retains a strong sense of the national. In the Balkans, the homogenizing potential of globalization is countervailed by the heavy promotion of national differences on television. No transnational Balkan news programmes exist yet – and there have been no serious attempts in the past to create pan-Balkan television news programmes. Romania's first niche news channel, Realitatea, planned to launch a cable and satellite Balkan Television Network with the aspiration of creating a Balkan version of Euronews. The goal was to start a pan-Balkan lifestyle and news network that would bring together 'people from the Balkans to get to know each other', but the project has never been realized (Holdsworth 2006). A more successful attempt was made by Vebi Velija in Macedonia and Albania with his AlSat-M television, which started its bilingual broadcasting service in 2006 to 'cultivate multi-ethnic coexistence among the Balkan people' (personal interview, Macedonian journalist, 3 May 2008). Velija also owns TV ALSAT, which broadcasts programmes in the Albanian language to Albanians in Albania, Kosovo, Macedonia, Montenegro and Europe on terrestrial and satellite routes 24 hours a day. The result, according to some critics, is that the AlSat-M project is not so much a pan-Balkan broadcaster as it is an attempt to extend the pan-Albanian reach of Velija's other channel. As one Macedonian TV producer put it, voicing the suspicion with which the divided populace in the Balkans view one another, the AlSat-M project 'really fosters a plan for a greater Albania, and not regional collaboration. AlSat-M masquerades as a cross-border project, but, in reality, pursues Albanian ideas and interests.'

Pink TV may turn out to be the first 'really successful and powerful' Balkan regional player, thanks to its development of the spinoff channels TV Pink BIH (Bosnia and Herzegovina), TV Pink M (Montenegro) and Pink International. In addition to reaching over 90 per cent of Serbian homes, and becoming the most popular national television station in Serbia (Tarlac 2003), Pink TV is now available on satellite throughout the former Yugoslav region. In both BIH and Montenegro, TV Pink became one of the most popular channels. Its satellite and cable programmes are also heavily watched in Slovenia, Macedonia and Bulgaria. The odd paradox of Pink TV – one that might be attributed to what I am describing as its populist version of commercial nationalism – is that it has proven to have broad appeal beyond Serb audiences even as it continues to reproduce the Serbian cultural nationalism it honed during the Milosevic era.

Despite the introduction of news, Pink TV maintains a predominantly entertainment-oriented profile: it offers a combination of quiz shows, fashion programmes, reality shows, Latin American telenovelas, turbo-folk music videos and Hollywood films. The most watched programmes on Pink TV are local productions with a distinctive national character: sports, domestic entertainment shows (e.g. *Grand Stars*, a turbo-folk version of *Pop Idol*) and dramas (such as the first Serbian soap opera, *Seljaci* (Farmers)). Recurring programming themes include the portrayal of forms of identity that are anchored in some immutable past, where the use of local dialects and scenes of rural life become the bulwarks of a fortress that cannot be demolished by any other culture. TV programmes on local cuisines and natural resources, but also hip urban culture, promote an atemporal vision of Serbian national culture, where the passage of time has been suspended in favour of an idealized identity, unspoiled by troubled histories. In this regard, Pink TV offers a new version of national identity in which different global formats intermingle with traditional nationalistic stereotypes, myths and rituals. The paradoxical result is to represent the diversity of hybrid forms of identity while helping to produce a sense of deeply traditional, nationalistic identity.

Pink TV still relies on cheap formats, including a range of reality shows, talk shows and studio interviews. In general, Balkan producers have turned to Western programming to copy profitable formulas, and this has led to numerous licensed formats, including game-show and reality TV formats. The increasing popularity of reality television formats worldwide has influenced producers in the region; almost every station offers an Endemol production. In Slovenia, both Kanal A and Pop TV, the most popular commercial channels, offer locally produced copies of international formats such as *The Bachelor*, *Big Brother* and *Popstars*. In the Republic of Macedonia, the most watched programme in 2006 was the quiz show *Who Wants to Be a Millionaire?* The advantage of these formats is that they can be 'glocalized' (Aslama and Pantti

2007): global formats can be built around local cast members and thereby incorporate relevant themes.

The way global programming is appropriated on Balkan TV leads one to question not the obvious impact of globalization on national identity, but the extent to which accepted discourses about the nation-state may conceal the primacy of commercial considerations in new cultural formations of national (istic) identity. As one Pink TV producer asserted: 'If our programming consists of reality shows, local entertainment, advertising and quiz shows ... it is characteristic that we tend to assert national belonging in these global formats. Our production practices become heavily localized.' Glocalization doesn't just provide elements of local 'flavour'; it also becomes a tool for the promulgation of a post-socialist, commercially supported version of nationalism.

Three ingredients of commercial nationalism

The aesthetic of commercial nationalism blends elements of the authoritarian spectacles of socialist-era broadcasting with the fast-paced celebrity focus of the post-MTV sound-bite era. The result is a combination of the idealization and Manichaeism of the socialist-era with the predictable entertainment formulas and stereotypes developed by commercial broadcasters. There are three dominant and sometimes overlapping elements of what I am describing as television's version of commercial nationalism. It is worth explaining these in more detail and offering some specific examples.

The first is the replacement of an emphasis on the state and state-oriented politics by a patriotically inflected focus on national and religious identity. If state broadcasting in the communist era attempted to promote solidarity in explicitly political terms by appealing to a trans-ethnic sense of shared class identity, in the post-socialist era national unity is couched in less overtly political terms – namely, those of ethnic belonging and religious identity. This is not to say that such categories are apolitical in the sense of being without political impact; rather that they tend to trump political deliberation with visceral appeals to faith and blood, to a shared sense of 'natural' cultural identity that transcends political community. These appeals resonate with the well-known shift in advertising strategies associated with the rise of the marketing industry: from information-based ads to emotional and associational appeals (Marchand 1985). Commercial broadcasters understand the ratings appeal of highly charged ethnic and religious topics, and do little to translate them into more deliberative forums, rather seeking to stoke their visceral, emotional character to attract audiences. Consider, for example, an episode of the popular Slovene 'political' talk show *Trenja* (Friction), which featured a debate over the construction of a mosque in the predominantly Catholic country. Despite the fact that there is a Muslim population of some 55,000 people in the nation of only two million, there are no mosques in the country, since municipalities have refused building permits for their construction. For those who imagined that the advent of a Western model of commercial journalism might raise the level of political discourse in a nation once dominated by a tightly controlled state monopoly, the level of discussion on *Trenja* would come as a disappointment. The structure and tone of the show worked hard to reinforce nationalist prejudices by appealing to religious and ethnic anxieties. One of the guests, a theology professor, captured the tone of the show with his observation that 'We Slovenes, as a small nation, have survived here for the last thousand years ... The mosque does not fit into Slovene landscape, and is strictly a political institution ... you cannot compare it to the Catholic Church.'

This is perhaps a classic example of how commercial nationalism functions: since the goal is not political or ideological per se – to foster a sense of class unity, for example, or to rally the nation around a set of political reforms – but purely economic, pre-existing prejudices are exploited rather than challenged. If one might fault state broadcasting for narrowing down the discourse by ruling out opposing viewpoints, commercial nationalism achieves a similar goal through different means. It limits the discourse by playing to dominant sets of prejudices, reproducing and amplifying them – not because of a fear of political reprisals, but rather out of a concern that any such challenge might threaten ratings.

The second ingredient of commercial nationalism is the emergence of a hybrid aesthetic that draws on the similarity between the rituals of authoritarian state spectacle and commercial extravaganzas: 'the May Day Parade meets the Super Bowl'. The paradoxical, but perhaps familiar, result of a commercially depoliticized culture is that politicians are represented through the discourses of celebrity, while celebrities are invited to comment on the political. To put it in slightly different terms, what counts as the political is not so much the nuts and bolts of political self-governance as the glamour of power, the lifestyles of the powerful and wealthy. Think *Fox News* meets *Entertainment Tonight*, with a dash of *Lifestyles of the Rich and Famous*. This aesthetic was nurtured in the shadows of Milosevic's authoritarian regime, when Pink TV honed its aesthetics of kitschy celebrity nationalism with celebrity talk shows and turbo-folk extravaganzas. Perhaps because of the ostensibly apolitical character of its blatantly commercial approach, and perhaps because of post-political nationalism, Pink TV outlasted Milosevic, serving as the first broadcaster to carry the voices of his democratically elected successors. This does not mean that Milosevic-era sentiments were banished from the programming, rather that they were able to cloak themselves, as before, in the guise of entertainment. Serbian turbo-folk star and Pink TV stalwart Ceca invokes – albeit in indirect ways – her ties with Milosovic's nationalism and the Serbian paramilitary soldiers, called the Tigers, led by her now deceased husband Arkan, who were responsible for some of the worst killings in Bosnia. In 2002 she appeared in a television advertising spot for coffee C, posing in a seductive way, surrounded by tigers.

The third ingredient is a reliance on style, glamour and entertainment (and in particular on national music, sports and self-help programming) to displace overtly political coverage and debates. Commercial nationalism, unsurprisingly, neatly aligns itself with incipient forms of neoliberalization in Balkan region. Insofar as the neoliberal agenda is to transpose politics into the register of the market – to transform governance into a series of markets (for education, health care, etc.) – commercial nationalism might be understood as the form of nationalism most appropriate to the neoliberal era. To the extent that neoliberalism relies on strategies of individualization and responsibilization – devolving functions once understood as collective, and in this sense political – onto self-actualized, 'responsible' individuals, the proliferation of self-help discourses on Balkan TV fits neatly with the emergent model of commercial nationalism. During times of social change associated with profound risk and anxiety, self-help discourses provide citizens with instructions on how to understand these changes, and how to adjust and empower themselves. In this regard, they fashion a version of post-political (that is to say, market-based) citizenship for the neoliberal era.

In the last decade or so, books and magazines emphasizing popular spiritual themes have been on the rise: parapsychology, astrology, natural health, holistic healing, massage, chiropractics, bio-energy and self-help. Television stations regularly broadcast spiritual self-help shows, including programmes (with names like *Z nami* (With Us) and *Duša* (Soul)) that promulgate 'therapeutic self-help discourses' to advise and encourage viewers to modify their (personal) behaviour in order to better fit within society. Some hosts of these shows claim to be blessed with an uncommon gift. They are perceived as being spiritually strong and independent because they draw their energy from the deep well of tradition – a tradition that increasingly has come to be understood in deeply nationalistic terms. Although such shows profess to transcend the 'merely political' through recourse to more profound realms of spirituality, their concerns include political topics. The famous Serbian 'seer' Kleopatra, for example, had her own show on Pink TV, with a clear political mission: she would predict Serbian military victories, and would claim she also advised the 'great leader', Milosevic, who was, according to her, a 'living saint'.

Conclusions

Balkan TV, because of its transition straight from what might be described as a state propaganda model to a largely deregulated commercial one, represents an interesting and perhaps unique combination of nationalist tendencies with market imperatives. In some ways, the transition from state spectacle to commercial diversion, epitomized by the entertainment-oriented programming of a channel like Pink TV, is not as large a shift as it might initially seem to be. Pink TV did avoid explicitly political programming, but it also incorporated elements of the folk music and dance that were familiar to viewers from the era of day-long festivals of unity and culture. With the failure of the Yugoslav project, these cultural celebrations, rather than attempting to transcend regional and national prejudices, started to capitalize on them – that is, to cater to them for largely commercial purposes. The function of the cultural spectacle shifts – thanks in part to commercial imperatives – from serving the ends of pan-Slavic socialist solidarity to exploiting suppressed nationalisms. But it does so not in the overt, politically propagandistic style familiar to the socialist era, but rather in the guise of popular entertainment that mobilizes a nationalist discourse of ethnic belonging, superiority and entitlement. This is expressed through, for instance, the music and style of turbo-folk, the observations of commentators and the cultivation of a nationalist celebrity culture.

The version of commercial nationalism described in this chapter may be distinctive to the Balkans, but some elements will be recognizable in other contexts. The Fox News Channel in the United States, for example, relies on a blend of news-as-entertainment and entertainment-as-news, with a strongly nationalist slant. Its close ties to the Bush administration give it the feel of a pseudo-state organ that uses the news to distract attention and mobilize a visceral, patriotic response. It would be interesting to compare the formats, style and tone of Balkan commercial nationalism with other broadcasting systems in the process of navigating the historical shift from state and public broadcasting to increasing commercial competition. It is at the moment when a state propaganda system combines with a commercial one that variants of commercial nationalism seem to appear. The nationalistic framework that characterizes most prime-time television programmes in the region, I suggest, is characteristic of the confluence of global and local trends, which ultimately aims at reinforcing (rather than resisting) stereotypical visions of 'being' Slovene, Croatian, Macedonian or Serbian.

Notes

1 Another example of an over-saturated broadcasting environment is Serbia, where licences were given away as political favours throughout the 1990s, or broadcasters worked with no licence. During most of the 1990s (Milosevic's regime), the total number of media outlets in Serbia was unknown (Djoric 2002). Today, it is argued that besides national broadcaster RTS, there are 755 broadcasters in Serbia: 543 radio stations, 73 television stations and 139 stations broadcasting both radio and television programmes (*Politika* 2005).

2 The result, even after the rise of commercial broadcasting, is that news is the genre in which television stations compete directly, in terms of both content and the number of journalists.

Chapter 12

Anachronism, apologetics and *Robin Hood*

Televisual nationhood after TV

Stephanie Hemelryk Donald

Anachronisms, power and class

Television studies post-television is a project that announces two problems for contemporary media research. First, what is 'post' in one place may be current in another; and second, the appellation 'post-anything' is generally a signal of intent to revision rather than to abandon an intellectual or political project. It is therefore wise to warn the reader that we may stray immediately into the past in our efforts to explain disquiet with the present.

Two examples, politically and geographically removed from one another, illustrate these points of departure. In China, while the central television service retains strong aspects of social management and governmental control, nonetheless the television as a widespread platform for entertainment and information is a contemporary lifestyle benefit for millions of new viewers or newly modernizing viewers. China is a post-socialist television mediascape, but it is not post-television per se. Although the blogosphere is the foremost domain of sometimes untrammelled discursive mayhem, much of what is debated has been initially communicated via television. The reference points for national and intra-national opinion are televisual. The Opening Ceremony of the 29th Olympiad in Beijing, directed by Zhang Yimou and approved by the Central Committee of the Politburo, was all about the deep past, although it used the cinematic technology of the present and the mass-line aesthetics of the last 60 years of authoritarian rule to make its points. Its meaning and values (discrete qualities – one obvious, the other absent) immediately became the topic of blogs throughout Chinese cyberspace. Everyone watched it because it was a greatly anticipated statement from China to the world, but more exactly, it was a defensive directive from the party-state to its people. Television was at its most relevant, but as a reference point for the rest of the conversation, not as a place where that conversation could develop.

Television in (or from) the United Kingdom, which is the main subject of this discussion, has long moved beyond its 'public service (BBC) plus easy-viewing (ITV)' model. The set-top box, multi-channel, interactive model of television has been incorporated into households' daily routines. At the same

time, TV is now a rabid dog in the British middle-class imagination: car-
icatured as a domain of the tabloid, comprising celebrity nonsense, reality
combat and the carnage of a working class allowed to go, oh so utterly, to
moral seed.[1] As the Scottish essayist Andrew O'Hagan has put it, even while
decrying the class cruelties of post-Thatcher New Labour: 'George Orwell
would whiten to address the mob that now scans the *Daily Mirror* and each
night flicks between the bouts of gladiatorial combat happening on every
other channel' (2008: 6).

Thus we are dealing with a media platform that is digitally advanced in
delivery options, but mediaeval in the ferocity of its content. TV in the
United Kingdom depends on both characteristics for its (anti)-social potency
and the maintenance of its 'mob' of dedicated viewers and professional
detractors. TV in China is about entertaining and informing (to a point) a
working middle class, with the maintenance of state power a final priority.
British TV is not a managed ideology per se, but it is nonetheless an instru-
ment of class and transitory national cohesions. I do not refer to the many
ways in which television may now be downloaded, streamed and merchan-
dised, but to the very old-fashioned box in a home living space. Watching the
DVD of the Australian comedy *Summer Heights High* in a flat in Paris was a
hilarious night's entertainment for my hitherto innocent (of Australian
humour) English brother, but it only really mattered when it was screened on
British TV later that year, and he could share his discovery with a nation of
similarly bemused Brits. Of course, the new hit was debated and played out in
new media forums, in the now classic convergence model of multi-platform
bridges, broadcast audience figures and after-show spin.

So television is neither simply a pliable mouthpiece of Reithian or communist propaganda nor a bastion of democratic principle and informed debate.
But it is related to both realms. A somewhat old-fashioned medium, required
to literally broadcast symptoms, statements and standpoints of the nation's
ontological system, television draws heavily on the past to stage its grip on the
present. Thus, TV lends anachronism a peculiar legitimacy. The great anachronism at the heart of much of what happens on television is the presiding,
organizing power of the nation-state. As Zhu (2008) argues in her excellent
study of television in the post-reform era in China, even escapist historical
drama is often an iteration of the political reality of its viewers (Zhu 2008:
62ff). As determinedly as television drama locates its narratives in imagined and
self-confident versions of the past, so does it inevitably articulate the dominant
anxieties, hopes and truisms of the national present.

Britain

There are then good reasons why the spirit as opposed to the hollow
letter of such hopes, articulated on the eve of the New Labour victory of
1997, will struggle to be realized without an appreciation that they

require not just the parliamentary defeat of the new Right, but a full understanding of the obstructive powers of the capitalist marketplace. Of course this is precisely what the ideology of New Labour forbids.

(Dave 2006: 137, on Keiller)

When the British media scholar Roger Silverstone (1993) compared television to a transitional object for grown-ups, he was speaking within a national context – albeit a complicated one. His observation added to the over-whelming sense of those growing up in Britain of the 1970s and 1980s that television was what united us in our disparities. In British media studies, at least in the early 1990s, there seemed little dispute that television was a fundamental player in the maintenance of national life. Through its affect, its class positioning and its scheduling, television made Britain legible to itself and, in Silverstone's metaphor, gave it the wherewithal to grow in mutuality if not maturity. The 'transitioning' national viewers were conceived as already and always British, although migrancy in the form of post-colonial, 'raced' subjects hovered on the edge of the agenda.

In the late 1980s, as production was increasingly outsourced from the broadcasters to smaller creative houses, the marketing of British television to the world became a major cost-offset activity for the big buyers in the BBC. Contemporary British television is now known internationally for its attachment to reality television and celebrity culture, its global children's programming and its worldwide sales of blockbuster serials. In Australia, the programming of British shows and stories is commonplace on the ABC, and has been noted as a form of Australian folk memory (Malouf 2003: 13). Malouf writes of the generations of Australians who were caught between settlement and cultural cringe. The perspective of the migrant viewer is a necessary factor in seeing the national in contemporary television. The address to the national subject is recognized by the migrant, but it is vulnerable to their outsider status, both in the place of settlement and in their relation to origins.

Proximate nationalism

Serials and floating lives were discussed in Audrey Yue and Gay Hawkins' essay 'Going South' (2000), where the relation between timing and space in the flow of Chinese-language media to Australia was reiterated as crucial to identity management among *huaqiao*, migrant Chinese populations (Chu et al. 2003; Donald 2001; see also Cunningham and Sinclair 2001). Proximate time-presence allows the viewing subject (the migrant) to imagine their relation to a sending culture and society through events, images and discussions created in that other place. The media perform the role of transitional object from loss of one place to the possibility of surviving as a subject somewhere else. At the same time, the media-as-transitional object allows the subject to maintain an imaginary access to home. Such access – usually partial and decontextualized – provides points of connection and reference which string together across linear time in an attenuated, uprooted parody of place-memory and experienced time. In order to develop this thinly populated account of what has happened in her absence, the migrant must make, and remake, the imaginative leap of temporal proximity.

Active proximity was hyper-realized in the Chinese blogosphere and in the international circulation of emails and visual materials in the wake of the Olympic torch demonstrations around the Tibet uprising in March–April 2008. Television was apparently less important than the internet in this furore of nationalism, resistance and counter-resistance, but in fact CNN and other Western television news outlets were the key object of much of the criticism. On Olympics TV in China, the connections were consciously played out through shots of Tibetans in their homes watching the medal tally rise as bloggers noted that this would put CNN nay-sayers in their collective place.

This also relates to the opportunity to enact proximate time-presence. For overseas Chinese, rallying to the Torch was rallying against someone else's national TV (CNN). This was possible because, for once, there was a reason and an opportunity to be physically co-present with a significant event (the international progress of the Torch). Proximity could be performed for the sending culture's consumption rather than the other way around. What other chances does one usually have? This discussion will also be my own performance after all.

Blowing through

Given the history of invasion and settlement by the British, the emotive term 'migrant' is problematic to apply to more recent arrivals from the United Kingdom, or 'Yookay'. We're not really allowed to be migrants, because that entails a certain vulnerability, which Poms cannot claim. The decade 1997–2007 marked the first 10 years of my family's migration, but also the 10 years of Howard's power in Australia (he was elected in 1996) and Tony Blair's period as prime minister in the United Kingdom. Of course, the Blair years were strangely elusive while fascinating to my experience, because I missed them entirely. He was elected on 2 May 1997 and I left the country on 5 June of the same year.

The importance of British television exports to migrant populations of English-speaking Brits is, at least anecdotally, as crucial to settlement and identity management as Mainland Chinese, Taiwanese and Hong Kong serials, films and print media are to Chinese-speaking populations around the world. In Australia, there is a constant flow of Friday-night crime and espionage shows from the BBC and Channel 4 to the ABC, and the several other serials that come from the United Kingdom (including the classic adaptations referred to in Malouf's essay on Australia and Englishness (2003), and contemporary serial-dramas such as *Skins* and *The Bill*). The free-to-air access reiterates the allowable and hence privileged proximity of British culture in a non-British environment. The shows also, however, foster a shifting relationship between the sending culture and their migrant audiences, predicated both on time away from the United Kingdom and the depth of settlement in the receiving country. Whereas on first arrival the BBC imports represent a continuity of cultural reference to set against the unsettling illegibility of a new televisual world, as time progresses they become a reverse mirror on an increasingly unfamiliar place, and a source of surprise at what might be taken as ordinary in the sending country. As time progresses, watching British programming becomes more about nostalgia than about local knowledge. Migrant television is personal television, a transitional object in which the dyadic split is forced, or rejected, by the migrant's response to national solipsism in television-from-home.

Robin Hood and anachronism

> 'He perverted the course of justice, and attacked the very fabric of our state.'
> 'You're not Englishmen, you're not the England we fought for.'
> (*Robin Hood*, Series One)

The recent (2007–8) phenomenon of *Robin Hood* is a series based on an English myth of class reversal, on national precepts of fairness and justice, and on rugged masculinity in the English soul. Insofar as the series engages with these myths, it is an anachronistic account of the English. Moreover, in Dominic Minghella's Series One it also becomes a paean to British good sense, as the narratives spin an anti-war scenario and commentary on the Iraq conflict (2003–) through the tale of Robin of Locksley's unhappy return from Palestine.

The series provided Sunday-evening Britishness in a way that exceeds the regional crime thrillers (*Dalziel and Pascoe*, *Midsomer Murders*, *Foyle's War*) or the conservative masculinity of *Spooks*. Like its senior companion in the family timeslot of early Sunday evening, *Doctor Who*, *Robin Hood* uses forms of tonal and performative anachronism to achieve the currency of contemporary British cool. Both shows rely on their status as a brand product of Blair's Britain, even as they eschew its mistakes. Similarly, while their version of British gender relations is at once refreshingly equivalent, it recoups the British male as the most likely saviour (and solver) of intransigent world problems, which we remember have been in no small part caused or exacerbated by previous Crusades and by the Bush–Blair Crusade of 2003. *Robin Hood*'s sentiments make good television satire in a national context perhaps, but, once viewed outside of the United Kingdom, the anachronism of sending in an English hero to avenge and moralize on 'the England we fought for' (*pace* in Iraq) is difficult to take.

But perhaps we need to see UK television in its local cultural context to better understand what is happening in *Robin Hood*. The casting of Keith Allen as the Sheriff of Nottingham is a clue:

> 'Say farewell to your friend Mulch.' 'His name is Much.' 'Well, he'll be mulch in a minute.'
>
> (Series One)

This is panto.

Pantomime is a staple mode of British entertainment. It finds its way through the cultural system like a flag. From Christmas pantos in rep, to hip comedy on Channel 4, to outdoors Shakespeare, the patter, libido and excess of the parochial panto is rampant. I'll take a detour to a theatre job I once did in 1989, touring across England in the heyday of the poll tax and Thatcher's Britain. The play we were touring was *Cymbeline*. This comic-history is Shakespeare's foray into ancient Britain and is of similar ilk to *Robin Hood* in its vague evocation of an English past. In the outdoors production there was very little attention paid to history and the costumes made the actors look and feel like extras from an older *Robin Hood*, but not as dashing. The sartorial compacting of ancient Britain with the Crusades was an anachronistic answer to the company's straitened finances, but, dressed in Maid Marian garb aka Robin Hood disguise (see Figure 12.1), one knew, as performance strayed into overkill, that this was also about the national passion for pantomime. Such confusions were compounded by the venues, which included late-seventeenth- and eighteenth-century stately homes (including the pile in Keswick where Keir Hardie discussed the founding of the Labour Party with his unlikely aristocratic patrons), Peel Castle (a ruin on the Isle of Man, dating back to the Vikings), and an Elizabethan moated manor in Suffolk. The latter venue was best remembered for the (recently minted) owner/ Lord of the Manor's request that the actors eat in the kitchen. This was a tour and a production of quite enormous anachronistic propensities.

The company convened in May in 1989, rehearsing in a park in north London with a director-manager who, I remember, adored the local Conservative MP, Michael Portillo.[2] It rains quite a lot in the English summer, so much of the time we shouted our lines, through the pouring rain, at happy locals peering from under tarpaulins, or staring through the windowed walls of the Orangery. The only thing that kept the cast and audience going were the unintended puns on the weather that Shakespeare obligingly provided for such downpours:

> ... but if there be
> Yet left in heaven as small a drop of pity
> As a wren's eye, fear'd gods, a part of it!
>
> (Act IV, Imogen)

etc.

Anachronism and apologetics

I had put aside these memories until recently, when the project of this book made me consider the role of anachronism both in the text and in the reception of exported British television. Television before TV came to mind. *Robin Hood* has been a success story for the producers (three series and international sales). The retelling of a semi-mythical tale of the essential British class warrior – who is also a member of the ruling classes (Robin, Earl of Locksley) – was now couched in the anxieties of the Iraq War, and of how to talk about Englishness without resorting to bombast or Blairite fundamentalism. Sensitive masculinity was an important ingredient, as were the fashion choices of Marian (whose solidly curvaceous body shape made a statement about firm, fleshly, female beauty that was as politically right on as the replacement of Friar Tuck with a female Muslim healer, Djak (Anjali Rose), disguised as a boy). Thus the excitement of the Gisbourne/Hood competition for Marian's affections swept through expat culture, as grown men self-defined their sexual competitiveness in black leather or rural brown. Even my students were humming LDN.[3] Perhaps the casting director realized that these connections would make the series unbeatable – or perhaps cool celebrity Britannia really is inescapable in pop culture.

In the 2006–8 version of *Robin Hood*, anachronism is more than an underlying necessity of how all stories are told to new generations: it is the presiding trope of the script. This is apparently the twelfth century, but men's sexual politics are, well, not bad really; when faced with death at the hands of a rough diamond from Brookside (see Series Two – 'Robin's Birthday'), they can even talk about their feelings (or at least seem inept when they can't), and of course the overriding concerns of the heroes are for social justice in a class-ridden society which is facing the challenges of an unjust war and inward migration from the Middle East. Women in the series are feisty and politically sound, but with more than a hint of post-feminist sexiness. British multiculturalism is given a slight appropriative nod in the form of Djak, who eventually marries Will Scarlett. She is matched with Marian, who combines passion with philanthropy. There is also some attempt in the first series to persuade us that Robin has been turned off killing by his unhappy experiences in an early Gulf War. This is the *Guardian Weekly* in moving pictures, not *Morte d'Arthur* or *The Greene Knight*.

Anachronism is an appropriate term through which to describe the tone and modality of the series' moral structure, and its metaphorical allusions to the here and now. Historians of folk stories would point out that a national myth is always anachronistic insofar as it is brought into the service of the present to give depth and legitimacy to current ways of doing, being and seeing the nation. So perhaps I should qualify my stating of the obvious by adding that when a nation confidently turns political navel-gazing into a mediaeval folk drama on global television, it surely has a profound confidence about its place in the world. It also lays itself open to critical interpretation by its own

Figure 12.1

migrants – those most concerned to savour the series' national nostalgia, while sufficiently separated from the centrifugal impulse of the national to question the version of anti-salvationism it offers as salve in a troubled world. Indeed, the sense that Robin Hood's ultimate failure to defend England (*pace* all of us civilized folks) from John and the Sheriff is nonetheless a valuable heroic response reads from a distance as a hubristic misunderstanding of other diplomatic possibilities the world over.

> Nothing sorts out memories from ordinary moments. Later on they do claim remembrance when they show their scars.
>
> (Chris Marker, cited in Lindroos 1998: 224)

> The view of another culture went hand in hand with the belief that our technologized gaze was equivalent to the gaze of God, which should have made murder impossible.
>
> (Chow 1993: 166)

The troubling sense of déjà vu which I feel when I compare this contemporary, classy production of *Robin Hood* with the rough *Cymbeline* of 1989, or even the stagey historical dramas on Chinese television, is something to do with sorting out memories. Taking the lead from the film-maker Chris Marker's observations, there are memories which are made for us by the media, and deeper memories which sort themselves out from the unexpected conjunction of ordinary moments, which may or may not be mediated. Furthermore, for many of us these are memories strung along the thin skein of displaced migrant experience, and their skinny vulnerability is raw. Too little context and too much distance cause one to react against (or in tune with, depending on one's own contextual needs) national presumptions of interiority, of uninterrupted history and of heroic response.

> Robin Hood, Robin Hood,
> Riding through the glen.
> Robin Hood, Robin Hood,
> With his band of men.
> Feared by the bad, loved by the good.
> Robin Hood, Robin Hood, Robin Hood.
>
> (*The Adventures of Robin Hood* 1955)

So, as I watch the nice, cohesive, anti-war version of Britain re-enact a folded double entendre of the Thatcher years of the poll tax (the Sheriff's crude taxation enforcement system) within the grip of Blair's war on terror (the Crusades), I see a nation playing away its guilt. Cool Britannia is a little confused by being too rich, too rough and too gung-ho for its own brand. It has maintained and grown both the economic success that was embarrassingly founded in the social vacuum of the 1980s (an economy that dismissed with a shrug the victims of the 1989 crash and has seemingly lasted until the credit crunch of 2008), and the continuing aggression of its foreign policy. The angst is relieved for the nation by Robin Hood, England's stalwart, returning hero.[4] This is television after war and after new media. It is both the start of debate and the statement of the nation's best practice. Like the equally anachronistic sci-fi hero in *Doctor Who*, Robin is regenerated and reincarnated for England, Yookay, the Universe, the World and its conscience. And suddenly I remember that, while rehearsing the brave Imogen in *Cymbeline*, dressed up like Robin Hood in Enfield in May and early June 1989, Tiananmen was happening elsewhere. It has taken many years to get a clearer view of what occurred in the Square and across China over those few weeks, but the news of the massacre on 4 June was astounding at the time, partly because the media – our media – had been 'there', watching and protecting the demonstrators by their presence. But, as Rey Chow has written in her analysis of the US media's coverage of televisual events, CNN was, even before its wartime role in the Gulf War of 1990–91, making history but without understanding it. I will leave others to draw the ironic relationship to Marx's famous one-liner. The stark truth was that there was nothing that global television news services, or any of us, could do, and we totally mistook what reaction overseas mediation would provoke from the Chinese leadership. This demonstration was really nothing to do with us, and yet everything to do with our collective and misplaced sense of potency. To mix my metaphors, we were dressed up for a pantomime with nowhere to go on the world stage.

Cultural studies thinkers have recently agreed that the parochial is a good thing, but this insight is somewhat offset by social science theorists who argue that cultures of migration must also be grounded in the space of arrival. This produces a cosmopolitanism that is grounded, or 'actually existing' (Robbins 1998; Kofman 2005; Roudometof 2005), and which challenges the parochial on its own turf. The two perspectives may be brought into a different focus if we add the notion of actually existing cosmopolitan migrants. They are progressively ungrounded in the parochial cultures from which they come, and face new, resistant parochialisms in the place of settlement. Televisual nationalism offers both respite and, through its bland insistence on the place – England, the Yookay, China – as the place where historical truth resides, further evidence of their shrinking roots.

Chow (1993) may or may not be accurate in her interpretation of CNN's effects in China in 1989. Maybe the leadership just didn't care. Certainly in the CNN fallout in 2008, the angry reaction of Chinese audiences worldwide to perceived bias suggests that the leadership won the nationalistic argument. It is fair comment, then, that CNN's attempts 20 years ago to commandeer for Western democracy the struggle in the Square itself and in demonstrations across eastern China were both futile and counter-productive. I don't blame *Robin Hood* for Tiananmen, but I do wonder why a global migrant audience buys so passionately into a narrative of salvation, where leadership is provided by a British landowning-soldier-monarchist just back from the Crusades. Isn't that kind of apologetic class confusion in the same vein as the Western media's confusion over national loyalties that characterized the run-up to the Beijing Olympics? A man with a bow and arrow and a lopsided smile won't necessarily wipe out or transcend the histories with which we arrive wherever we go.

Or maybe what I am debating through the prism of anachronism is better described as yet another set of apologetics for past and present:

> Celebration or apologetics aims to smooth over the revolutionary moments of the historical process. Its concern is to construct a continuity. It accentuates only those elements of a work, which have already entered posterity. What it misses are the jagged edges which offer a foothold to someone who wants to get beyond that work.
>
> (Benjamin, quoted in Wohlfarth 1998: 15)

In 1989, the *Cymbeline* show went to Chester, to a very small twelfth-century manor in a large park. Our venue was a small stone house with a small hall and a small minstrels' gallery. Unlike most National Trust properties today, it had not yet been 'dressed'. This made the place seem closer to its own past than it might have, had it been draped in authentic tapestry and carefully placed wooden settles. The show that night was interrupted when a baby bat fell down the chimney and was rescued by the ranger – maybe this gives a sense of the scale of the place. The building was not, of course, of *Cymbeline*'s era – but it was not far off the *Robin Hood* period, even if Nottingham is on the wrong side of the country (and the series itself filmed in Hungary). Think of the scenes in Series Two when Gisbourne and Marian are trapped in Nottingham, waiting for Prince John's henchmen to destroy the town. Well, it was a much smaller hall even than that.

And so finally I find a memory that in Benjamin's terms begins to get beyond – to make a transition perhaps – the hubris of national mythologies, and the confidence of national statements and expectations of proximity after television but through TV. Hood's lost manor in Nottingham was minute, local and muddy, and nested by protected bats. If only his desire to win it back did not so easily fall prey to the excessive, obese national imaginary that stalks global television. If only the makers of *Robin Hood* could see that their well-meaning metaphor of anti-war sentiment was nonetheless founded in free-to-air British cool and sovereign righteousness. If only television could find a national voice that was muddy underfoot, and scaled to size, then the reverberations after TV is switched off might be less troubling. But of course, it is hard to resist nonetheless. I still prefer *Robin Hood*, Series One and Two, to much else on TV – pretty much anything, really. So maybe my transitional object is still clutched close, even though I have noticed that it is just a teddy bear with a lopsided grin, and it's not going to make being English more British, or being Australian less so.

The question of television studies after TV is ultimately still problematic. New media compete with TV for the attention of, and relevance to, the users, but they are still also in an intense dialogic relationship with television's hold over the national imaginary, off and on shore. This is nowhere more apparent than in the mediation of national belonging, state politics and nationalism. China provides a certain kind of case study, but Britain is also looping its image and its anxieties through anachronistic reruns of core mythologies. One produces spectacular massed drummers, and the other goes for panto.

Notes

1 Bev Skeggs's comments on snobbism in British television at a CRN meeting in Melbourne in 2007 reassured me that this is not a lone opinion.

2 Michael Portillo was a Conservative Member of Parliament (Enfield Southgate), whose electoral defeat in 1997 was replayed on video in many homes for several weeks. The clip is available on YouTube: www.youtube.com/watch?v = mdKexAVIUY4. Theatre Set-Up (the name of the company) was based in Enfield. The company still exists, with the same director, and – if the website is accurate – one of the same actors, wearing the same red cloak. See www.ts-u.co.uk.

3 From Keith Allen's daughter Lily Allen's 2006 release, *Alright Still* (Regal Zonophone Records).

4 *The Adventures of Robin Hood*, 1955 (Sapphire Films/BBC), with Richard Greene, was a major home-grown adventure series screened on British TV, and has arguably had a

strong effect on the imagination of two generations of baby boomer Brits, most of whom can still sing the theme song. On the blog PopMatters, Brian Holcomb notes that the series was produced by Lew Grade; he also points out the nice irony that it was sometimes scripted by blacklisted members of the American Communist Party (www. popmatters.com/pm/review/8840/adventures-of-robin-hood-vol-15, accessed 20 July 2008). Note on continuity: a slightly earlier attempt at *Robin Hood* (1953, BBC) starred Patrick Troughton (later to be the star of *Doctor Who*, and grandfather of Sam Troughton, who plays Much in the 2006 series). These connections matter to the baby boomers as much as to the casting system in British theatre royalty.

Part Four

Television content: what's on now?

Introduction

The chapters in this Part focus on the content of television – what is watched, what is produced, and who does the watching and producing. Among the issues underlying the analyses here are the international trade in formats influenced by the competing forces of globalization and localization; the rise of the geo-linguistic and diasporic markets coupled with the emergence of new content suppliers such as Mexico; and the corresponding decline in the importance of Hollywood in markets such as India and China. Once more, as is the case throughout this book, the accounts in this Part present versions of 'what's on television' that emphasize the need to recognize the variety of platforms, formats, production and audience histories currently in play in contemporary television studies.

This variety acknowledged, it is nonetheless true that locally produced drama and reality television formats tend to top the national ratings tables around the world. While often the result of the trade in global formats, the individual programmes are usually, as Anthony Fung and Albert Moran both demonstrate, the outcome of a strong process of localization. While there is a clear trend to be observed in the kind of popular fare that achieves ratings success internationally, there are also significant patterns of difference in the actual content available to each local or national community. While four of the five chapters in this Part insist on the presence of a strong national audience, three of these four argue that this audience connects to a nationalized popular culture built on the provision of entertainment that can as easily serve a political as a cultural purpose.

Anthony Fung's chapter provides an exemplary account of how, for the rapidly growing Chinese television audience, there is a close connection between popular culture and state pedagogies. Fung looks closely at how a global format such as *Survivor* has been modified for Chinese audiences in order to meet the twin objectives of Chinese mainland television producers: providing successful commercial entertainment and at the same time maintaining their alignment with state political and cultural agendas. As Fung demonstrates, the Chinese versions of international reality television genres mediate the state imperatives of inculcating soft nationalism while encasing the programme in a format that is highly globalized and thus fashionable and new. While the format may be new, the blending of popular culture and nationalism is not. Fung – like Volcic in her chapter earlier in this book – explains how state ideologies have managed surreptitiously to insert themselves into the national popular culture, and thus how television has played a major part in infusing the popular sphere with nationalist nostalgia as a means of stabilizing the powers of the state.

However, the reassertion of the national within the processes of format localization can be assessed differently in other political contexts. Albert Moran's chapter presents a more positive reading of the changing political economies of the global television production industries under the influence of the expansion of the trade in television formats. This is an industrially focused account of the processes through which this international trade is managed. While Moran's initial interest is in the international dimensions of this trade, his close attention to the modification and localization of the traded format provides us with a demonstration of the countervailing effect of the local industry and its audience. Paradoxically, Moran concludes, it appears as if the advent of the global trade in TV formats, rather than displacing the local industry, has demonstrated the 'endurance or even reappearance' of the national element within the broader economy of a globalizing television industry.

While so many accounts of television in the current era see it as a declining technology, Adrian Athique's discussion of the Indian and neighbouring markets turns that on its head by talking about the contemporary moment – with its proliferation of local broadcast stations and a massively expanding popular audience – as constituting the region's 'age of television'. According to his account, the rise of broadcast television has only just begun. It is significant that this has occurred through the deregulation of state TV and the expansion of commercial broadcasters whose programming has aggregated an audience by linking film and television in a reciprocal loop to produce a highly distinctive nationalized popular culture – of Bollywood gossip, entertainment and talk show programmes. The growth of this audience is further enhanced through the proliferation of cable and satellite television to regional Sri Lanka, Bangladesh and Pakistan and internationally – and the circulation of the other regional broadcasters corroborates Athique's account of a regionalizing television scene that is expanding.

What seems to be driving this new audience, in both the Indian and Arab markets, is the emerging freedom from traditional, state-controlled pedagogic television. In both instances, we can see the shift from highly politicized content towards a more 'feminized' form of entertainment that is redirected at issues located within private and domestic spaces. As Naomi Sakr's piece explains in relation to Arab satellite talk show programming, this is emotionally charged television dedicated to the public expression of private grievances (even if the audience prefers to watch rather than to tell, or to watch in private). As is the case with many of the contributions to this book, Naomi Sakr points to the influence of the usual shifts and trends – convergence, globalization of programming, fragmenting audiences and so on – but the detail of her account is a compelling demonstration of the need to look closely at the specific contexts in which these shifts play out. The development of talk shows for the Arab market dealing with sex, family life, premarital sex, divorce and drug use has captured a growing audience whose active participation is assisted by the fact that they are also becoming adept at using the internet and mobile telephony. Breaking the taboos that inhibit direct and public discussion of such issues is to some extent enabled by the level of privacy and anonymity made possible by these new modes of participation, which have in turn opened up new spaces for the use of new media technologies. The story Sakr has to tell about the success of these programmes, as well as about the difficult issues to be dealt with before they can be produced or screened, is highly specific to the large and growing market for Arab-language programming, but it reminds us of the contingency of the relations between television and the nation, television and the commercial audience, television and culture.

The rise of the Latin American production industries is yet another case in point. In relation to the television experience available in this geo-linguistic region, many of the standard patterns do not apply. Structurally, John Sinclair suggests, it is 'not yet the post-broadcast era', as the industrial giants Televisa and Globo maintain their dominance of free-to-air broadcasting and as the continuing income equalities among the audience affect the demand for subscription-based services. At the level of reception, Sinclair also argues, the consumption of television has remained a family ritual and so its social and cultural function is further differentiated from many of the factors used to mark the post-broadcast era. However, the region's nationally based but interrelated industries are major players in the world's media markets and at the leading edge of the globalization of content. The telenovelas are a case in point. Their popularity is robust enough to return 80 per cent of production costs within their home markets, thus allowing export prices to be adjusted for different markets; in turn, this makes the telenovelas a cheap alternative for importing countries. More significantly, however, the international success of the telenovelas – both in their original form and in remakes and adaptations – runs against the grain of the standard orthodoxy on the importance of cultural proximity. The telenovela format has been successful even in non-culturally proximate locations such as China, Russia and Eastern Europe, and Sinclair examines some of the reasons why this has occurred.

Rather than chronicling the death and decline of television, or rather than simply providing another element in the apparently irresistible narrative of globalization and convergence, the chapters in this Part demonstrate that 'what is on' television is rapidly reinventing itself in these markets: within new

formats, new audiences and new technologies, and while establishing productive conversations with other media such as film, new media, internet and
mobile phones. However, what is conclusive is that these chapters provide
entry points for us to reconsider what television is constitutively *becoming* in
these largest television markets in the world, and the need to understand the
functions of new genres and formats in their specific cultural contexts.

Chapter 13

Latin America's impact on world television markets

John Sinclair

As far as television is concerned, the Latin American region has some unique characteristics. First, whereas most countries of the world began their television systems on the state-owned, usually public-service model exemplified by the BBC, almost all Latin American countries adopted the privately owned, commercial model of their influential northern neighbour. Second, Latin America was the first world region to experience colonialism on a continental scale, the legacy of which is that Spanish is the language of nearly all countries in that region, with a significant exception: Portuguese is the language of what is by far its largest and most populous nation, Brazil. This common linguistic, and to a large extent cultural, heritage from the colonial past has allowed programme exchange to flourish throughout the continent. Indeed, Latin America forms the greater part of the geo-linguistic regions of both Spanish and Portuguese, which include Spain and Portugal as well as the Spanish-speaking United States and Portugal's former colonies respectively. A geo-linguistic region, therefore, is defined not necessarily by geographical connectedness, but virtually: by commonalities of language and culture. Such regions have been a crucial touchstone for the internationalization of the media, particularly of television programmes and services (Sinclair et al. 1996).

Just as in the geo-linguistic region of English, where the United States, as the one-time colony, now harbours a much larger number of speakers (304 million) than the erstwhile colonial power (61 million), and indeed challenges its hegemony over the language, so it is in Latin America where Mexico, with its 110 million, is nearly three times Spain's 40.5 million, while Brazil's 192 million swamp Portugal's 10.7 million (*World Factbook* 2008). In terms of television production, having the world's largest domestic market in English has been one major factor in allowing the United States to come to dominate the television trade in the Anglosphere (and beyond), and this is correspondingly true also for Mexico and Brazil in their respective geo-linguistic regions.

In other words, Mexico and Brazil stand in the same relation to the rest of the Spanish-speaking and Portuguese-speaking worlds as the United States does to the English-speaking world. The economics are such that a large domestic market allows television producers to recoup all or most of their costs in the home market, so that programme exports can earn relatively cost-free profits. In addition to the economies of scale and scope that large domestic producers enjoy, the key Latin American producers have the additional advantage of being able to integrate production and distribution – that is, the dominant networks produce their own programming, which minimizes costs even further.

Language is the vehicle of culture, so it is not similarities of language alone that give access to foreign markets, but culture more broadly. This has been conceived as 'cultural proximity', which includes, as Joseph Straubhaar (2007) has formulated it most recently, 'cultural elements – dress, ethnic types, gestures, body language, definitions of humour, ideas about story pacing, music traditions, religious elements – that are often shared across national borders' (2007: 237). Straubhaar argues that these factors incline audiences to prefer programmes from their own culture – or, when these are not available, from cultures similar to their own, not necessarily with the same language.

This would suggest that, in addition to language, there are 'pan-Latin' characteristics of successfully exported programming. Taken in conjunction with the economics of large markets, similarities of language and culture certainly seem to account for the success of Mexican and Brazilian programmes. This is most evident in the case of the telenovela genre, the melodramatic serials that still form the bulk of programme exports from these countries. However, as we shall see, the fact that such programmes have also found eager audiences in linguistically and culturally remote countries like Russia and China makes it clear that the geo-linguistic regions and cultural proximity explanations only go so far in explaining the success of telenovela exports.

This is the major issue to be addressed in this chapter, but first it is appropriate to outline the major exporters of the region and note how they have built their markets, and then to provide some understanding of the telenovela as a genre. To follow Rafael Roncagliolo's (1995) classification, Mexico and Brazil are pre-eminent as 'net exporters' within the region, for the reasons indicated, but Venezuela and Argentina must be acknowledged as 'new exporters', with Colombia, Chile and Peru seeking to join them, but coming from far behind. The rest of the nations in the region – mainly the smaller nations of Central America and the Caribbean – are 'net importers' (ibid. 1995: 337).

Mexico's Televisa

The development of television in Mexico is defined by the emergence of Televisa, a quasi-monopolistic, cross-media conglomerate that, under the direction of three generations of the Azcárraga family, not only came to dominate the national television market, but went on to become conspicuous in pursuing its international ambitions as the world's largest producer of television programming in Spanish.

Televisa was one of the first media corporations in the world to see the advantages of satellite for the distribution of programmes to far-flung and dispersed audiences outside its borders which shared linguistic and cultural similarities with the programming's nation of origin. The name Televisa, in fact, is a contraction of Televisión vía Satélite and, true to its name, Televisa has used satellite technology to leverage its pre-eminence in the world's largest Spanish-speaking domestic market into the rest of the Spanish-speaking world. Satellite distribution has been used to augment the role of Protele, Televisa's sales division, which exists to sell programme rights and physically distribute programmes on an international basis through its foreign offices. Crucially, Televisa used satellite technology to build a national Spanish-speaking television network in the United States, Univisión, in the 1970s. Again, it used its satellite-to-cable service, Galavisión, as the basis of an international news and entertainment service in the late 1980s, and was instrumental in the launch of one of the world's first commercial international satellite systems, PanAmSat (Sinclair 1999).

At one stage in the early 1990s, Televisa was making direct investments, notably in stations in Peru and Chile. As well, it was seeking a toehold in Spain, but the Mexican peso crisis obliged it to drastically sell off or diminish its stake in all its direct foreign holdings, including PanAmSat and Univisión. Around the same time, Televisa became faced for the first time with serious competition in its domestic market when, in 1993, the government sold the licences for its own networks to a private group, TV Azteca (Sinclair 1999).

Since then, Azteca has gone on to become Televisa's only serious competitor in Mexico, and also with international ambitions – notably via Azteca America, a Spanish-language network it has developed in the United States. Even with only half Televisa's output and a quarter share of the domestic market, Azteca is said to be the world's second-biggest producer of Spanish-language programming (Hecht 2005). The domestic market remains the crucial battle-ground for Televisa to defend – for all its export activity, Televisa still derives nearly two-thirds of its revenue there (Dickerson 2005), while more than half of its export earnings come from its most important foreign market, the 44 million 'Hispanics' or 'Latinos' in the United States (US Census Bureau 2007). Nevertheless, both producers are selling their programmes worldwide, in over 100 countries from Slovenia to Indonesia (Hecht 2005). While Televisa's only recent direct investment has been within its own geo-linguistic region – Spain – it continues to supply programming to significant markets outside it, notably China, while at home it co-produces in English and in Spanish with global majors like Endemol and Fremantle Media (Carugati 2006).

Brazil's TV Globo

In Brazil, the dominant broadcaster and producer, TV Globo, began in the 1960s as the television division of the integrated media holdings of the Marinho family, which still controls Globo today. Although it had been Globo's competitors who had developed the Brazilian telenovela as a genre, it was Globo that commercialized it as the staple of domestic programming, and built it into an export product in the 1970s (Mattelart and Mattelart 1990: 14–17). The lusophone, or Portuguese-speaking, geo-linguistic region is far smaller than the Spanish one, as there are fewer people in fewer countries, and they are also more dispersed and less affluent as markets. Thus, Globo and the other Brazilian television producers have had tighter options in developing overseas markets than has Televisa. Although Brazil is the biggest lusophone country in the world, and absolutely the biggest country in Latin America, it is the only one in its region that speaks Portuguese. Furthermore, Brazilian programmes for the Latin American market have to be transcodified into the NTSC transmission standard used everywhere else in the Americas, as well as being dubbed into Spanish, adding a level of cost which Spanish-language competitors don't have. Therefore, Globo has been more oriented to Europe in its export efforts than to its Spanish-speaking neighbours (Marques De Melo 1988: 41–3).

Thus Portugal assumed a strategic significance for Globo – much more than Spain has ever done correspondingly for Televisa. Globo sold several telenovelas to Rádio e Televisão Portuguesa (RTP) in the 1970s and 1980s and, with the creation of private channels in the 1990s, secured a stake in one of them, Sociedade Independente de Comunicação (SIC), and went on to build it into the leading network (Sousa 1997). Globo programmes proved popular with Portuguese audiences, who joked about 'colonialism in reverse'. Globo also concentrated on those European countries that were culturally similar, by virtue of a common Latin heritage, and which were also more accustomed to watching dubbed programmes. In the mid-1980s Globo started a vogue in Italy for Brazilian and other Latin American telenovelas, and also sold several telenovelas to Canal Plus and other channels in France. Just as US exporters always have done, Globo's practice was to set different prices for different markets, and at different stages of market penetration – though in general it has been able to charge more in European than in Latin American markets (Marques De Melo 1992: 9).

While linguistic and cultural similarities may have helped to open up some initial markets for Globo – and, it should be added, for some of its competitors – the sale of Brazilian telenovelas certainly has not been restricted to what Roncagliolo calls the 'Latin-European countries' (1995: 340). By the end of the 1980s, telenovelas were being discovered by audiences in such culturally and geographically remote countries as the former Soviet Union, Poland and China, as well as the United Kingdom, Australia and New Zealand. Although international sales at the beginning of the 1990s were only 3 per cent of total revenue (Marques De Melo 1992: 8) – even less a proportion of income for Globo than for Televisa – Globo has continued to seek to develop programme exports as a major area of activity, and it continues to be a production-driven organization. Like Televisa, Globo also has an international satellite service, but satellite technology has been rather less instrumental for Globo in the internationalization of its programming (Rêgo and La Pastina 2007).

Interestingly, given that Globo and other telenovela producers in Brazil rely on initial domestic market success as the basis for subsequent export strategies, there is a tension between such 'Brazilianization' of the genre and the broad acceptability of the products to international audiences (Lopez 1995). This has meant that not all telenovelas can be exported, while those that are exported may have to shed or at least play down precisely those more familiar characteristics that make them appealing to Brazilians. This dilemma is not a problem for Televisa – indeed, perhaps it is even an advantage, at least insofar as its main market in the United States is concerned, given the Mexican origins of the majority of US Hispanics. On the other hand, Televisa was not able to develop a market for its telenovelas in Spain, where their more Mexican qualities were seen as a liability, while in Portugal Brazilian popular culture was readily embraced. Globo, like Televisa, is seeking to further internationalize its production – and not just of telenovelas – via co-production, and productions with international casts in languages other than Portuguese (Carugati 2004).

New exporters

While companies like Telefé in Argentina and RCN in Colombia are active in exporting their programmes, the most significant Spanish-language player outside of Mexico is Venevisión, owned by the Cisneros industrial group (CGC). Like Televisa and Globo, CGC is a conglomerate in which media are integrated both vertically – notably through its television network and an international sales division – and horizontally – incorporating companies ranging across several media fields. CGC has direct interests in television networks in other Spanish-speaking countries, and supplies telenovelas and other programmes under contract to Univisión in the United States. Yet, unlike Televisa and Globo, Venevisión does not have a large domestic market in its home country of Venezuela, and so is much more dependent on its international activities, which include extensive film and television production and distribution from its offices in Miami, and most recently format and programme sales to China and India, not to mention co-productions with those countries (Carugati 2008). Once again, the pattern has been for Venevisión to have cultivated export markets which have linguistic and cultural similarities in the first instance, and later to gain entry to alien ones further afield.

The telenovela as a genre

The commercialization of popular culture in the media of Latin America is deeply entrenched and long standing: the telenovelas that form the backbone of television programming in Latin America today have descended from the radionovelas that were expressly developed as cultural vehicles for advertising in the region by sponsors such as Procter & Gamble and Colgate-Palmolive in Cuba in the decades between the two world wars, and subsequently diffused to continental Latin America, ultimately migrating to television (Luis López 1998). In spite of its capture by the same companies who fostered the soap opera in the United States, scholars of the telenovela are careful to distinguish between the two genres: whereas the soap opera can run for years, the tele-novela is finite, usually running for 6 to 12 months, and having a discernible narrative structure of beginning, middle and end. There are also thematic distinctions to be drawn: telenovelas often take dramatic motivation from contemporary social conflicts and issues, while the soap opera rests more on individual characters and conventional plots. Furthermore, aficionados like to draw attention to national differences in telenovelas: Brazilian ones have rela-tively high production values and more complex plots, while the Mexican telenovelas tend to go for more obvious melodramatic and sentimental effects (Lopez 1995).

Markets beyond geo-linguistic regions

We have seen that the exploitation of comparative advantage within a geo-linguistic region, and the cultural proximity which accompanies it, offers an adequate – though not comprehensive – explanation for the success of Tele-visa, Globo and Venevisión in building their export markets within Latin America, Latin Europe and the Spanish-speaking United States. However, such linguistic-cultural theories seem mute and helpless in the face of the enthusiastic take-up of the telenovela in Eastern Europe, Russia, China and elsewhere far beyond the boundaries of the Latin world.

There are three quite different kinds of explanation on offer for this phenom-enon: these are respectively anthropological, economic and temporal. The anthropological one argues that the telenovela as a genre is based on themes which are universal in their appeal, and that their simple melodramatic narrative mode can be understood and appreciated by audiences everywhere. While this line of thought may suggest the archetypes theorized by Jung or the mythic structures of Lévi-Strauss, there are less abstract approaches available. Notably, Straubhaar (2007) has recently modified his cultural proximity concept to take account of 'genre proximity', where the programmes have resonance with traditional forms of storytelling in the receiving society; 'thematic proximity', where audiences are responding to stories built around the universal experience of urbanization and modernization in general; and 'value proximity', which is where traditional values, including religion, triumph over their tension with modernity as a global phenomenon (ibid. 2007: 196–202). Thus, to take an example of value proximity, or its absence, programme exporters report that US series 'don't work' with Chinese audiences because they are more about individual than collective experience (Bielby and Harrington 2002: 229n), whereas telenovelas have thematic proximity in that they reflect more of the realities of life in societies undergoing industrialization (Madden 2008).

The second kind of explanation is much more mundane, having to do with the economics of the international programme trade. The annual value of telenovelas has recently been estimated at US$2 billion, but only around US $340 million of that value is in exports (Bardasano, cited in TVMASNOVE-LAS 2004). In other words, sales of advertising carried by the programmes in their home markets generate close to 80 per cent of revenue for the producers/distributors. This means that they can sell telenovelas to foreign markets at much less than the cost of production. As well, they can calibrate the price in accordance with the size and purchasing power of the particular market (Mato, cited in Ortíz de Urbana and López 1999). Furthermore, costs of production are low in any case. While there is a big variation between the higher production values of Brazilian telenovelas as against their Mexican counterparts, as of the mid-2000s the cost range was put at between US $40,000 and US$70,000 per hour (TVMASNOVELAS 2004). This compares with US$2 million for an hour of drama in the United States, where even reality shows were around US$700,000 per episode (Entertainment Industry Development Corporation 2005).

Thus, from the point of view of the importing countries, telenovelas are cheap programming in the first place, and come with the bonus of proven success in their home markets – however alien they may be! The spread of telenovelas out of their geo-linguistic regions and into Eastern Europe and Asia in the 1980s and 1990s therefore has a ready economic explanation in that these were then fairly poor markets with relatively little production capacity of their own, and telenovelas offered a very affordable option with which to fill expanding schedules.

However, as these markets have matured over the last decade, they have begun to produce their own serial fiction, and audiences have proved responsive. If television is a cultural industry, we can think of this development as a kind of import substitution process, as in the manufacturing industry: reducing dependency on imports by making local adaptations of them. This is the significance of the Latin producers' ventures into co-production and format trading noted earlier. The receiving markets are now more sophisticated – at least in that audiences are demanding programmes that reflect their own culture and are in their own language, there is now advertising better able to pay for domestic programming, and local production capacity is increasing. The paradigm case is the series that English-speakers know in its US version as *Ugly Betty*, but which was originally a Colombian production, subsequently remade in India, Russia, Germany, Hungary, Greece and Belgium, and even in Mexico and Spain (Mikos 2008). Most recently, a Chinese version has been produced (Madden 2008).

Finally, the temporal explanation lays its emphasis on the intrinsic daily rhythm of the scheduling of telenovelas, and the habitual everyday shared ritual quality of watching and discussing them in specific social settings (González 1994). Traditionally, telenovelas are 'strip-programmed' – that is, they occupy the same timeslot each day of the week, and one telenovela follows another throughout prime time. This practice has been followed in many of the markets where they are shown, and anecdotes abound as to how the streets fall silent at the time when the latest telenovela is being shown.

Not yet the post-broadcast era

Even before the end of the 1990s, the concept of 'post-broadcast' television was being used to take account of new means of television delivery such as direct-to-home (DTH) satellite, and the challenge that cable subscription services presented to the traditional, free-to-air, mass media model in Latin America (Sinclair 1999: 162). Both Televisa and Globo had reinforced their broadcast market dominance with strategic stakes in cable television in their respective markets, and survived when challenged in the early 1990s by the advent of Spanish-language satellite-to-cable channels from US companies such as HBO, CNN, CBS and MTV. Indeed, their respective prime positions were recognized in the strategic alliances formed by the US-based companies that introduced DTH to the region in the mid-1990s (Sinclair 1999), so that today Liberty Media and News Corporation operate their DTH services Sky Mexico in conjunction with Televisa, and Sky Brazil with Globo (News Corporation 2008). Yet the penetration of pay TV, cable and DTH, is limited – 25 per cent in Mexico (which includes only 1.2 million DTH subscribers in a nation of 20 million television households) and 10 per cent of 48 million households in Brazil (*Broadcast* 2007; TV Telco Latam 2008). Clearly, the base of both Televisa and Globo remains their pre-eminence in their free-to-air domestic markets in countries marked by severe income inequalities between the globalized elites and the common people, *la gente corriente*, who just love their telenovelas. So, while these programmes have achieved a global impact in markets far beyond the Latin world, their production and distribution grow out of a regional media ecology in which deeply entrenched nationally based oligopolies continue to thrive on revenue from advertisers paying to reach the traditional mass audiences for broadcast television.

Chapter 14

Reasserting the national?

Programme formats, international television and domestic culture

Albert Moran

Introduction

It is now 10 years since the *Big Brother* TV programme format was devised in the Netherlands by producer John de Mol for his production company Endemol. As Bazalgette (2005) has shown, the programme was ground-breaking in terms of its premise of bringing together a group of young people and having them live in a confined space where they were filmed by a battery of hidden cameras. Beginning in the Netherlands, and soon giving rise to a string of franchised productions around the world, *Big Brother* has become the most watched programme in world television history. The accumulated global audience for its various national versions regularly produced up to 2005 was estimated at 740 million viewers. It has also proved to be an extremely valuable franchise around the world, generating more than US$4.7 billion in profits for its owner in the same period (Bazalgette 2005).

But the phenomenal success of the programme also heralded the maturation of TV formats. This way of doing television is now a highly significant component of industry and cultural practice in modern television, at both the national and international levels. Whether in the form of reality, game show, infotainment programming, makeover, talent show, sitcom or drama, the advent of the television programme format seems to signal the triumph of media globalization, even while asserting the continued importance of local or domestic programming (Moran and Malbon 2006). What does this paradox imply? How can the TV programme format best be understood in the rapidly changing mediascape of present-day international television?

This chapter explores the practice and meaning of TV format programming. It is divided into six sections. The first sketches the notion of a global television system. In the next two sections, I outline the main features of format programming, including its evolution as an industry practice. The following two sections develop an understanding of adaptation, drawing on semiotics and translation theory. In the concluding section, I consider this customizing of formats for home audiences under the label of nationalization.

Global television?

Since the late 1980s, television in many parts of the world has found itself in a new era (cf. Moran 2005). This has come about via a unique intersection of new technologies of transmission and reception, innovative forms of financing, fresh means of imaging the audience, novel forms of content provision and new constructions of the television commodity. Technological digital convergence has become a dominant notion, with new players entering the distribution arena, including companies based in the telecommunications and computer sectors. Alongside the move to privatize much of television broadcasting services, there has been a parallel shift towards the use of independent production companies. Hollywood is no longer the dominant centre for the global production of popular television output. Other media capitals, including London, Hong Kong, Tokyo, Beijing and Mexico City, are becoming prominent hubs of a more international structure. Genres that once were marginal in popularity, such as game shows, talent contests, self- and home-improvement programmes, and hidden camera 'documentary', have now become mainstream forms of programming output. Several of these programme types highlight the capacity of the 'ordinary' person to go on television, and are part of a neo-liberal zeitgeist. The abundant multi-channel services offered by technology share the same outlook. These are complementary to the information and entertainment provisions of broadcasters, and are increasingly more interactive than the older services. Producers and broadcasters are also finding fresh ways of tapping income. The new structures of finance include not only the incidental commercial services available through domestic technologies of telephone and computer, but especially have to do with intellectual property (IP) rights.

This wave of development has been occurring with television in the West, but has also been apparent elsewhere. Many scholars see this increasing uniformity as evidence of an evolving global order in television (Waisbord 2004; Chalaby 2005; Tunstall 2008). In any case, it is worth recalling that an older term, 'world television', remains a valid label for such a configuration (Tunstall 1970). A nascent world or global system of television has existed for some time, but may now be gathering strength. Chalaby identifies four interconnected components of a planetary television system that is complexly interrelated and changing (Chalaby 2005: 9). First, there is the media industry component, itself constituted by seven giant transnational television corporations. In addition, there are also other multinational organizations with strong regional sales or those with global reach, specializing in niche markets. Second, there is a technological infrastructure in the shape of worldwide communication networks that include cable, satellite and the internet. This technical matrix facilitates and maintains the operation of these organizations. News and entertainment content and associated data and services that circulate through the system make up a third realm of global television. Finally, there is the world regulatory regime that includes various international bodies, technical and trade agreements, and legal decisions and ordinances.

Such a scheme of a global television system is at best rudimentary, and various other interconnected sectors could and should be added. One such domain, for example, is the vital matter of television and media labour, with associated issues such as employment, worker associations, new technology, skill and craft matters which are in constant flux and contestation (Miller et al. 2001; Wasko and Erickson 2008). It should also be added that the reach of this system of a global television is far from global, with many television viewers and television systems outside its operation (Tunstall 2008: vii–xii). Chalaby's (2005) own particular focus of interest has to do with transnational satellite television. This is an important component of this complex, evolving jigsaw of world television, but so too are other developments. One of these is especially important for this chapter. It can be approached in terms of the content and related services that Chalaby identifies as the third of his four interrelated components.

Format programmes

Aside from the home-grown provision of television output, two different forms of programming distribution and production now characterize international and national television (Waisbord 2004). The first of these modes is the more familiar and traditional. It has been labelled 'canned' programming and it describes a programme devised, produced and broadcast in one territory, which is then shipped in cans or other containers for rebroadcast elsewhere. The canned programme is always already nationalized, whether it has originated in the United States, the United Kingdom, Japan or elsewhere. When it plays in foreign-language territories, the canned programme can be customized for home audiences, up to a point, by dubbing or subtitling.

The second, more recent mode has to do with format programming (Moran 1998; Moran and Malbon 2006). Under this system, a programme is devised, produced and broadcast in one territory. Subsequently, the programme's format is made available as a set of services or franchised knowledges which allow the programme to be adapted and produced for broadcast in another territory. Mostly, the format programme constitutes a flexible template or empty mould awaiting particular social inflexion and accent in other television territories to appeal to home audiences in that place. In this sense, the television format programme might be said to be unbounded and universal. It offers itself as possible evidence of an emerging global television system.

As part of television format remaking, the programme is usually modified in such a way as to seem local or national in origin. Whether or not the programme is 'live' or scripted, the stories it tells will tend to deal with the audience's world. Moreover, its performers and participants will, for the most part, be ethnically familiar, speak one or other of the dominant territorial languages, be pictured in recurring, everyday locations dealing with recognizable situations, and behave in customary and familiar ways. Home audiences are seen to prefer a programme that is attuned to their sense of who they are (Tunstall 2008: x). One might treat this form of programme adaptation as one of format customization or indigenization. However, further qualification is in order as a means of sharpening our sense of the intriguing, paradoxical significance of programme formats in the era of new television. For on the one hand they seem to have a go-anywhere quality that is not a part of the make-up of canned programming, yet on the other hand they also appear to have a capacity to take root and nativize themselves in different television territories.

Format origins and development

Although TV format franchising reached its commercial zenith with *Big Brother*, nonetheless this form of programme provision is not new. Elsewhere, for example, I have noted that the practice of translating the Bible from Latin into indigenous languages appeared in north-west Europe as early as the fifteenth and early sixteenth centuries (Moran 1998: 22). Similarly, the borrowing of radio programme ideas for adaptation in other places happened from the 1930s onwards. However, systematically facilitating broadcast programme adaptation was something else, a new business departure. Take the example of the children's television programme *Romper Room* (Hyatt 1997: 364). This show first appeared on a local US television station in Baltimore in 1953. The year was an auspicious one, as US small-business organization was beginning to undergo a transformation with the emergence of a new kind of franchising operation (Dicke 1982: 218–44). Hitherto, franchising had been organized around the distribution of material goods or products. In the 1950s a new kind of franchising emerged, relating to the distribution of services or tertiary products. One of the most spectacular examples of this kind of distribution arrangement had to do with new fast-food restaurant franchising, including those of Burger King, Kentucky Fried Chicken (now KFC) and McDonald's (Dicke 1982).

Although the Baltimore version of the *Romper Room* programme was reasonably successful, its creators turned down an offer from the CBS network to buy the programme. Instead, they packaged a range of relevant services and resources that they licensed out to a string of local television stations across the country. By 1957, 22 stations were licensing the format and producing their own local versions of the programme. Six years later, 119 US stations had their own *Romper Room*. By then, the franchise was being distributed internationally, and included several versions of the programme being made in Australia and Japan.

Over the next half century, the practice of TV programme format franchising slowly came to be accepted in the international television industry. Since around 2000, format programming has been a mainstay of television output in many different territories around the world. It tends to operate in the higher-budget end of markets and complements the import of canned programming. More importantly, the TV programme format helps to give popular transnational shows an indigenous or domestic look and sound. But how exactly does this format customizing come about? The next two sections examine this kind of adaptation, first in terms of two polar types of customization or translation, and then in terms of the process of modification and variation.

'Closed' and 'open' adaptations

Adapting and producing a format programme is usually an interactive process involving a centrally located format licensor and a licensee company based in a peripheral television territory. The former has extensive knowledge of the format and its inception in other places, and is fully aware of its pitfalls and difficulties as well as its triumphs and successes. The latter has a more intimate sense of the home audience culture – that is, a greater intuitive sense of what will be suitable for viewers. A particular adaptation will generally represent a compromise between these two parties. However, in rare instances the licensing company will insist that the adaptation follow a standardized pattern that makes little or no concession to the interests and sensibility of a home audience.

With the international licensed adaptation and production of different national versions of *Who Wants to Be a Millionaire?* for instance, the United Kingdom-based Celador, which owned the format, insisted that these adhere closely to the template created around the first incarnation of the programme in the United Kingdom (Spenser 2006). This was certainly the case in India. To maintain the success of the programme and to enhance the value of the brand and the franchise, Celador put a great deal of work into the collaborative activity of training local production personnel in the style and form that it wanted in *Kaun Banega Crorepat*, the Indian version of the format. To this end, three staff members were sent out from the London office to India to train the local production team, while four Indians went to the United Kingdom for further training (Spenser 2006).

This kind of TV programme format adaptation might be called McDonaldization. However, it has by and large been the exception rather than the rule. The experience of *Who Wants to Be a Millionaire?* has been repeated with the international adaptation of only one other TV format, *The Weakest Link*. In both cases, the licensed owners of the formats, Celador and the BBC, insisted that adaptations follow a highly standardized formula so far as the form and style of each adaptation was concerned (Spenser 2006; Cousins 2006; Jarvis 2006). This kind of decision making, where local input and inflection were discounted entirely, is unique in the international TV format business, although cases have occurred elsewhere in the culture industries. Burston (2000), for example, has reported a parallel process of international reproduction of cultural look-alikes in the case of large-scale live musical theatre in such markets as New York, London, Toronto and Sydney.

Elsewhere, drawing on semiotics and literary translation theory, I have labelled this kind of format programme remaking situation a 'closed' adaptation (Lotman 1990; Lefebvre 1993). What is required in any particular remake in any territory is a close approximation of the original version of the programme. Head office has taken this crucial decision, and local production personnel must follow this course of action. As in literary translation, the aim is to produce a 'literal' approximation of the original version of the format programme. This look-alike, equivalent translation process emphasizes a high degree of fidelity to an original, even if the new version makes little concession to the interests and tastes of a new audience.

Usually with TV programme reproduction, however, a more 'open' adaptation is tolerated, even welcomed. Semiotics speaks of a more 'poetic' translation (Biguemer and Shulte 1990; Lotman 1990; Lefebvre 1993). Further necessary changes have been introduced in a new version of a text in the interests of cultural audience intelligibility and access. In the case of TV programme format adaptation, the creative sovereignty of the local production team is greatly enhanced in the process of adaptation and production. New versions of the format are likely not to be copies or look-alikes of earlier versions, and are far less substitutable for one another. Hence, for example, a loose adaptation of *Survivor* in China, *Into Shangrila*, seemed only a distant cousin to the format original, the Swedish *Castaway Robinson*, and to its most successful remake, the US programme *Survivor*, although the latter two had more of a sibling resemblance to one another (Keane 2004).

Levels of format adaptation

As well as understanding this kind of transproduction of formats as a tug of war between serving a source and serving an audience, one can also grasp the process in terms of a trail of individual adaptation decisions about various elements of the format. When a TV format programme is being tailored to suit a home audience, various levels of production determination come into play. Heylen (1994) has usefully suggested a tripartite scheme for understanding levels of activity in relation to a literary or written work that must be taken into account in translation. These involve linguistic codes, intertextual codes and cultural codes (Heylen 1994: 1–15).

Of course, television programmes do not operate with linguistic codes. Instead, the poetics of television can be located in matters of form and style (Bordwell and Thompson 2004). The latter consists of staging, shooting, editing and sound. Form involves elements of extended organization and sequencing, such as storytelling and magazine-type arrangements. These categories are complex and involve numerous individual elements that can be manipulated. One example of this kind of textual coding can be cited. Colour is a component of television's *mise en scène* that is frequently deemed to be nationally sensitive in game shows and other format genres. This element often necessitates cultural decision making in order to give a format pro-gramme a recognizable 'look' so far as domestic audiences are concerned (Cousins 2006).

Meanwhile, the manipulation of intertextual elements belongs to a second level of adaptation. These codes are not necessarily as discrete or self-contained as those discussed in the previous paragraph. Instead, they appear to connect with specific bodies of knowledge held by particular communities, including both local production teams and segments of the home audience. At least three different sets of intertextual elements can come into play in a format adaptation. One set has to do with television production industries. Formats carry the imprint of the institutions within which they were first devised and developed. Frequently, the adaptation and production of a format will neces-sitate a significant readjustment in a national television production milieu, in part drawing this institution into the norms and practices of a more interna-tional or global TV industry. Intertextual knowledges can come into play in a second way, relating to the particular format programme modes or genres that are being adapted. Elsewhere, I have suggested that the adaptation of a drama series format offers more opportunities for creative improvisation than does a game show format (Moran 1998: 107). Third, a local adaptation may herald the introduction of a new television genre to a particular national television culture and industry. This happened with the establishment of Australian soap formats in Western Europe in the 1990s, the inauguration of reality formats in many parts of the world after 2000, and the more recent introduction of tel-enovela templates in territories as diverse as India and Israel. Intertextual codes also operate in relation to performer persona knowledge in local television cultures. Hence, in the Netherlands and Germany, particular casting decisions soon brought about narrative deviations in the remakes of the Australian soap operas already mentioned (Kolle 1995).

A third level affecting format adaptation is that combination of factors making for communal and national difference. Broadly, these have to do with social matters of language, ethnicity, history, religion, geography and culture. Irrespective of the genre involved, a format programme will carry particular situations, figures, subject matters and issues. The extent to which these will be recognizable and acceptable within particular cultural settings may vary considerably. Hence, the lack of continuing popular success of *The Weakest Link* in East and South-East Asia was attributed to the dominatrix and the public shaming of contestants, while *Big Brother* in Saudi Arabia excited a good deal of outcry, which caused its cancellation (Spenser 2006). More usually, though, successful domestication does occur with formats. Attempting to explain the 1990s success of the Polish adaptation of the 1950s US television sitcom *The Honeymooners*, one UK consultant specialist emphasized both a timeless element that might appeal to the Polish female audience as well as a more specific social appeal to a post-Communist Polish audience (Cousins 2006).

Of course, while producers frequently speculate as to whether or not a format has undergone sufficient adaptation of the right kind, it is the home audience that is best equipped to deliver a verdict about its domestication. The same consultant producer told a story in which the customization of *The Honeymooners'* format seemed so complete as to persuade one of the members of the local audience that the Polish programme was not an adaptation based on an overseas format import, but was, rather, a programme that was completely indigenous and home grown to Polish culture:

> I was talking to a continuity girl and I said, 'Have you watched *The Honeymooners?*' And she said, 'Of course, it's very funny, I watch it every week. Why are you interested?' So I said that the company licensed out the scripts and she said, 'No, no, this is a Polish show.' This is the greatest accolade when they believe one of our shows is 'local'.
>
> (Cousins 2006)

The three levels of adaptation outlined are not separate in practice. Rather, most decisions in the process of adapting and producing a format programme in a home territory are multilayered and shot through with many of the social values of a home community. To pay attention to these values is to tailor or customize the format for home audiences, always recognizing that this kind of construction of a television localism or nationalism is a negotiated one. It is a matrix of particular choices that may suit the inclination and preferences of some members of the home audiences, while perhaps challenging, offending or even seeming irrelevant to the tastes and sensibility of others in that population. This, in turn, raises the matter of the larger social implications of TV formats and their cultural adaptation in particular territories.

National persistence

Up to this point, I have used several terms to indicate the modifications introduced when a TV format programme is inflected towards the taste and sensibility of a home audience in a particular territory. 'Adapt', 'tailor' and 'customize' are deliberately neutral terms insofar as their larger cultural implications are concerned. Even the label 'indigenizing' is only the loosest of social approximations when it comes to the translation of a format into an acceptable domestic idiom. In an era of increasingly larger movements of populations around the globe, it is impossible to designate a kind of majority television viewership of native origin and ancestry. Home audiences are likely to be mixed, heterogeneous and diverse in their interests and tastes. The term 'localize' also makes little real sense as a means of understanding processes taking place when a TV format is customized. Television programmes attempt to maximize the population reach of their programming. Hence, even where specific choices have to be made regarding language, accent, ethnicity, religion

and so on that will discriminate against various groups in a viewing population, format programming implicitly suggests that its address and appeal
extends beyond local communities and attempts to talk to a national audience
(Moran 1998).

In fact, a related difficulty with the label 'local' should be noted in passing.
This has to do with its use in conjunction with the term 'global' as a way of
encapsulating the dual spatialities of the TV format. The latter appears to be
universal or global in its marketing and circulation, even while it seems to be
local and distinctive in its production and reception. Yet formats are not
global in their circulation, although the international television industry claims
that they are. While TV formats frequently achieve impressive numbers of
licensings into many territories across the world, there are inevitably numerous
other markets where they are not licensed, adapted or even noticed (Tunstall
2008: xi–xiv). Elsewhere, for instance, I have noted that Africa, parts of the
Middle East, most of the former Soviet Union territories, and various parts of
South and South-East Asia are all sparsely represented at the international TV
format fairs (Moran 2008). Hence, TV formats are better thought of as transnational rather than global in their commercial circulation. Similarly, as has
also been pointed out, formats are better thought of as national rather than
local in their cultural adaptation and appeal.

In other words, the advent of TV formats as a central element in the new
television landscape appears to signal not the disappearance of the national in
favour of the global and the local, but its emphatic endurance or even reappearance. The TV format industry's maturation as a mainstay of an international system of cultural exchange seems to point not to a strengthening of the
global and the local at the expense of the national, but to an enhancement of
the national that may be to the detriment of those other two levels. As a
transnational business system, TV formats are intimately dependent on the
national, even if that persistence is frequently ignored and mistaken in favour
of its own seeming disappearance. This apparent withering is strikingly in line
with postmodernist claims about the increasing irrelevance and disappearance
of the national sovereign state (Hirst and Thompson 1995; Weiss 1998). But,
just as the latter is a myth that suits various power interests in such areas as
politics and economics, so the dissolution of the national into the local and the
global, so far as TV format adaptation is concerned, also seems illusory.

To understand this apparent vanishing, it is helpful to turn to a recent work
of social science. Billig (1995) has usefully coined the term 'banal nationalism'
to indicate precisely this visible invisibility of an ideological superstructure in
everyday life. The kind of mundane, taken-for-granted representations of the
nation that are found in particular incarnations of TV programme formats are
the means by which the nation is reproduced as a hegemonic form. This
ideological project is constant and ongoing across a series of different fronts in
many arenas of social life, including that of television. At the same time, such
work is subtle, unobtrusive, banal. Of course, most TV format programming

appears to be about almost everything else other than the power within which the aura of nationhood exists. Nevertheless, nationhood continues to be inconspicuously suggested in the interstices of format adaptations – in a detail of colour, a quiz question, an outdoor setting, a story situation, an accent, a theme song and so on. Billig sees these small, unobtrusive gestures and details as so many daily unnoticed 'flaggings', or reminders of nationalism. As he puts it:

> Banally, they address 'us' as a national first person plural; and they situate 'us' in the homeland within a world of nations. Nationhood is the context which must be assumed to understand so many banal utterances.
>
> (Billig 1995: 175)

How better, then, to cloak this persistent nationalism in the case of TV format programming than by cultivating the myth of its dissolution into globalism and localism? Nationalism has constituted a bedrock of television in the past. As this exploration of the phenomenon and meaning of TV format commerce and culture has suggested, this task is by no means superseded by the cultivation of other formations. Instead, in an era of a rapidly changing international television landscape, TV formats continue to anchor their adaptations in the ongoing reality of the national.

Chapter 15

From monopoly to polyphony

India in the era of television

Adrian Mabbott Athique

Introduction

For the first four decades after independence in 1947, the Indian media industries provided an illustration both of the mixed-economy model established by the Congress Party and of the federal structure of the country. Unlike the various Indian film industries, which supplied different language groups across the country with populist fare at the cinema, the realms of radio and television were state monopolies that remained under tight central control. Nation-building agendas and didactic imperatives dictated the wider purpose and content of television broadcasting in India, giving the national broadcaster Doordarshan a justified reputation as a state mouthpiece with an aversion to entertainment. Following the political upheavals of 1991, one of the most visible symptoms of the subsequent 'liberalization era' was the progressive opening up of the media sector. The rapid growth of 'multinational' television in the country has been paralleled by even more spectacular growth in the numbers, size and scope of commercial Indian broadcasters. Deregulation has instigated the emergence of a vibrant multi-vocal mediasphere in South Asia, more than capable of balancing the presence of foreign operators. Since, unlike the reaction to the commercialization of broadcasting in Europe, few commentators in India today have lamented the displacement of Doordarshan, this chapter will argue that the Indian experience indicates the need for a new critical understanding of the potentials of television in Asia after the era of state monopoly.

The era of monopoly

Almost alone among the countries that emerged from decolonization, India reached independence in 1947 already in possession of one of the world's flourishing cinema industries. The popularity of this medium had expanded steadily since the advent of local film production three decades before independence, with the coming of sound in 1931 leading to the development of several production centres (in effect, distinct regional industries) serving the major language groups. However, the post-colonial government of India was not favourably disposed towards Indian cinema. Cultural nationalists were suspicious of the cinema as a source of Westernization and moral decay, while India's modernizing socialists were equally antipathetic to a popular film industry funded by the black economy and directed towards visceral escapism, romantic fantasy and emotional manipulation. As such, commercial Indian cinema was deemed unsuitable for the nation-building project. Television broadcasts, from their humble beginnings in 1959, remained under the government umbrella of All India Radio and the formal jurisdiction of the Department of Information and Broadcasting.

Television, which was at that time being deployed as a mass medium in the Northern Hemisphere, was regarded by India's first prime minister, Jawaharlal Nehru, as an expensive luxury for a country where famine, illiteracy and destitution defined the existence of millions of people. Only nominal experiments in broadcasting took place during the 17 years of his premiership (1947–64). Nehru's antipathy towards the development of television was expressed in largely practical terms: his insistence that all of the emerging state media should eschew trivial entertainments and 'foster a scientific temper' among the population revealed much of the ideological programme that would define Indian television during the era of state monopoly (Manchanda 1998: 137). To be fair, Nehru's attitudes were far from controversial. During the 1950s and 1960s, the role of the mass media in the decolonizing world was understood overwhelmingly in terms of a developmental logic (see Sparks 2007).

For the post-colonial elites, this development mission was twofold. The explicit goal was the pursuit of an industrialized economy, with a modernized population equipped to operate it. Equally important, however, was the development of a state apparatus whose hegemony over social life was recognized and to which the population was loyal and committed. This twin project of constructing state hegemony over the modernizing nation encouraged moves towards the institutionalization of the economy, with the parallel influence upon cultural production at a policy level being the promotion of state-sponsored social realism. Accordingly, India's state media celebrated scientific progress and state policy, along with what the government regarded as authentic Indian lives – heavily biased in favour of rural India. All of this was consciously directed towards winning the loyalty of the labouring classes for the scientific Marxism of the Congress Party (Roy 2008). This agenda shaped the contours of television programming in India when broadcasting was eventually extended beyond Delhi in the early 1970s. TV broadcasts started in Bombay metro in 1972 and five other broadcast stations, or Kendras, were in operation by 1975. Television was separated from All India Radio in 1976 and constituted as a separate government-run entity named Doordarshan (meaning literally 'television'). Since television as a medium has probably done more worldwide to define what it is to be middle class than any other technology or cultural form, it is of some significance that TV was consciously deployed in

India by Doordarshan in such a way as to circumvent the entertainment of the middle classes. From the ambitious satellite television experiment of 1975–76 and the subsequent planning of a national terrestrial network, Doordarshan's programming was intended to forge a direct connection between the ruling elite and the labouring classes, conceived overwhelmingly as a rural population (Rajagopal 1993). All of this was deeply paradoxical in a situation where only the affluent were able to afford television sets, and where broadcast capacity did not reach beyond the metropolitan areas (Manchanda 1998: 141).

The great irony of India's massive National Network, when it finally arrived (along with colour broadcasts) in the 1980s, was that the growth in technical capacity that had made it possible had also been paralleled by the steady decline of state legitimacy since the idealism of the Nehru era. While the European social democracies had developed national TV systems during the high tide of the political legitimacy of public institutions in the 1950s, India only achieved a national broadcast television network three decades later, in an era when its political system, its ruling elites and its public institutions were held in low regard by the general population. Doordarshan was widely perceived as a condescending state mouthpiece with scant regard for the interests of its audiences – and not without cause. Furthermore, the use of the National Network to impose Hindi-language programming on non-Hindi-speaking regions was clearly resented – despite the obvious popularity of Doordarshan's concession to entertainment (and to private sponsorship) in the form of Hindi soaps from the mid-1980s onwards (Ninan 1995).

Throughout the four decades of state monopoly over broadcasting, the intractable popularity of the commercial cinema always provided a counterfoil to the state media. Taken together, the two alternative voices of modern India provided a useful illustration of the contradictions of the mixed economy model. Indian state television provided a procession of benign politicians and tame journalists saluting state personnel, venerable classical artistes, worthy scientists and academics, along with countless dancing children and grateful villagers. By contrast, India's biggest films were populated by angry urban youths, corrupt politicians, jaded policemen, vile gangsters, kindly prostitutes and weeping mothers. This popular circus thus provided an alternative narration of India's encounter with modernity. Ultimately, it would take a new historical epoch to bring them into direct conversation.

The era of polyphony

The abrupt shift from the era of monopoly into the era of polyphony is generally seen as being marked by regulatory changes sparked by a massive technological intervention from outside the national space: Rupert Murdoch's STAR TV, broadcasting via ASIASAT across South Asia from its uplink station in Hong Kong (Butcher 2003; Thussu 2007). However, the transformative effects of new media technologies directed by global capital were assisted by favourable conditions created in India prior to this intervention. Faced with Doordarshan's didactic programming, the urban middle classes in Mumbai had been forming small-scale illegal neighbourhood cable TV systems from the early 1980s (Kohli-Khandekar 2006: 68–70). Their primary motivation was the lack of entertainment enshrined in Doordarshan programming. Accordingly, programming for these grass-roots operations was drawn from pirated and foreign-sourced video cassettes, typically offering popular Indian films and international soap operas. This alternative, localized and unofficial television culture was to prove crucial when what was in many ways its global opposite revolutionized broadcasting across the subcontinent in 1991.

With the arrival of transnational satellite content from CNN, Prime Sports, BBC and MTV along with STAR's own entertainment channel, India's affluent English-speaking urban elite was finally able to consume 'international' entertainment and news sourced directly from the developed anglophone world. Nonetheless, despite numbering some 10 million households, STAR still had a very small audience in proportional terms, less than 5 per cent of the Indian total (Thussu 2007: 595). However, the rapid augmentation of pirated video films with downlinked satellite broadcasts by canny neighbourhood cable operators quickly led to a much larger market for imported television. By 1993, urban Indians were able to access a growing range of international TV channels for as little as US$1 per month. Neighbourhood-specific cable networks were providing this international content to their subscribers along with the latest Indian films and live cricket matches, interspersed with intensely local events such as weddings and religious festivals within the neighbourhood itself – all of this unregulated and plastered with the advertisements of local businesses (Mishra 1999). This grass-roots TV system pushed the satellite revolution beyond the confines of its business model and simultaneously exploded the cherished national ambitions of Doordarshan, going simultaneously both local and global.

With no effective legislative or technical defence against what was known as the 'invasion from the skies', the cultural influence of foreign television that had been so effectively restricted for three decades was a major source of concern for India's officials (Manchanda 1998). Unable to restrict access to foreign media content, regulators quickly became far more amenable to the idea of privately owned television in India. Indeed, the Congress Party was rapidly reconsidering its overall economic and ideological position in the light of the collapse of the socialist world in the very same year that STAR arrived in India. It was clearly untenable to prevent the emergence of indigenous commercial television, to the advantage of foreign-owned networks that operated beyond any state regulation. Accordingly, the state monopoly on television in India was abruptly terminated, opening the field for commercial television stations. If one thing was going to survive the demise of the socialist dream, it was India's long-standing commitment to import substitution (Chadha and Kavoori 2000: 419–21).

Looking on in 1991, Subhash Chandra, the imaginative chairman of an Indian toothpaste tube manufacturer, was quick to realize that locally produced content would be the key to success in the Indian market. What Chandra understood was the pent-up demand for a middle-brow, indigenous television aesthetic of the kind that Doordarshan had never pursued or wanted, and which international recyclers of content did not adequately understand. Put simply, what was needed was a vulgar Indian popular that was readily available to Chandra through the massive cultural capital of the Indian film industries. The launch of Chandra's Hindi-language ZEE TV in October 1992 heralded one of the great business successes of the Indian 1990s. Making deals with the film world, Chandra was able to rely heavily on the back catalogue of the Indian cinema. ZEE TV was thus able to cater to the 90 per cent of the Indian television audience who identified popular films as their preferred content. The importation of the Bollywood A-list into a new range of talk shows, gossip spots and celebrity panels was an obvious move towards a new popular form of television. Further, the distinctive song-and-dance sequences of the Indian film came of age once more in this new era of television. The final ingredient was the introduction of new Hindi soaps that mixed Bollywood and Hollywood clichés to enormous effect. The programming mix in the family of ZEE TV channels drove a further massive expansion of television ownership among the lower middle classes, transforming the cultural make-up of the satellite audience.

Hot on the heels of the multinationals and the big Hindi networks, the deregulation of television also opened the way for the rapid emergence of regional language broadcasters across India. Just as sound pictures had led to multiple production centres and distinct vernacular markets for cinema in the 1930 and 1940s, the freeing of television from the Hindi-centric policies of Doordarshan paved the way for the emergence of large regional players in Indian television. Tamil-language channels Sun TV and JJTV both used the complex map of private cable networks to go on air in 1993. Within two years, AsiaNet, Eenadu TV, Udaya TV and others launched to provide services in the other major South Indian languages (Malayalam, Telugu and Kannada). Their massive popularity in their regional markets led to a further wave of local competitors. It was rapidly apparent that commercial television in India was not only to be national, international and intensely local – it was also to acquire a distinctly regional dimension (McMillin 2001). This, then, is the new era of polyphony: a time for the fulfilment of pleasures that were long suppressed in the name of national integration, such as desires for regional expression, consumer durables or banal audiovisual entertainment of a suitably international standard.

A final aspect of this era that warrants a mention here is the international reach of the Indian television revolution. The political make-up of the subcontinent means that regional broadcasters are effectively transnational broadcasters. For example, Kolkata-based Bengali broadcasters are seeking bigger audiences in neighbouring Bangladesh, where the majority of Bengali speakers are found. Tamil-language channels reach Tamil-speaking audiences in Sri Lanka and, despite a blanket ban on Indian-produced media in Pakistan, all of the Indian Hindi channels access substantial audiences there via satellite or cable operations. In this respect, the linguistically driven regionalization of Indian TV has created transnational television audiences within the region.

Further afield, the success of ZEE UK and ZEE US was always an important component of Chandra's operations (Dudrah 2002; Thussu 2005). Since splitting with Murdoch's STAR in 1999, ZEE has also launched its own pan-Asian service to compete directly with its former partner, not just in India but across the entire region. On a more modest scale, Sun TV reaches its Tamil-speaking viewers not just in the state of Tamil Nadu and in neighbouring Sri Lanka, but also in Malaysia and Singapore, and in London and Vancouver – not to mention the large numbers of Tamil migrants dispersed across the different regions of India itself. New Delhi Television (NDTV), which used to provide English-language local news for STAR, has become a major independent player in the emerging South Asian news market (Thussu 2007). NDTV is also available to satellite subscribers around the world, and in 2006 launched its own overseas channel in Indonesia (Mehta 2006).

The era of television?

This narrative provides a very important historical lesson for understanding the nature, purpose and future of television in Asia. After dragging its heels for a decade over the role of television in a country with so many pressing social and economic challenges to overcome, India consequently spent the next two decades failing to construct a national television address that could readily be accepted by its diverse population. It was by no means the technical obstacles that undermined India's great national television project, but rather an extraordinary failure of social imagination on the part of her decision makers.

Proponents of the free market can only take heart from the fact that the widely disparaged failure of the National Network to capture the public imagination was followed by a decade that saw the privatization of television drive India's emergence as a regional giant in transnational broadcasting – with one of the fastest growing television audiences in the world, served by over 200 channels. More cautious observers may note that the technical capacity behind India's television revolution remains firmly rooted in the technological efforts of India's socialist past. The fact remains, however, that in its long-running attempt to be everything that the popular cinema was not, Door-darshan failed to become popular. As such, Indian television today is not the dutiful daughter of developmental pedagogy, but rather the love-child of the brash Indian cinema and the seductive fashions of the trade in international TV formats (see Moran and Keane 2003). It is neither truly indigenous nor truly international, and could arguably be seen to represent everything that its erstwhile regulators sought to avoid. At the same time, the pivotal role played by contemporary television in promoting the aspirations at the heart of India's 'New Economy' appears to have won government sanction.

While the statistics produced during the era of monopoly told a story of the gradual extension of geographic coverage in an exact parallel of the discussion of Indian railways, the era of polyphony has been very much focused on the bums-on-seats ethos of commercial broadcasting. Indeed, this discursive shift from geographic to demographic conceptions of the audience is perhaps the best indicator of the success of the new television era. At 108 million house-holds, with an average household size of 5.3, the television audience in India today can be estimated at over half a billion people (Census of India 2001; Kohli-Khandekar 2006: 62). Cable and satellite channels reach 61 million households, growing at 10 per cent per annum (Thussu 2007: 594). Despite the runaway success of the private sector undoubtedly driving the growth of the medium, Doordarhan's stranglehold on the terrestrial network means that it retains its pre-eminence over the non-metropolitan audiences who make up almost half this total. However, it is equally clear that Doordarshan has had to follow the lead of the commercial broadcasters by belatedly launching its own range of entertainment-focused and regional-language channels, which in turn increase its reliance on advertising revenues to produce competitive content in a commercialized environment (Ohm 1999).

It is in urban India that the new era of television is most readily apparent, and the bias in content reflects this (Thussu 2005: 170). In 1990, visitors to India were unlikely to see a television broadcast unless they had affluent Indian hosts or stayed in 5-star hotels. Televisions, where you did see them, seemed to be used almost entirely for watching popular films on video cas-settes. Ten years later, however, you wouldn't expect to take a $10 hotel room in a regional town without getting access to at least 50 channels of colour TV. The crucial point here is not the comfort of the habitual tourist, but rather the fact that 15 years ago most Indians remained outside of the global mediascape, while today television pours information in constantly from every other part of the globe, and from across India itself. India is clearly now part of the new world of globalization, and for the urban citizen the proof positive of this is that India is now part of the world of global TV.

In a wider sense, the Indian experience with television in the contemporary period must of necessity contribute to the reformulation of our understanding of the medium. Over the period of the television explosion in India, the Western world has been very much more concerned with the transformative potentials of computer networks, the 'new media'. We have been encouraged to think about a convergence of multimedia, an exciting new spectrum of digital television and a personalized, hand-held, on-demand smörgåsbord of imagery that will come to define what Spigel and Olsson (2004) have called 'television after TV'. In light of the Indian situation, however, we should remain wary of the pronouncements of a post-TV era. Television has increased its audiences in India by hundreds of millions since 1991 and is arguably only now beginning to realize its true potential as it passes the half-way mark in reaching India's 1.1 billion-strong population. With an estimated 108 million TV connections as opposed to 7.5 million internet connections, the reach and revolutionary potential of the two media hardly seem comparable at this moment (Kohli-Khandekar 2006: 22).

It could, in fact, be argued that the era of TV has only just arrived in India, since the era of state monopoly from 1959–91 largely corresponds with a lengthy extension of the government newsreel by other means – as opposed to TV in the way that we have come to understand it in other parts of the world. From this perspective, the rapid leap made by Indian television from that age into the era of competitive multi-channel, multi-format, transnational broadcasting is even more impressive – but this is a leap into the TV age rather than into any post-TV epoch. Since the Indian experience is not so far removed from what has occurred in most of Southern Asia in terms of broadcast content over the same period, this would imply that the era of TV is far from over in this region. Indeed, massive growth in those geo-linguistic markets over the same period serves to indicate that TV is only now realizing its potential as a global system (Bannerjee 2002; Chadha and Kavoori 2000). If TV is not over for more than a half of the world's population, we may be wise to assume that it may not be over at all.

What is over, then, if not television? What is over, indubitably, is the era of high-handed, developmentalist state broadcasting in Asia. As the story of Door-darshan in India demonstrates, even when you are in firm possession of both medium and message, a willing audience is required. In that sense, the audi-ence for the current television revolution in South Asia was born during the 1970s, when the moral authority of autocratic, statist nationalism reached its nadir. Since then, a growing suspicion of the governing elites, a sense of entitlement stemming from the democratic experiment and the desire to actually reap the promised fruits of development have transformed the relationship of the post-colonial state with its public. Perhaps this is why, in the larger scheme of things, the worthy, illiterate Asian peasant of developmental discourse has been so comprehensively overwritten by the increasingly cosmopolitan and globalized 'emerging consumer' of the Asian century. They are both media fictions, but the impact of such imagined communities upon the formulation of media policy and broadcast content should not be underestimated.

In the academic discussion of the internationalization of television in recent years, it has been the concentrations of production and the trajectories of transmission that have received the greatest attention (Curtin 2003). In terms of this mapping of 'hubs' and 'flows', we can readily see that India has various media production hubs that are locally, nationally, regionally and globally significant. In terms of flow, India sends out streams of content to every corner of the globe. On this basis, it is immediately obvious that India is a regional media power. This has been the case with film for decades, and the dispersal of television in recent years is broadly comparable. What television studies must now attempt to do in India is to investigate how the complex media sphere arising from the overlapping footprints of television both differentiates and interlaces so many publics within the national space. As such, we must rethink the role of TV in an era after the state broadcast model, where transmission is simultaneously both globalized and narrowcasted. It follows, then, that if we are to understand television in India today, we would be wise to turn our attention to the complex forms of social imagination now being forged among the numerous sub-national television audiences that are being so powerfully reconfigured by the changing environment.

Given the scale of television in Asia today, this is a programme likely to keep scholars busy for a very long time (see Butcher 2003; Mankekar 1999; McMillin 2002; Scrase 2002). At this early point, it nonetheless seems reasonable to say that what defines the era of polyphony is that the Indian television viewer is no longer confined to one homogenized, national space that is described for them. Instead, TV audiences simultaneously experience many Indias, in an environment where popular culture is being generated across the full spectrum of the local-global. From this perspective, it becomes apparent that from here on, with no single source of programming but with many, there will be no single national audience but, rather, multiple and shifting coalitions of spectatorship. Only in the circuses of Test cricket or in moments of great national crisis will the big national publics envisaged by South Asia's erstwhile state planners be likely to be formed.

There is a loss here, perhaps, but also a gain, since India is undeniably the heavyweight in the emerging media sphere in South Asia. Despite its critics, cross-border television and formal partnerships between Indian and Pakistani broadcasters have already greatly increased the scale of cultural exchange across the region. Recent years have seen the rapid emergence of a fourth estate in the subcontinent, with transnational reach and interests, operating from what have long been state-dominated and frequently hostile national spaces. The growth of commercial non-state media therefore has great potential to enhance empathic interaction between the South Asian nations. In that sense, the growing reach and complexity of television serve the interests of the entire region and are able to do so precisely because of the eclipse of the statist paradigm. It is a matter of no small importance that the greatest allegiance of contemporary Indian television is to television itself. If we are to move beyond the old nationalist models of broadcast television, we may need to further apply this lesson to understanding the era of global television.

Chapter 16

Fragmentation or consolidation?

Factors in the *Oprah*-ization of social talk on multi-channel Arab TV

Naomi Sakr

The number of Arab-owned television channels has increased so rapidly in recent years that most people have lost count. A 2007 prediction that there would be 500 satellite channels by the end of 2008 (PARC 2007: 14–15) turned out to be an underestimate. Nevertheless, that round figure conveys, at least statistically, what 'multi-channel environment' means in the context of Arab television. The implications of such proliferation are the same in Arab countries as elsewhere. Arab analysts comment repeatedly on fragmentation of audiences, insufficient growth in television advertising, and dilemmas about how to supply viewers with new content. Yet Arab television in the post-broadcast era also has characteristics of its own. Arabic-language programming easily crosses borders within the region, from Morocco to Oman, and other countries with Arabic-speaking populations. Although this large transnational market could be an economic blessing, the unstable nature of Arab politics, both within and between countries, tends to politicize pan-Arab media. Public statements by representatives of authoritarian Arab governments show that they still see television – whether publicly or privately owned – not as a creative industry but as a tool of domestic propaganda and foreign policy.

It might be conjectured that the demise of the captive audience, brought about by multiplying channels and diversifying modes of content distribution, would undermine television's usefulness to ruling elites. Indeed, commentators have suggested that innovative content on competing channels is of 'potentially enormous significance for the democratization of Arab societies' (Kraidy 2007: 55), that it helps to 'eviscerate the legitimacy of the Arab status quo' (Lynch 2005: 150–52) and nurture 'public dissent in a culture that has long prized consensus' (Power 2005). On the other hand, harsher assessments of global media transformations in the digital age highlight forms of business elite consolidation hiding behind a façade of diversity. Convergence of television, mobile telephony and the internet presents investors with opportunities as well as challenges. Dan Schiller (2007: 114) points out that 'increasingly variegated' sources of revenue have helped the largest media conglomerates both to absorb the rising costs of programming and to try out new cultural commodities. Media executives have come to regard different kinds of cultural material simply as 'content' that can be repackaged or 'repurposed' for delivery across different kinds of media outlet (ibid. 2007: 115). In other words, a mass audience may still exist if figures for all forms of access to the same item are aggregated. It just depends how questions about audience fragmentation are posed. For W. Russell Neumann, who studied the impact of 1980s cable television in the United States, they constitute a 'continuing and central problematic of political communications' – the key question being about balance: between centre and periphery, between different interest factions, between competing elites, and between central authority and the 'conflicting demands of the broader electorate' (Neumann 1991: 167). That is to say, media users may fragment or coalesce at different times and places, which calls for continual weighing of the power balance between cultural producers and consumers (Garnham 2000: 118–19).

Post-convergence television in the Arab world raises questions about the relative power of media businesses and media users, both as individuals and as groups. This chapter looks at changes on the business side, in channel expansion and strategies for retaining viewers, and on the user side, in access not only to television but to the internet and mobile phones as well. It then takes television talk about social issues as a testing ground for whether experimentation with new content owes more to the business motives of media owners or to the demands of ordinary viewers, intent on discussing shared social concerns. These alternatives align with the manipulation/empowerment axis that often underlies analysis of audience participation in television talk. Whereas political debates may be specific to a particular locality or social group, talk about personal and family relationships has the potential for mass appeal because it involves what Graham Murdock (2000: 199) calls the 'bedrock experiences of everyday life'. In the confessional genre of social talk associated with the US presenter Oprah Winfrey, there is tension between excessive personalization of social problems, which cuts them off from wider social structures and possibilities for collective action, and ratings imperatives, which oblige presenters to make audiences feel empowered by setting talk about personal experiences in a wider social frame (Shattuc 1997: 96). At the same time, the business of creating low-cost drama by getting 'ordinary people' to 'open up' on television presents a myriad of issues about who is really in control (e.g. Carpentier 2001; Couldry 2003; Ytreberg 2004). Therefore, the final section of this chapter briefly probes ways of understanding moves towards unprecedented levels of self-disclosure on Arab talk shows in the post-broadcast era.

Channel proliferation and viewer choice

Multiple factors explain the various phases of expansion in Arab television since the first Arab satellite channels started, separately backed by the Egyptian and Saudi Arabian governments, in 1990–91. The motivation then was to

provide Arabic-language programmes approved by political leaders allied to
the United States-led effort to end Iraq's invasion of Kuwait (Sakr 2001).
Thereafter, channel numbers increased quickly, boosted by the advent of two
Saudi-owned bouquets of encrypted channels in 1994 and another run as a
Kuwaiti joint venture with the US giant Viacom in 1996. When the idea of
an Arabic-language news channel was tried, first by the Saudi pay TV network Orbit and then on a free-to-air basis by Al-Jazeera, the copycat habit
took hold. But infrastructural developments were also decisive in the expansion process, because a sudden surge in satellite capacity greatly reduced
transmission costs. Egypt launched two satellites equipped with digital technology in 1998 and 2000, while the pan-Arab organization Arabsat, based in
Saudi Arabia, did likewise in 1999. Anxious to generate business for its Nilesat
fleet, in 2000 the Egyptian government allowed private television companies
to transmit from inside Egypt for the first time, provided they did so by
satellite.

From then on, upheavals across the region spurred interest groups to vali-
date themselves by controlling a satellite channel. In the turmoil unleashed by
the United States-led invasion of Iraq in 2003, more countries made modest
moves towards licensing private satellite ventures (Sakr 2007: 24–32). In
October 2003, the number of free-to-air channels stood at 86. Three years
later, it had trebled to 263 (Chahine et al. 2007: 2). In April 2008, an
Amman-based consultancy counted 377 free-to-air channels in the Arab
world, alongside a combined total of 140 subscription channels, mostly operated by the three Arab pay TV providers that had started in the mid-1990s.
On top of this were 120 terrestrial channels broadcasting in 19 Arab countries,
including a few privately owned terrestrial stations allowed in Lebanon,
Palestine, Jordan, Tunisia and Iraq (Arab Advisors Group 2008a, 2008b,
2008c).

It might sound from these numbers as though Arab viewers, after nearly
two decades of Arab television expansion, were spoilt for choice. The range of
offerings was so varied that one report classified them under 14 different
headings, running alphabetically through business and finance, children and
youth, documentaries and education, general channels, health, nutrition and
cooking, interactive channels, movies and series, music, news and current
affairs, promotional channels for tourism and real estate, religious channels,
'specialized' channels and sports channels (Arab Advisors Group 2008a). Spe-
cialization had reached the point where a whole channel was dedicated solely
to horse-racing. News channels numbered well over a dozen. Thirty or more
religious channels, Christian as well as Muslim, included at least 11 based in
Saudi Arabia (Saleh 2007).

Choice, however, implies that what is available is at least partly based on
research into what viewers want. In Arab television, that was not the case. On
the contrary, according to a consensus of industry insiders in 2008, audience
research in the region was 'still at its infant stage: subjective and ego driven'

(Boulos 2007: 36), lacking any 'common and bona fide audience measurement methodology' (PARC 2007: 11). The egos referred to were those of top executives, who were said to rely on their own assumptions instead of research (Malas 2008: 15). Whereas, in other parts of the world, Nielsen-style electronic people meters yield daily television ratings, in the Arab world a lack of data had fed a climate of suspicion about any statistical claims. With leading Arab networks resisting people meters, research companies continued to rely on computer-assisted telephone interviewing, even in countries where the privacy of telephone conversations is not assured. They would deliver unaudited interview data to media clients at monthly intervals for Saudi Arabia and at three-monthly or even annual intervals for countries with smaller or less affluent populations. Although a group of advertisers and advertising agencies had joined forces in 2004 to try to install people meters in the Gulf, an official at MBC Group – the region's top television conglomerate – suggested the installation could take until 2010 (*Emirates Business 24/7* 2008).

A disregard for transparency on the part of a few key companies can be explained by these companies' market dominance and interconnections. It was reported in 2007 that just nine media groups, operating 28 channels, together controlled more than 80 per cent of advertising revenue (Booz Allen Hamilton 2007). An even smaller number, consisting of MBC, Saudi TV, Dubai Media Incorporated, Rotana and LBC, were said to account for over half of all Arab ratings points (Booz Allen Hamilton 2006: 20). Al-Jazeera, despite its large viewership, stood apart from the other market leaders because it had been dropped by the single powerful media marketing agency that serves most of the others, and which is said to handle some 60 per cent of all advertising expenditure directed to Arab TV (Sakr 2007: 184–85). That agency, Lebanon's Choueiri Group, is so closely linked to MBC through the latter's own media sales house that it is practically a stakeholder in the company. MBC Group is headed by a close relative of Saudi Arabia's ruling family. Dubai TV, owned by the ruler of Dubai through Dubai Media Incorporated, has a vested interest in the success of Dubai Media City, where MBC is based. Rotana Group, based in Beirut and Riyadh, belongs to Saudi Arabia's biggest media mogul, the billionaire global investor Prince Alwaleed bin Talal. Alwaleed also owns most of Lebanon's LBC-Sat. He took a 49 per cent a stake in it in 2003, merged it with Rotana in 2007, and provided enough new capital to raise his stake in the LBC Group to 85 per cent in 2008.

In the absence of data that would be accepted as credible by all sides, advertisers remained wary of devoting big budgets to television. MBC, Rotana, Dubai TV, Al-Jazeera and Saudi TV, drawing on finance from outside the television business, expanded from single channels to multi-channel networks in 2003–6. Some of these provided foreign films, series and sitcoms, sports and music of a kind that had previously been the preserve of pay TV. As this happened, advertising money was spread increasingly thinly, despite huge discounts offered to advertisers, which rose from 70 per cent in 2002 to

85 per cent by 2004 (Booz Allen Hamilton 2006: 20). Scope for future increases in television advertising could be gauged by comparing statistics from Arab countries with the rest of the world. In 2004 television advertising reached US$175 per head of the population in the United States and US$87 in the United Kingdom; in Saudi Arabia, the United Arab Emirates (UAE) and Kuwait, the figures were US$52, US$30 and US$6 respectively (Booz Allen Hamilton 2006: 20).

Impact of convergence on programming

For all their nonchalance about low advertising revenues and credible audience measurement, the market leaders were nonetheless intent on building audiences. Given the extremely high proportion of young people in Arab populations, and given the declared mission of key Arab television executives to de-radicalize young people in the name of eradicating terrorism (Sakr 2008), it was imperative for serious market contenders to exploit emerging alternative platforms for delivering television content. Many ideas for linking television with mobile phones or the internet were imported, along with the programme formats mentioned below. Nevertheless, local take-up of mobile phones and the internet was influenced by local factors. Just as the management side of Arab television has its own historically specific dynamics, which make the sheer number of channels a fairly meaningless statistic, the same applies to the reception side: official data for access to communication technologies are often misleading. Indicators of access to free-to-air channels are relatively uncontentious, with many Arab countries reaching levels of 89–97 per cent (Eutelsat 2007; Forrester 2008). But access to pay TV is a different story. Officially, the percentage of Egyptian households with pay TV is in single digits. Unofficially, it is around 43 per cent (Arab Advisors Group 2008d). That is because neighbourhood cabling systems and signal piracy enable many low-income households in countries like Algeria, Egypt and Lebanon to watch pay TV channels on the cheap. When ART, one of the big three pay TV providers, monopolized regional rights to screen 2006 World Cup football matches to subscribers only, the signal pirates had other ideas (Sakr 2007: 190–92).

With satellite access becoming the norm, the next step for satellite channel operators was to benefit from the spread of mobile phones. The landmark event here was the deft acquisition by Lebanon's Future TV of *Pop Idol*, FremantleMedia's singing contest-cum-reality show format, just after it had broken viewing records in the United Kingdom and United States. Crucially, besides offering drama, home-grown celebrity and suspense, this format (renamed *Super Star*[1] by Future TV) had proved that telephone voting for contestants could siphon telecoms revenues into television. When the last show in the 2003 series of *Super Star* attracted nearly five million votes, a figure that was to double in the second series and treble in the third (Sakr

2007: 114), other Arab channels rushed to import or create formats that would have the same financial effect. Before long, analysts and audiences were getting a strong sense of déjà vu. Yet some formats simply could not be ignored. One or two, like *Al-Rais*, MBC's 2004 adaptation of Endemol's *Big Brother*, were too much at odds with local social conventions to survive. One or two others, led by LBC's *Star Academy* (also acquired from Endemol), became compulsory viewing and a regular talking point among a whole generation of fans and critics across the Arab world (Kraidy 2007).

Telephone voting for Arab TV shows took off at a time when mobile phones were becoming more widespread in some Arab countries than in Europe or the United States. In societies where everyone's conduct is watched and judged by everyone else, the mobile phone affords at least a measure of privacy. After WTO-related telecoms liberalization in the Arab region started to push prices down, mobile phone subscriptions rose by 70 per cent in 2005 alone (Madar Research 2006). By the end of 2007, the number of mobile phone subscribers far exceeded the number of inhabitants in Bahrain, Qatar, Saudi Arabia and the UAE, with the UAE's penetration rate of 173 per cent more than three times the Arab average of 50.8 per cent and the world average of 49.3 per cent (Kawach 2008). The ubiquity of phones helps to explain the rise of Arab television channels devoted to music video accompanied by SMS text messages displayed along the bottom of the screen. An absence of regulatory constraints made SMS traffic potentially even more lucrative for channel owners, which may be one reason why the number of Nilesat channels dependent solely on music video and SMS jumped to around 60 in little more than two years after Prince Alwaleed launched his first music channel under the Rotana brand (Battah 2006: 21). In this way, a new form of user-generated content was cultivated alongside that already long familiar to Arab viewers from live phone-in talk shows, which had been a feature of Arab satellite television for at least the past 10 years. Meanwhile, television companies' moves to deliver news and sports content to mobile phones brought the launch of the Al-Jazeera Mobile channel in 2003. Later, MBC started making 'mobisodes' of its drama serials and claimed to have achieved 100,000 downloads during the fasting and peak-viewing month of Ramadan in 2007 (*Emirates Business 24/7* 2008).

Any early agonizing over content adaptation eased when television streaming made viewing via the internet an everyday reality in Arab countries, as elsewhere. By 2008, nearly two-thirds of Arab channels had established an online presence in the form of a website or portal, and a quarter of all channels claimed to be using this presence to bolster revenues (Arab Advisors Group 2008a). Their eagerness reinforces other evidence that official figures for internet penetration among Arab populations need to be interpreted carefully, just like those for access to pay TV. In Egypt, for example, 10 per cent of the population are said to have internet access and only 0.5 per cent have broadband.[2] Yet large numbers of Egyptians use the internet not at home but in internet cafés – in some cases, for as much as 30 hours a week (Wheeler 2007: 7) – while over 63 per cent of Egyptian households with a broadband connection share it with neighbours (Forrester 2008). The marked rise of Arab blogging in 2005 and enthusiastic use of video sharing and social networking websites can be seen in this light. Amateur clips posted on YouTube, from cameraphone images of torture in Egyptian jails to video of a woman breaking the Saudi ban on women driving, have their counterparts on Arab sites such as Video Forum, a website run by MBC's 24-hour news channel Al-Arabiya. Some user-generated material from these sites is carried over to Arab television channels, but not all. Al-Arabiya refrained from airing the torture videos, or clips showing mobs of men assaulting women on the streets of Cairo, or one that appeared to show a man in Saudi Arabia throwing a terrified woman from an apartment window (Battah 2007).

Self-disclosure on Arab television: marketing ploy or social breakthrough?

It was against this background of partial mobility of content between television, telephones and the internet that apparently significant developments took place in the evolution of the talk show on Arab channels. Live phone-in talk shows were a key ingredient of success for Arab satellite channels from the early days. Orbit and ART were initially the most daring, but Al-Jazeera famously broke the mould with its no-holds-barred political debates. Al-Jazeera's competitors recognized in the late 1990s that they could differentiate themselves by means of talk shows that were more social than political. Yet there are several reasons for locating the turning point in social talk on Arab television later than this, somewhere in the period 2003–4, during which network expansion by MBC and others was at its peak. This was a time when taboo-breaking talk about sex and other personal matters became more commonplace on Arab television, in imported US series of *The Oprah Winfrey Show* and *Dr Phil*, or Arabic-language shows like *Sire w'Infatahit* (A Way of Life Revealed), hosted by Zaven Kouyoumdjian on Future TV, and *Kalam Nawaem* (Soft Talk), a women's round-table discussion programme that MBC modelled on ABC's *The View*.

Drawing on contrasting approaches identified in the introduction to this chapter and the themes emerging from the two previous sections, the story of this development in television content could be recounted in two different ways. One would focus on its business rationale in the face of media–telecoms' convergence; the other would look at a new generation of programme makers who had been trying for some time to use television to promote social change. The first account would start by tracing MBC's marketing strategy to the moment when it explicitly targeted the purchasing power and growing assertiveness of young Saudi women. The strategy crystallized after MBC's management had made a bid to attract young audiences in 2003 by creating

MBC2 as a vehicle for screening English-language movies, sit-coms and other imported content with Arabic subtitles, free-to-air, round the clock. MBC3, a children's channel, followed in 2004 along with MBC4, at which point MBC2 became a full-time film channel and other material was transferred to MBC4. 'Everything in the marketing world' is about 'horizontal' and 'vertical' segmentation, an MBC executive said later. 'Vertical', he explained, meant catching viewers for MBC3 and encouraging them to graduate to MBC2, then MBC4 and then Al-Arabiya. 'Horizontal' meant encouraging viewers to move around between channels during commercial breaks (El-Hamamsy 2005). The transfer of *Oprah* to MBC4 seemed to vindicate the segmentation strategy because, as another MBC representative boasted, the large number of young Saudi Arabian women found to be watching the show, and chatting about it by mobile phone and email, revealed the under-exploited potential of this market segment (El-Rashidi 2005). The discovery – which anecdotal evidence suggests was also valid for women in other Arab countries – indicated that Arab viewers were keen to watch Oprah coaxing guests to talk about emotionally charged subjects – so much so that MBC4 screened *Oprah* twice a day, five days a week, and added *Dr Phil*, an *Oprah* spin-off, to its schedules. Taken together with MBC1's *Kalam Nawaem*, which had tackled sexual topics unfamiliar to Arab television, and whose presenters had used the show to share their own intimate experiences of divorce, childbirth and so on, the new talk show diet was judged to be a commercial success because it tapped into the 'core of the human experience' (Malas 2008: 17).

A second, alternative, account of the same phenomenon would feature Oprah Winfrey, the public therapist, as an acknowledged role model for aspiring Arab presenters, and stress the long history of those presenters' attempts to stimulate public talk about 'private' issues on Arab media. Sensitive family matters may still have been considered daring by the mid-2000s, but they were not unheard of in the early days of terrestrial television in Qatar and Kuwait, and had been broached on Egyptian radio in a programme called *I'tarafat Lailiyya* (Night Confessions), which ran from 1990 to 1996. Thus the stage was already set for the talk show *Ya Hala*, launched by ART in the mid-1990s, to discuss pre-marital sex, drug use, male impotence and divorce. It was also set for Saja, a private production company set up in Jordan in 1996, to plan on including sensitive topics in several talk show series it produced for ART. The company's young staff, conversant with the *Oprah* ethos, regarded controversy and lively discussion as essential both commercially and in the interests of social change. In practice, however, they found studio audience members so reluctant to provide personal testimony, for fear of embarrassing themselves and implicating family and friends, that they had to resort to indirect sources to illustrate the topics discussed (former Saja producer 2007). Over time, the programme makers found it so hard to inject drama into audience discussions about social topics that they started to avoid these topics altogether (ibid. 2007). That their experience was not unusual is underlined by

MBC's recourse to subtitling foreign versions of the confessional talk show. In Lebanon, however, others were ready to pursue the goal of domestic self-disclosure to promote social debate. Zaven, who later became known as a 'male Arab Oprah', started *Sire w'Infatahit* on Future TV at the end of the 1990s, modelling his own performance on Oprah's technique of 'opening up' herself so as to persuade guests to follow suit. Aware of resistance to his subject matter, Zaven told an interviewer: 'Change needs time ... People aren't ready to hear everything yet ... We can't rush things' (Armeniangate 2006). Even so, in 2004 new precedents were set. In one show, four people talked on camera about their lives as AIDS sufferers. In another, the discussion centred on sexual behaviour. Episodes like this arguably helped to lay the groundwork for *Kalam Kabeer* (Serious Talk), a sexual health advice show that ran on Egypt's privately owned El Mehwar channel in Ramadan 2006, similar to Dr Ruth Westheimer's programme on US cable television 20 years earlier.

Although there are obvious differences of emphasis in these two accounts of what is effectively the same programming trajectory, it is important to acknowledge that, in Arab television at least, commercial preoccupations and an interest in social change are not mutually exclusive. Asked to respond to allegations that MBC was trying to change Saudi customs and traditions, MBC Group Chairman Walid al-Ibrahim was categoric. It was his generation's duty to break 'obsolete traditions', he said, if by doing so it could make Saudi Arabia 'more open to the world with all its progress and modernity' (Dossari 2006). Zaven, meanwhile, has declared that he 'die[s] for ratings' (Malas 2008).

Conclusion

It may be no coincidence that the number of televised conversations about intimate human experiences increased in the Arab world at a time when not only was the number of television channels increasing, but so too were the possibilities for individuals to gain access to the content of these conversations through media other than the family television set. As for who or what was driving this phenomenon, the particularities of post-broadcast television in the Arab context suggest that it would be a mistake to overemphasize either commercialism or popular demands for social change. Media executives' policy statements, quoted here, do highlight a push for growth by the region's dominant media groups. But the chapter also showed that these groups' dominant position was already secured through opaque advertising fixes, implying that the political agenda behind their operations should also be taken into account. Other evidence points to a distinct reluctance on the part of Arab publics to take part in self-disclosure, for fear of embarrassment or shame. But those same people also showed resourcefulness in connecting to media that would give them access to taboo-breaking conversations conducted on television. This combination of give and take bears out Neumann's (1991) argument that questions about the fragmentation of television channels and audiences need to be answered by reference to deeper power balances between competing interest groups and elites.

Notes

1 The English words 'Super Star' are written in Arabic letters.
2 According to March 2008 data from the International Telecommunication Union (ITU), available at www.internetworldstats.com/africa.htm#eg (accessed 21 August 2008).

Chapter 17

Globalizing televised culture

The case of China

Anthony Y.H. Fung

A global world without freedom

Once we believed that globalization of culture could bring hope to people who live in worlds deprived of freedom, democracy and equality. Among the various processes of globalization, new forms of television – in the form of either hardware (such as satellite television and the internet) or software (television dramas, shows and formats sold internationally) – were supposed to play a major role in 'flattening' international differences and opening up politically closed regimes. However, what I am going to describe in the case of China tells an opposite story: the globalization of television genres does not seem to confirm the liberalizing thesis. In this chapter, I focus on the growing trend of the cultural adoption or 'cloning' of global television genres and formats in the People's Republic of China (PRC). The explication of how these global television genres or formats have been localized, nationalized or infused with state ideologies, and the rationale behind such modification, illustrates the role today's new television plays in a developing state. It also explains how, while globalizing television may connect worlds that are poles apart, the implications and the consequences for different cultures and states can be very different.

In this chapter, based on ethnographic observations from a selection of major Chinese television stations (including Chinese Central TV (CCTV), Shanghai TV, Hunan TV, Wuhan TV, Guangdong TV and Shenzhen TV), I provide a concrete illustration of how global genres or formats are being appended to, cloned into or adapted to local productions. Informed by interviews (necessarily remaining anonymous) with producers from these stations over 2005–8, this discussion examines the rationales and philosophies behind the localization of global television genres. Global culture has inspired hundreds of Chinese television programmes, and so it is impossible to give a comprehensive account of all the global television genres being adopted or localized. Therefore I will concentrate on some important globally adopted examples, television genres such as quiz shows, game shows and idol shows, to illustrate the situation (see Table 17.1).

Reforms of Chinese television: from structural changes to pragmatics

As China reforms and modernizes, the Chinese television industry has moved along the path of commercialization. As a legacy of communist rule, Chinese television stations are still state owned, serving as the mouthpiece of the authorities. However, since the 1980s and China's Open Door Policy, in addition to their political obligations, television controllers have also had to consider audience ratings and advertising revenues. A major paradigm shift occurred in 1983, when the Chinese authorities started to loosen their monopolistic control of the television stations; market consideration was suddenly important because the authorities terminated the subsidies for local and provincial television stations as part of a philosophy that allocated 'dual functions' to the media.

Ran Wei (2000: 332–3) has suggested that both domestic and external pressures were implicated in the commercialization of the Chinese media. The key domestic factor was the restructuring of China's archaic planned economy into a socialist market economy after the former Chinese leader Deng Xiaoping's symbolic tour to the comparatively capitalist southern China. In the wave of the reform that followed, the media had to respond to government's demand that they create media business enterprises. This new policy did not imply that the previous role of the media as the mouthpiece of the government had become obsolete, but it did require that the media address market needs in order to become more financially self-reliant. It was, in sum, a national policy of media commercialization that prompted media outlets to respond to the audience's desires and generate advertising revenue. The result was that the media explored new avenues – new programme types, the importation of programmes and the creation of new channels to name a few – to maximize profits within the ideological confines of a compromise between political and economic imperatives (Guo and Chen 1997).

In terms of external pressures, Wei (2000) suggests that technological advancement has been most significant for Chinese television. The abundance of media choices made available by the more relaxed policy for newcomers to China, mainly in the form of satellite television, created a highly competitive platform for media industries, particularly after the 1990s. Now, after some years of incremental development, there are 60 domestic regional satellite broadcasters and 31 legal foreign satellite channels (including both the non-encrypted ones such as Phoenix TV, and encrypted ones such as Xing Kong of STAR) competing with the Chinese national, provincial and city television stations (Huang 2007) – a scale of competition larger than any other market in the world (Fung 2008).

Nowadays, many provincial and local television stations provide access to avenues of information, along with a steady stream of light-hearted and sensational entertainment in the form of romance, sex, crime, tragedies, violence,

Table 17.1 Selected Chinese foreign-genre cloned programmes

Chinese programme	Chinese TV station	Global TV format adopted/models	Starting year
I Shouldn't Be Alive (Shengcundatiaozhan)	Guangdong TV	Survivors	2000
Canyon Survival Camp (Xiagushengcunying)	Guizhou TV	Survivors	2003
Gold Apple (Jin Pingguo)	CCTV-1	Survivors	2003
Happy Dictionary (Kaixincidian)	CCTV-2	Who Wants to Be a Millionaire?	2000
Mobilizing the Brave (Yongzhezongdongyuan)	Beijing Joymedia Group	Fear Factor	2004
Super Female Voice (Chaojilusheng)	Hunan Satellite TV	American Idol	2004
The Perfect Holiday (Wanmeijiaqi)	Beijing Vhand Culture CommunicationHunan Economic TV	Big Brother	2002
Who Will Tell Beijing Olympics (Shuijiangjieshuobeijingaoyun)	CCTV-5	The Apprentice	2004
Rose(Meiguizhiyue)	Hunan TV	The Love Boat	1999
Feichang 6+1	CCTV-2	The Simple Life	2003
AbsoluteChallenge (Jueduitiaozhan)	CCTV-2	The Apprentice	2003
Supermarket Champion (Chaoshidayingjia)	CCTV-2	What Not to Wear	2004
Go into Shangri-la (Zouruxianggelila)	Beijing Vhand Culture Communication	Survivor/Amazing Race	2001

star gossip and celebrity scandal. The political content of the media is diluted. Occasionally, the media may cover important political events but they do so in compliance with state orders. The intriguing question concerns how the television stations remain in touch with public sentiment by branding themselves as commercial entertainment, but without being seen as having entirely abandoned their political obligations and relevance. The failure to meet the political needs of the state is not just a matter of political correctness. It could lead to serious social consequences. In James Lull's ethnographies of Chinese television in 1989, he described the 'implacable contradictions existing in the popular consciousness', which are the results of interactions between the cultural promotion of consumption through the media and the harsh economic and political realities of the everyday lives of the public (Lull 1997: 260). Should those contradictions remain unresolved, it not only cripples the entire progress of television reform, but also undermines the legitimacy of the state. For the Chinese television industry, then, its role is not only to enhance a seamless fusion between market and state, but also to be able to resolve the contradictions felt by the populace. There must be some feasible ways to minimize the dialectics and enhance harmonic containment and accommodation (Zhao 1998: 21). What is argued in this chapter is that the media are now wiser, more flexible and more 'advanced'; as a result, Chinese television is able to produce programmes that specifically accommodate this purpose.

Global television genres in China

New television genres have reached unprecedented popularity in China, and the pleasure and entertainment they generate have overshadowed the prevailing social problems – that is, they have helped to play down, minimize or resolve the contradictions sensed by the population. However, the tested and almost guaranteed popularity of such globally inspired programmes – occasionally creating a state of frenzy among the public – can backfire, generating new social and even political problems. Often, the State Administration of Radio, Film and Television (SARFT) has had to intervene, either calling for a halt to certain programme types, or demanding that the stations modify the liberalizing tendency that is seen to accompany the Western modernity represented by such programmes.

At this point, I would like to re-emphasize this crucial principle underlying the operation of the media in China: the state has not given up its control of the media. Nor does the state implicitly allow the commercialization of the industry to displace its political mandate. Now and then, international and national media may conjure up the fantasy that the Chinese government is incapable of resisting the trend towards globalization that brings in the values of liberalism, freedom, democracy and so forth. However, I argue that this is unrealistic. During the entire process of globalization, the party tenets of the PRC have never been secondary to economic policy; rather, the state utilizes global forms of entertainment to reinforce the efficacy of its governance. To put it in another way, it is actually the force of globalization, in parallel with the notions of neoliberalism and capitalism, that indirectly strengthens the ruling powers in China.

The PRC has created a dual system of television programming: first, the core programmes explicitly planned for nationalist and other political purposes; and second, the globally tinted entertainment programmes. The former orthodox format, together with the obsolete theme of the 'main rhythm' programmes (historical or modern dramas with a very positive national and didactic theme), claims prime time; outside that timeslot, television stations are quite free to amuse the audience with the razzamatazz of showbiz and entertainment programmes.

For the latter, usually, they are a miscellany of foreign entertainment programmes and local production that attempts to reflect global taste. They are powerful enough to help the state to inculcate cultural values into the everyday life and experience of the audience. Under the veil of entertainment and pleasures derived from the programme, Ma suggests, the audiences are oblivious to their own indoctrination, temporarily sidelining their long-acquired anti-hegemonic read-between-the-lines skills to continue to indulge in the romance, comfort and fantasy on the screen (cf. Ma 2000: 29). In other words, exposure to mediated entertainment becomes a digression from politics. Hence, while these new global cultural forms are not supercharged with a political mission, the outcomes of the reading of these cultural contents can have political consequences.

After the mid-1990s, because of the circulation of the foreign television formats or the purchase of television programme franchises in different Asian regions (e.g. Hong Kong and Taiwan) (Keane et al. 2007), new international genres became visible to Chinese producers, who are permitted to travel overseas quite frequently to 'learn from the West'. Of course, while many delegates of Chinese stations ended up only with a pleasant tourist memory, producers in Hunan Television were bold enough to experiment with their new television formats when Hunan started to beam its signal across the country via AsiaSat2 in January 1997. In support of the leadership's objective of branding the station as the entertainment hub of China, many Western genres – the *Idol* format, quiz shows, game shows and reality TV formats – first appeared on Hunan Satellite Television. Programmes included *Happy Camp* (1997), *Rose* (1998) and *Super Female Voice* (2004).[1] Many other television channels, including the leader of the industry, CCTV, soon followed suit. In the keenly competitive international media environment, these global cultural forms are new vehicles through which stations compete with each other. In the following section, I will discuss some cases that highlight the problematics involved in this competition.

Social norms and gatekeeping

There have been many varieties of Western television formats cloned or adopted in recent years, but not all of them could reach the 'Chinese standard' required. Apart from considering market profit and political needs, the Chinese stations are gatekeepers charged with ensuring that cloned or adopted programmes do not contravene national norms and values. Thus there is no surprise that the French version of the *Big Brother* format, *Loft Story*, that portrays sexual and romantic relationships between female and male participants locked in a closed room, or Fox TV's *Temptation Island*, in which participants are seduced by overly sexy girls, are not cloned for the Chinese audience. The television stations do self-censor, rejecting global cultural content that might be regarded as perverting the morality of the Chinese public.

Whenever adopted, the genres must be translated into cultural forms that accommodate the specific social characteristics of Chinese society. A typical example was *Happy Dictionary* (*Kaixincidian*) (2000), inspired by ITV's *Who Wants to Be a Millionaire?* (UK). Though the original question-and-answer format was kept and money remained the major incentive for the contestants, the content of the questions and the prize system were localized. First, all the quiz content was designed to educate the public, thereby excluding questions about entertainment, celebrity gossip or hobbies that a Western audience might well have deemed interesting. Second, to avoid excessive competition between television stations, as well as an unacceptable promotion of materialism, the SARFT limited the monetary award to a maximum of RMB5,000; the television stations replaced the money with prizes, ranging from home appliances (for example, televisions and notebook computers) to household consumables. This modification altered the original intent and orientation of the programme – that taps into the individual aspiration for wealth – towards addressing family relationships, household necessities and social harmony.[2] Chinese society recognizes the family, not the individual, as the basic unit of society. In 2007, a new set of rules was introduced for the new season of *Happy Dictionary*, in which a contestant who failed to answer correctly might lose all their prizes to a domestic viewer or to studio audience members. The new rules were aimed at reducing the likelihood of all the prizes falling into the hands of a single individual. In this case, then, format characteristics that embodied Western values contradictory to traditional norms, social expectations and state agendas were modified.

Entertainment is, of course, secondary to the interests of the state, so it is not uncommon for state interests to take precedence over market populism in deciding the schedule for televised programming. For instance, within the two-month period after the Sichuan earthquake, variety shows – including many new genres on all television stations – were cancelled by an interim decree issued by the SARFT. The authorities' intervention was intended to orchestrate sympathy for the victims of the tragedy. In place of the programmes that were withdrawn, television stations were obliged to use the available time to serve the state interest. For example, Hunan Television replaced the second season of its Hong Kong–China co-produced popular celebrity dancing contest *Come Dancing* (2008) with *Running Ahead Olympic*, an outdoor steeple-chase turned television show. The latter carried a theme that was in line with the national Olympic agenda for the summer.

Managing the global desire

Of course, not all the global entertainment formats are safe. Even if we assume that television stations seldom deviate from the state agenda, it is inevitable that the values, desires and ideologies of modernity that accompany the new forms of television will trigger the 'affect' of the audience. By this, I mean an irrational, spontaneous, unpredictable and impromptu feeling generated among the audience – as opposed to the 'managed affect' of the planned, restrained and deliberate response generated by propagandist promotions mobilizing nationalist speeches, representation of glorious military victories and the depiction of traditional forms of heroism. When the global formats do create an affective relation towards Western modernity, the authorities have to suddenly become more interventionist and manage the unexpected consequences.

Among the programmes these new genres introduced into China, *Super Voice Girl*, known as *Supergirl*, presented by Hunan Satellite Television in the summer of 2004, has posed the most severe threat to the authorities. *Supergirl* was cloned from ITV's *Pop Idol* (UK) and Fox's *American Idol* (USA). In its second season in 2005, the station incorporated the BBC's *Fame Academy* model of interactive audience participation. For the regional selection into the national contest, and in addition to the three professional judges, the programme invited the nationwide audience to vote for their favourite contestants via SMS. The 'crisis' of this case has been widely discussed since, and it derives from the 400 million-strong audience's choice of Chris Li, who was not the ideal representative of Chinese femininity. The 21-year-old Sichuan girl was soon picked up by *Time*'s Asian edition version, which featured her frizzy-haired close-up shot in a special issue headlined as 'Asian heroes'. Even apart from the moral and cultural controversies created by Chris Li's proud and public androgyny, the deliberative potential of this imitation of a democratic political system meant that popular culture had crossed a boundary: it now had some direct relation to the political (Jakes 2005). The issue caught the attention of major Western media, including the *New York Times*, which compared Chris Li with China's political leader Hu Jintao through the sarcastic headline 'The Chinese Get the Vote, if Only for "Super Girl"' (Yardley 2005).

Many recent academic studies (e.g. Yang 2006) have also echoed the media by drawing the connection between the *Supergirl* format and political participation. The act of sending a message supporting their favourite contestants by mobile phones was regarded as a preliminary form of election, and the popularity of *Supergirl* was said to reflect people's hidden desire for the right to vote. Though the analogy has its limits, this was the first time that members of a Chinese audience were able to hand-pick their idols in a transparent and fair contest. In the eyes of the general public, what was upheld was the principle of one vote, one value; this principle is in stark contrast to those implicated in current political appointments. The provenance of such televised phenomena and their public circulation is exactly what Liesbet Van Zoonen (2005) has described as the 'convergence of politics and popular culture'. Based on the fundamental similarities between the active participatory culture in entertainment and citizenship, Van Zoonen (2005: 145) argued that the natural enthusiasm of the people for popular culture could revitalize the political culture inasmuch as audiences will 'rehearse' the same narrative techniques or even principles in the political realm.

One might suspect that the state would not be able to resist the power of this new kind of television, as newspapers such as the *Beijing News*' attempts to deride *Supergirl*'s democratic fantasy failed to change the public mind (Da Xi 2005). However, I would argue that the cultural terrains colonized by the new and globally connected television always operate under the control of the state. In the authoritarian context, it is not difficult for the state to 'adjust' the direction and power of a television programme. Consequently, in 2006 the state promulgated new media regulations via the SARFT in order to reconstruct a 'harmonious socialist society' (Macartney 2006). According to these new rules, television programmes must 'avoid vulgar or gross styles' and safeguard the morals of the younger generation. Judges appointed must not 'embarrass or heckle' the contestants (Macartney 2006). *Supergirl*'s producer, however, interprets these regulations as the state's instruction to exclude SMS voting from all kinds of programme. Subsequently, all television stations nationwide complied with this order without any apparent opposition.[3] *Supergirl* thus does not illustrate the omnipotence of globalized influence or the power of the marketization of the television industry, as many other studies may have suggested. Rather, it demonstrates that the state had been closely monitoring the case and was ready to insist on the modification of global formats if they failed to match state agendas.

Global form, political message

While the election of an androgynous *Supergirl* in China created a row over the desirability of the *Idol* format, other genres such as the Chinese version of reality television have been designed in a way that closely matches the national agenda. For the reality shows I have in mind, although they are all derived from the CBS (US) programme *Survivor* – a game show format in which contestants (tribe members) compete against each other in the wilderness – China's vernacular versions, including *I Shouldn't Be Alive (Shengcundatiaozhan)* (Guangdong TV), *Canyon Survival Camp* (Guizhou TV), *Gold Apple* (CCTV-1) and *Go into Shangri-la* (Beijing Vhand Culture Communication) played down the 'survival of the fittest' rivalry. In its place were political messages to do with nationalism, patriotism, unity and multiculturalism.

The most explicit of the modifications occurred with *I Shouldn't Be Alive*, made by Guangdong Television (a station in south China which is receptive to Western influence from the former British colony of Hong Kong). When this Chinese version of *Survivor*, the first version of this format in China, was broadcast in 2000, it soon became the talk of the town. The popularity of the American *Survivor* had paved the way for this format in China. Since the first series, the programme has set the standard for this kind of reality show: the original focus on egotistic competition and individual belligerence was translated into a 'human versus nature' competition in which participants toured around the 40,000 kilometre-long border of the country over seven months. The local production deliberately diluted the dark side of humanity – the personal conceit, egoism and selfishness that characterized the American version. It cancelled the voting session, used in the original show to kick out 'the weak', and expunged shots that might provoke the issue of privacy, emphasizing the hardship and determination of the comrades-in-arms as they overcame obstacles along the journey.

Once the structure of this format was established and widely accepted by the public, the authorities further politicized it. In 2001, the 80th anniversary year of the Communist Party, Guangdong TV launched the second season of *I Shouldn't Be Alive: Walking the Long March Road*, in which 20 challengers walked the same 6,000-kilometre path taken by the Red Army of the Communist Party in exile, penetrating into deep forest, climbing snowy peaks and crossing rugged wilderness. That this globally inspired Chinese television programme attempted to insert first, a nationalistic ideology, and second, a social philosophy, into a commercial formula might seem absurd; however, it did have a strong appeal in the Chinese context. The reasons why need some elaboration.

Soft nationalism with pleasure

First, given *The Long March* as its title, the programme itself is very explicit about its political resonance. Nonetheless, Guangdong TV was able to retain its entertaining nature. As an entertainment, the programme focused on how participants restrained their temperaments, made judicious decisions and maintained their leadership in the face of extreme hardship. The competition of the 'New Red Army' conjured up excitement and laughter for the audience. At the same time, the state organ also aimed to demonstrate, even in these abysmal conditions, the importance not only of intimate relationships, fraternal friendship and basic altruistic values, but also of patriotism – not in abstract terms, but manifested through the practices of the young participants in the expedition.

As a consequence, the authorities were able to reinvigorate a modernized patriotic spirit, not simply one of nostalgic remembrance. The television programme demonstrated to the public that Chinese culture can still be the object of veneration by its people today. In this sense, television nowadays is not too much different from the propaganda of the old days. It is still a state apparatus. However, after years of media reform, the Communist media could now present a soft or banal nationalism that is naturally 'flagged' in the media through symbols, language and icons (cf. Billig 1995) that have taken on a more acceptable and modern form. While audiences can be entertained by such cultural representations and expressions, they also receive a sense of empowered nationalism, the same effect achieved when China hosted the Beijing Olympics.

To outsiders, a commercial programme burdened with political-economic purposes might seem a contradiction. However, in the highly politicized Chinese culture, the combination of commercialization and nationalism is not uncommon. From high art to popular culture, such fusion seems to be the legacy of Chinese rule. On the high art side, there is the well-known Chinese pianist Lang Lang playing the Yellow River Piano Concerto – a rearrangement of the Yellow River Cantata composed in protest at the Japanese occupation in the late 1930s – with the China Philharmonic Orchestra, and numerous contemporary Chinese painters of oil paintings, that include Liu Xiaodong's *Military Realism* and Yue Minjun's *Take the Plunge*, depicting symbols of the Cultural Revolution. In popular culture there are the persona of the most popular Chinese hip-hop singer Jay Chou, who dresses in public in Chinese robes bespangled with glistening golden dragon patterns (Fung 2008), and the award-winning movie *Hero* (2002), celebrating and justifying dictatorship in the name of cultural unity. The newly globally cloned television genre is one more entertaining cultural form used to creatively package politics.

Heroism within collectivism

Second, *Walking the Long March Road*, and more overtly another *Survivor*-cloned reality show titled *Canyon Survival Camp* (2003), prescribed a social philosophy of collectivism, a legacy of Confucian ethics. Ying Zhu (2008) has described how, even amid the worsening social conditions – namely increasing social inequalities, political corruption and local maladministration – the Chinese media can skilfully manufacture a popular genre, such as the dynasty drama, to justify Confucian leadership in order to neutralize public hostility towards the regime. These reality programmes operate in similar ways, but in new, globalized entertainment formats. In *Canyon Survival Camp*, 12 contestants aged from 20 to 40, drawn from different provinces, had to survive in the remote Guizhou Nanjiang Valley for 24 days. It is the closest reality show to the *Survivor* format, as the participants were divided into two tribes, and after each round of competition the losing tribe had to expel a member. The elimination of tribe members might appear intrinsically ruthless, but *Canyon Survival Camp* foregrounded the participants' companionship, forgiveness, encouragement and cooperativeness, in place of the conflicts, animosity, trickery, exclusion and conspiracy that mark the Western version. Even though participants were tempted to drive out opponents to win the RMB100,000 prize, Chinese participants still prefer to appear kind, sincere and cooperative in the eyes of the public, their friends and family. Listed as one of the nominees for the Best Life Programme for the official Chinese Television Chart in 2005, *Canyon Survival Camp* successfully reproduced a sense of Chinese collectivism that ranked social virtues and public goals above the personal.

However, one can imagine how such general preaching of collectivism might constitute another form of high-handed suppression of individuality, or indeed might rehearse an official rhetoric that, in their daily life, no one believes. To deal with that possibility, the television stations have made use of the generic features of the format, which highlight the achievements and attitudes of the survivor or the winner. Team leadership, self-sacrifice, compassion, thoughtfulness and so forth were all winning qualities that not only could be eulogized by the audience, but that the producers could exploit. As my informants emphasized, they were not unequivocally told by the authorities to present these people as heroes. But by exploiting the intrinsic potential of this new genre, the producers understood that they could tap into a deep-seated Chinese heroic tradition in a way that rendered the programme commercially viable while also favoured by the state.

Heroism has long been a construct of communist propaganda. The People's Liberation Army (PLA) used to have Lei Feng, an iconic self-sacrificing soldier who was devoted to Chairman Mao and the people. The takeup of global genres demonstrates the modernity of Chinese television; rather than commanding the audiences to 'learn from Comrade Lei Feng', the new global genres can simply present the vivid life experiences and altruistic acts of the contestants to the television audience. If the audience members internalize such heroism, the heroes and their values, they then become exemplars for this generation. With the media as socializing agents, the authorities are thus able to manufacture a version of heroism that sustains the *status quo*.

Conclusion: commercialization of political ideals

The case of Chinese television described above might help us to respond to a more fundamental question: in what ways is today's television 'new' to us? The packaging, format and 'feeling' of globally created, locally inflected television may be fresh to the audience, but the television content 'tuned' by the authorities may not be too much different from what preceded it in terms of its social and political functions. The globalization of television may bring in more entertainment, higher doses of material desires and more diversified cultural representations, as well as new and more advanced technology, but the socio-political role of television in China remains relatively unchanged. As illustrated in this chapter, similar to the role of the state apparatus, it extends its historical mission to reinstate the principles of cultural collectivism and at the same time uses traditional constructions of heroism as the strategy to effectively boost the former. What is even more advanced is that the global forms help fashion a soft nationalism that crystallizes the citizens, not in a forceful manner, but in an unconscious and subtle way that desensitizes their antagonism. In this sense, the new television in China is not the 'cult of newness' from outside that replaces the 'cult of history' (Beech 2002) and thus leads the Chinese away from communism. Nor is the new media television culture likely to liberalize the authoritarian state.

Notes

1 Author's interview with producer of Hunan Economic TV.
2 Author's interview with producer Zheng Wei.
3 Author's interview with producer of *Supergirl*.

Bibliography

Abu-Lughod, L. (2005) *Dramas of Nationhood: The Politics of Television in Egypt*, Chicago: University of Chicago Press.

Accenture (2008) 'Accenture Survey Finds Broad Agreement within Media and Entertainment Industry on Direction of Digital Market', company press release, 5 May. Online. Available http://newsroom.accenture.com/article_display.cfm?article_id = 4674 (accessed 10 May 2008).

Adalian, J. and Schneider, M. (2007) 'Strike May Force Rewrite', *Variety*, 409, 17 December: 28.

——2008 'Upfront Upheaval', *Variety*, 31 March: 14.

Agence France Press (2007) 'Facebook Users Listed for Search', *Australian*, 2 October: 36.

Alvarado, M. and Stewart, J. (1985) *Made for Television: Euston Films Limited*, London: BFI.

Anagnost, A. (2008) 'From "Class" to "Social Strata": Grasping the Social Totality in Reform-era China', *Third World Quarterly*, 29(3): 497–519.

Andrejevic, M. (2004) 'The Webcam Subculture and Digital Enclosure', in N. Couldry and A. McCarthy, eds *MediaSpace: Place, Scale and Culture in a Media Age*, London: Routledge, 193–208.

—— (2007) *iSpy: Surveillance and Power in the Interactive Era*, Lawrence, KA: University Press of Kansas.

Appadurai, A. (2006) *Fear of Small Numbers*, Durham, NC: Duke University Press.

Arab Advisors Group (2008a) 'Online Presence of FTA Satellite Channels in the Arab World', press release, Amman, 14 July.

—— (2008b) 'Satellite Pay TV Operators in the Arab World', press release, Amman, 14 January.

—— (2008c) 'Terrestrial TV in the Arab World', press release, Amman, 15 May.

—— (2008d) 'Egypt Media Survey 2008', press release, Amman, 20 May.

Armeniangate (2006) Interview with Zaven Kouyoumdjian. Online. Available www.armeniangate.com/2/Various/Interview-Zaven.html (accessed 19 August 2008).

ASEAN, 'ASEAN and India Seal Trade, Cooperation Pacts with Eye on "Asian Century"'. Online. Available www.aseansec.org/afp/87.htm (accessed 9 September 2008).

Aslama, M. and Pantti, M. (2007) 'Flagging Finnishness: Reproducing National Identity in Reality Television', *Television & New Media*, 8(1): 49–67.

Aurthur, K. (2005) 'Lifetime's Place in the House (and Senate)', *New York Times*, 16 October: 2.1.

Australian Communication and Media Authority (ACMA) (2008) 'IPTV and Internet Video Services', Canberra: Australian Government, April.

Ayres, I. (2007) *Super Crunchers: How Anything Can be Predicted*, London: John Murray.

Bachman, K. (2007) 'Candidates Still Favoring Local TV Ads', *MediaWeek*, 15 October. Online. Available www.mediaweek.com (accessed 15 May 2008).

Bakhshi, H., McVittie, E. and Simmie, J. (2008) *Creating Innovation: Do the Creative Industries Support Innovation in the Wider Economy?* NESTA, March. Online. Available www.nesta.org.uk/creating-innovation (accessed 8 August 2008).

Banham, R. (1962) '*Coronation Street*, Hoggartsborough', *New Statesman*, 9 February: 200–1.

Banerjee, I. (2002) 'The Locals Strike Back: Media Globalization and Localization in the New Asian Television Landscape', *Gazette: The International Journal for Communications Studies*, 64(6): 517–35.

Bar, F. and Taplin, J. (2007) 'Cable's Digital Future', in S. Banet-Weiser, C. Chris and A. Freitas, eds *Cable Visions: Television Beyond Broadcasting*, New York: New York University Press, 66–84.

Bardoel, J. and d'Haenens, L. (2008) 'Reinventing Public Service Broadcasting in Europe: Prospects, Promises and Problems', *Media, Culture & Society*, 30: 337–55.

Barr, C. (1977) *Ealing Studios*, London: Cameron & Tayleur.

Battah, H. (2006) 'The SMS Invasion', *Middle East Broadcasters Journal*, 6: 18–22.

—— (2007) 'In the Eye of the Beholder', *Middle East Broadcasters Journal*, 11: 18–21.

Bazalgette, P. (2005) *Billion Dollar Game: How Three Men Risked It All and Changed the Face of TV*, London: Time Warner.

Beaty, B. and Sullivan, R. (2006) *Canadian Television Today*, Calgary: University of Calgary Press.

Beech, H. (2002) 'Let One Hundred Cultures Bloom', *Time Asia*, 11 November. Online. Available www.time.com/time/asia/features/china_cul_rev/opener.html (accessed 20 July 2008).

Bennett, J. (2008) 'Television Studies Goes Digital', *Cinema Journal*, 47(3): 158–65.

Bielby, D. and Harrington, C. (2002) 'Markets and Meanings: The Global Syndication of Television Programming', in D. Crane, N. Kawashima and K. Kawasaki, eds *Global Culture: Media, Arts, Policy, and Globalization*, London: Routledge.

Biguemer, J. and Shulte, R. (1990) 'Introduction', in J. Biguemer and R. Shulte, eds *The Craft of Translation*, Chicago: University of Chicago Press.

Billig, M. (1995) *Banal Nationalism*, London: Sage.

Booz Allen Hamilton (2006) *Strategic Review of the Television Broadcasting Sector in the Middle East*, rev. edn, Dubai: Booz Allen Hamilton.

—— (2007) 'Booz Allen Hamilton Finds Television Programming Improving in the Arab World', press release, 13 November.

Bordwell, D. and Thompson, K. (2004) *Film Art: An Introduction*, New York: McGraw Hill.

Born, G. (2003) 'Strategy and Projection in Digital Television: Channel Four and the Commercialization of Public Broadcasting in the UK', *Media, Culture & Society*, 25: 773–99.

Born, G. and Prosser, T. (2001) 'Culture and Consumerism: Citizenship, Public Service Broadcasting and the BBC's Fair Trading Obligations', *The Modern Law Review*, 64: 657–87.

Boulos, P. (2007) 'What Revolution?' *Middle East Broadcasters Journal*, 15: 36.

Boyles, D. (2003) 'EuroPress Review: Some 2003 Bests', *National Review Online*, 30 December. Online. Available www.nationalreview.com/europress/boyles200312300000.asp (accessed 30 March 2008).

Breslin, S. (2006) 'Serving the Market or Serving the Party: Neo-liberalism in China', in R. Robison, ed. *The Neo-Liberal Revolution: Forging the Market State*, New York: Palgrave, 114–34.

Broadcast (2007) 'Latin America', 12 October. Online. Available www.broadcastnow.co.uk/international/latin_america/news/latin_america.html (accessed 18 June 2008).

Brown, M. (2007) *A Licence to Be Different: The Story of Channel 4*, London: BFI.

Bruns, A. (2008a) *Blogs, Wikipedia, Second Life, and Beyond: From Production to Produsage*, New York: Peter Lang.

—— (2008b) 'Reconfiguring Television for a Networked, Produsage Context', *Media International Australia*, 126: 82–94.

Budowsky, B. (2006). 'New Year: The Triumph of New Media, New Political Optimism and New Leadership', *Huffington Post*, 31 December. Online. Available www.huffingtonpost.com (accessed 30 March 2008).

Buonanno, M. (2008) *The Age of Television: Experiences and Theories*, trans. Jennifer Radice, Bristol: Intellect.

Burston, J. (2000) 'Spectacle, Synergy and Megamusicals: The Global-industrialisation of the Live-entertainment Economy', in J. Curran, ed. *Media Organisation and Society*, London: Oxford University Press, 44–63.

Butcher, M. (2003) *Transnational Television, Cultural Identity and Change: When STAR Came to India*, New Delhi: Sage.

Caldwell, J.T. (2003) 'Second Shift Media Aesthetics: Programming, Interactivity and User Flows', in A. Everett and J.T. Caldwell, eds *New Media: Theories and Practices of Digitextuality*, New York: Routledge, 127–44.

—— (2004) 'Convergence Television: Aggregating Form and Repurposing Content in the Culture of Conglomeration', in L. Spigel and J. Olsson, eds *Television After TV: Essays on a Medium in Transition*, Durham, NC: Duke University Press, 41–74.

Calhoun, C. (2007) *Nations Matter: Culture, History and the Cosmopolitan Dream*, London: Routledge.

Campaign Finance Institute (2008) 'Party Conventions' Financiers Have Spent Nearly $1.5 Billion on Federal Campaign Contributions and Lobbying since 2005', 20 July. Online. Available www.cfinst.org (accessed 10 August 2008).

Carpentier, N. (2001) 'Managing Audience Participation', *European Journal of Communication*, 16(2): 209–32.

Carugati, A. (2004) 'Globo's Roberto Irineu Marinho', *World Screen*, May. Online. Available www.worldscreen.com/print.php?filename = 0504marinho (accessed 8 August 2008).

—— (2006) 'Grupo Televisa's Emilio Azcárraga Jean', *World Screen*, January. Online. Available www.worldscreen.com/print.php?filename = azcarraga106.htm (accessed 8 August 2008).

—— (2008) 'Cisneros Group of Companies' Gustavo Cisneros', *World Screen*, January. Online. Available www.worldscreen.com/print.php?filename = cisneros0108.htm (accessed 1 May 2008).

CBC (2007) *Striking the Right Balance: CBC/Radio-Canada Annual Report 2005–6*, Ottawa: Government of Canada.

Census of India (2001) Online. Available www.censusindia.gov.in (accessed 12 June 2008).

Center for Media and Public Affairs (2008) 'Media Bash Barack (Not a Typo)', 28 July. Online. Available www.cmpa.com (accessed 6 August 2008).

CFTPA (2002) *The Canadian Film and Television Production Industry Profile 2002: Canadian Independent Production – the Challenges of Uncertainty*, Ottawa: CFTPA.

Chadha, K. and Kavoori, A. (2000) 'Media Imperialism Revisited: Some Findings from the Asian Case', *Media, Culture & Society*, 22(4): 415–32.

Chahine, G., El Sharkawy, A. and Mahmoud, H. (2007) *Trends in Middle Eastern Arabic Television Series Production*, Dubai: Booz Allen Hamilton.

Chalaby, J.K., ed. (2005) *Transnational Television Worldwide: Towards a New Media Order*, London: I.B. Tauris.

Chaudhry, L. (2006) 'Can Blogs Revolutionize Progressive Politics?' *In These Times*, February: 24–30.

Cheng, S. (2006) 'Cultural Proximity, Diasporic Identities, and Popular Symbolic Capital: Taiwan Cultural Worker Qiong Yao's Cultural Production in the Chinese Media Market', *Global Media Journal*, 5(8).

ChoiceStream (2008) 'Real Relevance, Real Results', corporate web page. Online. Available www.choicestream.com (accessed 28 August 2008).

Chow, R. (1993) *Writing Diaspora: Tactics of Intervention in Contemporary Cultural Studies*, Bloomington, IN: University of Indiana Press.

Chu, Y. (2008) 'The Emergence of Polyphony in Chinese Television Documentaries', in K. Sen and T. Lee, eds *Politics, Media and Regime Change in Asia*, London: Routledge, 49–69.

Chu, Y.C., Donald, S.H. and Witcomb, A. (2003) 'Children, Media, and the Public Sphere in Chinese Australia', in G. Rawnsley and M.-Y. Rawnsley, eds *Political Communications in Greater China: The Construction and Reflection of Identity*, London: RoutledgeCurzon, 261–74.

Chua, B.H. (2001) 'Pop Culture China', *Singapore Journal of Tropical Geography*, 22(2): 113–21.

CNN.com (2004) 'TiVo: Jackson Stunt most Replayed Moment Ever', 3 February. Online. Available www.cnn.com/2004/TECH/ptech/02/03/television.tivo.reut/index.html (accessed 20 July 2008).

Collins, S. (2008) 'Broadcast Networks under Siege', *Los Angeles Times*, 26 May. Online. Available www.latimes.com/entertainment/news/tv/la-et-channel26-2008may26,0,69241 (accessed 10 August 2008).

ComScore (2008a) Press release, 12 May. Online. Available www.comscore.com/press/release.asp?press = 2223 (accessed 20 August 2008).

—— (2008b) Press release, 25 June. Online. Available www.comscore.com/press/release.asp?press = 2292 (accessed 9 August 2008).

—— (2008c) 'Americans Viewed 12 Billion Videos Online in May 2008', press release, 14 July. Online. Available www.comscore.com/press/release.asp?press = 2324 (accessed 20 August 2008).

Coppens, T. and Saeys, F. (2006) 'Enforcing Performance: New Approaches to Govern Public Service Broadcasting', *Media, Culture & Society*, 28: 261–84.

Cornfield, M. (2006) 'The Internet and Politics: No Revolution, Yet', *Pew Internet & American Life Project*, 6 November. Online. Available www.pewresearch.org (accessed 20 August 2008).

Couldry, N. (2003) *Media Rituals: A Critical Approach*, London: Routledge.

Cousins, B. (2006) Interview with Albert Moran, FremantleMedia, London.

Crossick, G. (2006) *Knowledge Transfer Without Widgets: The Challenge of the Creative Economy*, London: Goldsmiths College, University of London.

CRTC (2008) 'CRTC Submits Report on the Canadian Television Fund'. Online. Available www.crtc.gc.ca/eng/NEWS/RELEASES/2008/r080605.htm (accessed 2 July 2008).

Crupi, A. (2008) 'AMC Offers New Sales Tools to Guarantee Upfront Buys', *Mediaweek*, 7 April.

Cummings, B. (2008) 'Addressable Advertising Gets Closer to Reality', *Brandweek*, 4 May.

Cunningham, S. (1988) 'Kennedy-Miller: House style in Australian Television', in E. Jacka and S. Dermody, eds *The Imaginary Industry*, Sydney: AFTRS. Republished in S.

Cunningham, ed. (2008) *In the Vernacular: A Generation of Cultural Criticism and Controversy*, Brisbane: University of Queensland Press, Ch. 6.

—— (2004) 'The Humanities, Creative Arts and International Innovation Agendas', in J. Kenway, E. Bullen and S. Robb, eds *Innovation and Tradition: The Arts, Humanities and the Knowledge Economy*, New York: Peter Lang, 113–24.

—— (2005) 'Culture, Services, Knowledge: Television between Policy Regimes', in J. Wasko, ed. *A Companion to Television*, Malden, MA: Blackwell, 199–213.

Cunningham, S. and Sinclair, J., eds (2001) *Floating Lives: The Media and Asian Diasporas*, Lanham, MD: Rowman & Littlefield.

Curtin, M. (1996) 'On Edge: Culture Industries in the Neo-network Era', in R. Ohmann, G. Averill, M. Curtin, D. Shumway and E. Traube, eds *Making and Selling Culture*, Middletown, CT: Wesleyan University Press.

—— (2003) 'Media Capital: Towards the Study of Spatial Flows', *International Journal of Cultural Studies*, 6(2): 202–28.

—— (2004) 'Media Capitals: Geographies of Global TV', in L. Spigel and J. Olsson, eds *Television After TV: Essays on a Medium in Transition*, Durham, NC: Duke University Press, 270–302.

—— (2007) *Playing to the World's Biggest Audience: The Globalisation of the Chinese Film and TV*, Berkeley, CA: University of California Press.

Da, Xi (2005) 'What Is the Meaning of Supergirl?' *Beijing News*, 18 August. Online. Available http://news.sohu.com/20050818/n226713336.shtml (accessed 17 July 2008).

Dan (n.d.) '*Friends* Ratings: The Only Complete Online *Friends* Ratings Archive!' Online. Available www.newmusicandmore.tripod.com/friendsratings.html (accessed 20 August 2008).

Dave, P. (2006). *Visions of England: Class and Culture in Contemporary Cinema*, Oxford: Berg.

Dawson, M. (2007) 'Little Players, Big Shows: Format, Narration, and Style on Television's New Smaller Screen', *Convergence*, 13(3): 231–50.

Deloitte Touche Tohmatsu (2007) 'Are You Ready for the Future of Media? State of the Media Democracy'. Online. Available www.deloitte.com/us (accessed 20 August 2008).

Dicke, T.S. (1982) *Franchising in America, 1840–1980: The Development of a Business Method*, Chapel Hill, NC: University of North Carolina Press.

Dickerson, M. (2005) 'Battle Intensifies over Control of Mexican TV', *Los Angeles Times*, 17 January. Online. Available http://articles.latimes.com/2005/jan/17/business/fi-mextv17 (accessed 5 August 2008).

Djoric, S. (2002) *Bela knjiga o radiodifuziji 1990–2000* (White Book of Broadcasting 1990–2000), Belgrade: Spektar.

Donald, S.H. (2001) 'History, Entertainment, Education and *jiaoyu*: A Western Australian Perspective on Australian Children's Media, and some Chinese Alternatives', *International Journal of Cultural Studies*, 4(3): 279–99.

Dossari, S. (2006) 'Q&A with Arab Media Mogul Waleed Al Ibrahim', *Asharq al-Awsat English*, 23 November. Online. Available www.asharqalawsat.com/english/news.asp?artid = id7129 (accessed 29 February 2008).

Dudrah, R. (2002) 'Zee TV-Europe and the Construction of a Pan-European South Asian Identity', *Contemporary South Asia*, 11: 163–81.

Dyer, Richard (1981) 'Introduction', in R. Dyer, ed. *Coronation Street*, London: BFI.

Economist, The (2006) 'A Fuzzy Picture: Mobile TV', 378(8459), 7 January: 57.

—— (2007) 'Screen Test: Mobile Television', 384(8545), 8 September: 76.

—— (2008) 'Flickring Here, Twittering There', 16 August: 30–1.

Eggerton, J. (2007) 'Pelosi to Meet C-SPAN about Camera Coverage of House', *Broadcasting & Cable*, 3 January. Online. Available www.broadcastingcable.com (accessed 20 August 2008).

—— (2008) 'McCain: Media-Lite', *Broadcasting & Cable*, 6 September. Online. Available www.broadcastingcable.com (accessed 20 August 2008).

Electronic NewsWeekly (2008) 'IPTV Deployments Double for the Second Year Running as Broadband Continues Strong Growth', 28 July.

El-Hamamsy, G. (2005) 'Carving up the Dish', *Business Today Egypt*, September. Online. Available www.businesstodayegypt.com/article.aspx?ArticleID = 5714 (accessed 2 March 2008).

Ellis, J. (1975) 'Made in Ealing', *Screen*, 16(1): 78–127.

—— (2002) *Seeing Things: Television in the Age of Uncertainty*, London: I.B. Tauris.

El-Rashidi, Y. (2005) '*Oprah* is Attracting Young, Female Viewers to TV in Saudi Arabia', *Wall Street Journal*, 1 December.

Emirates Business 24/7 (2008) 'Most Regional TV Channels Irrelevant', 29 January. Online. Available www.business24–27.ae/cs/article_show_mainh1_story.aspx?HeadlineID = 1594 (accessed 2 March 2008).

Entertainment Industry Development Corporation (2005) 'Television Sustains Los Angeles Entertainment Production', 19 August. Online. Available www.eidc.com/EIDC – Production_Trends_Release_081905.pdf (accessed 5 August 2008).

Eutelsat (2007) *Cable and Satellite TV Market: 2006*. Online. Available www.eutelsat.com/products/pdf/cable_satellite_tvmarket.pdf (accessed 8 May 2008).

Fenech, S. (2008) 'Australian TV Programs Available on iTunes', *Australian Online*, 25 June. Online. Available www.news.com.au/technology/story/0,25642,23921353–5014116,00.html (accessed 8 August 2008).

Feuer, J., Kerr, P. and Vahimagi, T., eds (1984) *MTM 'Quality Television'*, London: BFI.

Fitzgerald, A. (2008) 'TV Companies Work Hard at Targeting Their Audiences', *Australian*, 7 July: 34.

Fordin, H. (1975) *The World of Entertainment: Hollywood's Greatest Musicals*, New York: Doubleday.

Former Saja producer (2007) Author interview, Sharjah, 12 December.

Forrester, C. (2008) 'Free Satellite Winning in Mid-East', *Rapid TV News*, 8 June. Online. Available http://rapidtvnews.com/index.php/200806081369/free-satellite-winning-in-mid-east.html (accessed 11 June 2008).

Foser, J. (2008) 'Media Matters', *Media Matters for America*, 5 September. Online. Available www.mediamatters.org (accessed 8 September 2008).

Frey, B. (2007) 'The Future of Television Advertising', panel discussion at the Future of Television Conference, New York City, November. Audio online. Available www.televisionconference.com/audio2007.shtml (accessed 12 July 2008).

Friedman, W. (2008) 'Addressable TV Marketing Arrives', *Daily Variety*, 2 May: 20.

Fritz, B. (2008) 'Summer's "Grand" Slam', *Variety*, 410, 21–27 April: 1–2.

Fu, W.W. and Wildman, S. (2008) 'Economic Research on Asian Media Markets and Industries: A Critical Reflection', *Asian Journal of Communication*, 18(2): 92–101.

Fulgoni, G. (2008) 'Online Is the New Primetime', paper presented to Advertising Research Foundation Annual Summit, 31 March. Online. Available www.comscore.com/press/presentations.asp (accessed 10 August 2008).

Fung, A. (2003) 'Marketing Popular Culture in China: Andy Lau as a Pan-Chinese Icon', in C.C. Lee, ed. *Chinese Media, Global Contexts*, London: RoutledgeCurzon, 257–269.

—— (2004) 'From Republic of Letters to Television Republic? Citizen Readers in the Era of Broadcast Television', in L. Spigel and J. Olsson, eds *Television After TV: Essays on a Medium in Transition*, Durham, NC: Duke University Press, 386–417.

—— (2008a) *Television Truths*, Oxford: Blackwell.

—— (2008b) 'The Supremacy of Ignorance over Instruction and of Numbers over Knowledge: Journalism, Popular Culture and the English Constitution', *Journalism Studies*, 9(5): 679–91.

Harvey, D. (1990) *The Condition of Postmodernity*, Cambridge, MA: Blackwell.

—— (2005) *A Brief History of Neoliberalism*, Oxford: Oxford University Press.

He, J.S. (2007) Interview with He Ji Shen, National Communications Commission, October.

Hearn, A. (2007) '*Top Gear* Around the World', *AutoTrader*, 16 March. Online. Available www.autotrader.co.uk/EDITORIAL/CARS/FEATURES/33790.html (accessed 10 February 2008).

Hecht, J. (2005) 'Mexican Novelas Go Global', *Entertainment News Wire*. Online. Available www.allbusiness.com/services/amusement-recreation-services/4743820–21.html (accessed 5 August 2008).

Henderson, L. (2007) *Social Issues in Television Fiction*, Edinburgh: Edinburgh University Press.

Heng, L.L. (2007) Interview, Media Development Authority.

Heylen, R. (1994) *Translation Poetics and the Stage: Six French Hamlets*, London: Routledge.

Higgs, P., Cunningham, S. and Bakhshi, H. (2008) *Beyond the Creative Industries: Mapping the Creative Economy in the United Kingdom*. Online. Available www.nesta.org.uk/beyond-the-creative-industries (accessed 8 August 2008).

Hilmes, M. (2007) *Only Connect: A Cultural History of Broadcasting in the United States*, 2nd edn, Belmont, CA: Wadsworth.

Hirschorn, M. (2008) 'TV's Uncertain Future', *Australian Financial Review*, 11 April: 1.

Hirst, P. and Thompson, G. (1995) *Globalisation in Question: The International Economy and the Possibilities of Governance*, Cambridge: Polity Press.

Hobson, D. (2008) *Channel 4: The Early Years and the Jeremy Isaacs Legacy*, London: I.B. Tauris.

Hoffman, H. (2008) 'Two Steps Forward, One Step Back: NBC's Olympic Coverage', *Cnet News*, 28 June. Online. Available http://news.cnet.com/8301–10784_3-9979961-7.html (accessed 18 August 2008).

Hoggart, R. (1957) *The Uses of Literacy*, London: Chatto & Windus.

Holdsworth, N. (2006) 'Romania's "Bell" Tolls for New Era', *Hollywood Reporter*, 7, November.

Hong, J.H. (1993) 'China's TV Program Import 1958–88: Towards the Internationalization of Television?', *International Communication Gazette*, 52: 1. Online. Available www.pressreference.com/Sw-Ur/Taiwan.html (accessed 20 August 2008).

Hoskins, C., McFadyen, S. and Finn, A. (2001) 'Refocusing the CBC', *Canadian Journal of Communication*, 26: 17–30.

HRT Report (2003) 'Analiza slušanosti i gledanosti programa i emisija HRT-a u razdoblju od 1. siječnja do 30. studenog 2002 godine', Zagreb: HRT.

Huang, X. (2007) 'Who Seized the England League?' *Nanfang Daily*. Online. Available http://www1.nanfangdaily.com.cn/b5/www.nanfangdaily.com.cn/southnews/zmzg/200703150722.asp (accessed 21 July 2008).

Hyatt, W. (1997) *Encyclopedia of Daytime Television*, New York: Billboard.

—— (2008) *Global Capital, Local Culture: Transnational Media in China*, New York: P¢ Lang.

Fung, A. and Curtin, M. (2002) 'The Anomalies of Being Faye Wong', *International Jou of Cultural Studies*, 5(3): 263–90.

Galvin, N. (2008) 'Small Screen's Big Potential', *Sydney Morning Herald*, 22 May.

Gandy, O. (1990) 'Tracking the Audience: Personal Information and Privacy', in J.D Downing, A. Mohammadi and A. Sreberny, eds *Questioning the Media: A Critical Ir duction*, London: Sage, 207–20.

Garnham, N. (2000) *Emancipation, the Media, and Modernity*, Oxford: Oxford Unive Press.

—— (2003) 'A Response to Elizabeth Jacka's "Democracy as Defeat"', *Television & . Media*, 4: 193–200.

Garrett, D. (2008) 'Skeins Swim in Web Stream', *Variety*, 3 March: 16.

Gauntlett, D. (2007) 'Media Studies 2.0', 24 February, revised March. Online. Avail www.theory.org.uk/mediastudies2 (accessed 8 May 2008).

Georghiou, L. (2007) *Demanding Innovation: Lead Markets, Procurement and Innov* NESTA Provocation 02, February.

Gillian, L.E. (2004) 'We Didn't Flinch', *Daily News Halifax*, 7 October: 29.

Given, J. (1998) *The Death of Broadcasting: Media's Digital Future*, Sydney: UNSW Pres

Glaser, M. (2007) '2008 Candidates Jump Online with Early Blog Ads', *MediaShift*, 19 uary. Online. Available www.pbs.org/mediashift.

Global Media Journal (2006) 'Chinese Media Market', 5(8). Online. Available http:/ calumet.purdue.edu/cca/gmj/sp06/graduatesp06/gmj-sp06gradref-cheng.htm (acc 20 August 2008).

González, J. (1994) *Más (+) Cultura(s)*, Mexico DF: Consejo Nacional para la Cultura Artes.

Government Information Office (Taiwan) (2007) 'Overview of Taiwan's Broadca Industry, Republic of China (Taiwan)', 22 June. Online. Available http://open.nat tw/OpenFront/report/show_file.jsp?sysId = C09602367&fileNo = 002 (accesse February 2008).

Gray, J., Jones, J.P. and Thompson, E., eds (2009) *Satire TV: Politics and Comedy in the network Era*, New York: New York University Press.

Green, J. (2008) 'Why Do They Call It TV When It's Not on the Box? "New" Telev Services and "Old" Television Functions', *Media International Australia*, 126: 95–105

Gripsrud, J. (2004) 'Broadcast Television: The Chances of its Survival in a Digital Ag L. Spigel and J. Olsson, eds *Television After TV: Essays on a Medium in Tran* Durham, NC: Duke University Press, 210–23.

Gueorguieva, V. (2007) 'Voters, MySpace, and YouTube: The Impact of Altern Communication Channels on the 2006 Election Cycle and Beyond', *Social Science puter Review*, 26(3): 288–300.

Guevarra, V. and Lee, S.Y. (2008) 'Asian Telecoms Bet Big on IPTV to Lure Viev *Wall Street Journal* (Eastern Edition), 8 January.

Guo, Z. and Chen, H. (1997) 'China's Media Content under Commercialism', *Communication Review*, 24: 85–101.

Guth, R.A. and Delaney, K.J. (2007) 'Microsoft in Talks about Facebook Investment', *Jones News Service*, 25 September.

Halper, M. (2006) 'Hollywood Comes Calling on Mobiles', *Variety*, 20 February: 19.

Hartley, J. (1999) *Uses of Television*, London: Routledge.

Idato, M. (2005) 'Home Invasion', *Sydney Morning Herald*, 29 August.

Institute for Politics, Democracy & the Internet (2007)'New Media and the 2008 Presidential Election', 28 September. Online. Available www.ipdi.org (accessed 3 March 2008).

Iordanova, D. (2006) *The Cinema of the Balkans*, London: Wallflower Press.

Iwabuchi, Koichi (2002) *Recentering Globalization: Popular Culture and Japanese Transnationalism*, Durham, NC: Duke University Press.

Izkoff, D. (2007) 'A Brave New World for TV? Virtually', *New York Times Online*, 24 June. Online. Available www.nytimes.com/2007/06/24/arts/television/24itzk.html?_r = 2&oref = slogin&pagewanted = print&oref = slogin (accessed 10 February 2008).

Jacka, E. (2003) '"Democracy as Defeat": The Impotence of Arguments for Public Service Broadcasting', *Television & New Media*, 4: 177–91.

Jacka, T. (2006) *Rural Women in Urban China: Gender, Migration, and Social Change*, Armonk, NY: M.E. Sharpe.

Jakes, Susan (2005) 'Li Yuchun Loved for Being Oneself', *New York Times*. Online. Available www.time.com/time/asia/2005/heroes/li_yuchun.html (accessed 10 July 2008).

Jakubowicz, K. (2006) 'Keep the Essence, Change (Almost) Everything Else', in I. Banerjee and K. Seneviratne, eds *Public Service Broadcasting in the Age of Globalization*, Singapore: AMIC.

—— (2007) 'Public Service Broadcasting: A Pawn on an Ideological Chessboard', in E. de Bens, ed. *Media Between Culture and Commerce*, Chicago: Intellect.

Jarrett, K. (2008) 'Interactivity is Evil!: A Critical Investigation of Web 2.0', *First Monday*, 13(3), March. Online. Available www.uic.edu/htbin/cgiwrap/bin/ojs/index/php/fm/article/view/2140/1947 (accessed 10 April 2008).

Jarvis, C. (2006) Interview with Albert Moran, BBC World, London.

Jenkins, H. (2006) *Convergence Culture: Where Old and New Media Collide*, New York: New York University Press.

Joannou, M. (2000) *Contemporary Women's Writing: From the Golden Notebook to the Color Purple*, Manchester: Manchester University Press.

Johnston, K.M. (2008) 'The Coolest Way to Watch Movie Trailers in the World: Trailers in the Digital Age', *Convergence: The International Journal of Research into New Media Technologies*, 14(2): 145–60.

Joost internet television site. Available www.joost.com (accessed 29 August 2008).

Jovanovic, I. (2008) 'Save the Last Dance for Us', *TransitionsonLine*, 30 May.

Kawach, N. (2008) 'UAE has Highest Mobile Penetration in GCC', *Emirates Business 24/7*, 10 August.

Keane, M. (2001) 'Television Drama in China: Engineering Souls for the Market', in R. King and T. Craig, eds *Global Goes Local: Popular Culture in Asia*, Vancouver: University of British Columbia Press, 176–202.

—— (2002a) 'Send in the Clones: Television Formats and Content Creation in the People's Republic of China', in S.H. Donald, M. Keane and H. Yin, eds *Media in China: Consumption, Content and Crisis*, London: RoutledgeCurzon, 80–90.

—— (2002b) 'As a Hundred Television Formats Bloom, a Thousand Television Stations Contend', *Journal of Contemporary China*, 11(30): 5–16.

—— (2004) 'A Revolution in Television and a Great Leap Forward by China? China in the Global Television Format Business', in A. Moran and M. Keane, eds *Television Across Asia: Television Industries, Programme Formats and Globalization*, London: RoutledgeCurzon, 88–104.

—— (2005) 'Television Drama in China: Remaking the Market', *Media International Australia*, 115: 82–93.

Keane, M., Fung, A.Y.H. and Moran, A. (2007) *New Television, Globalisation and the East Asian Cultural Imagination*, Hong Kong: Hong Kong University Press.

Keeter, S. (2008) 'Cell Phones and the 2008 Vote: An Update.' Pew Research Center, 17 July. Online. Available www.pewresearch.org (accessed 6 August 2008).

Klaassen, A. and Hampp, A. (2008) 'CBS, Spike Kick Video up a Notch', *Advertising Age*, 79(22), 2 June: 8.

Klinger, B. (2006) *Beyond the Multiplex: Cinema, New Technologies, and the Home*, Berkeley, CA: University of California Press.

Kofman, E. (2005) 'Figures of the Cosmopolitan: Privileged Nationals and National Outsiders', *Innovation*, 18(1): 83–97.

Kohli-Khandekar, V. (2006) *The Indian Media Business*, New Delhi: Response Books.

Kolle, R. (1995) Interview with Albert Moran, Grundy World Wide, Sydney.

Kotz, D. (2003) 'Neoliberalism and the US Economic Expansion of the 1990s', *Monthly Review*, 54(11): 15–32.

Kraidy, M. (2007) 'Idioms of Contention: Star Academy in Lebanon and Kuwait', in N. Sakr, ed. *Arab Media and Political Renewal: Community, Legitimacy and Public Life*, London: I.B. Tauris, 44–55.

Kronja, I. (2001) *Smrtonosni sjaj: masovna psihologija i estetika turbo-folka*, Belgrade: Tehnokratia.

Lau, T.Y., Look, K., Atkin, D. and Lin, C. (2008) *Cross Media Ownership: An Analysis of Regulations and Practices in Australia, Hong Kong and Singapore*, Telecommunication Research Trends.

Leadbeater, C. and Oakley, K. (1999) *The Independents: Britain's New Cultural Entrepreneurs*, London: Demos, Institute of Contemporary Arts and the Smith Institute.

Lefebvre, A. (1993) 'Introduction', in A. Lefebvre, ed. *Translation/History/Culture*, London: Routledge, 1–13.

Lewis, J. (2007) 'The Media Mob', *American Thinker*, 21 August. Online. Available www.americanthinker.com (accessed 20 May 2008).

Lin, C. (2006) *The Transformation of Chinese Socialism*, Durham, NC: Duke University Press.

Lindroos, K. (1998) *Now-time, Image-space: Temporalization of Politics in Walter Benjamin's Philosophy of History and Art*, Jyväskylä: Sophi Publications.

Lopez, A. (1995) 'Our Welcomed Guests: Telenovelas in Latin America', in R. Allen, ed. *To Be Continued … Soap Operas Around the World*, London and New York: Routledge, 256–75.

Lopusina, M. (2003) *Ceca, Izmedu Ljubavi I Mrznje*, Beograd: Evro.

Lotman, Y. (1990) *Universe of the Mind: A Semiotic Theory of Culture*, Bloomington, IN: Indiana University Press.

Lotz, A. (2007) *The Television Will Be Revolutionized*, New York: New York University Press.

Lu, S. (2000) 'Soap Opera in China: The Transnational Politics of Visuality, Sexuality, and Masculinity', *Cinema Journal*, 40(1): 25–47.

Luis López, O. (1998) *La Radio en Cuba*, 2nd corr. edn, La Habana, Cuba: Editorial Letras Cubanas.

Lull, J. (1997) 'China Turned on (Revisited): Television, Reform and Resistance', in A. Sreberny-Mohammadi, D. Winseck, J. McKenna and O. Boyd-Barrett, eds *Media in Global Context: A Reader*, New York: Arnold, 259–68.

Lynch, M. (2005) 'Assessing the Democratizing Power of Arab Satellite TV', *Transnational Broadcasting Studies*, 1: 150–52.

Ma, E.K.W. (2000) 'Rethinking Media Studies: The Case of China', in J. Curran, ed. *De-Westernizing Media Studies*, London: Routledge, 21–34.

Macartney, J. (2006) '*Pop Idol* TV Show Stifled as Chinese Get Taste for Having a Vote', *Times*, 1 April. Online. Available www.timesonline.co.uk/tol/news/world/asia/article700649.ece (accessed 17 July 2008).

MacDonald, G. (2004) 'I Wanted … to Capture the Real Horror of It', *Globe and Mail*, 9 October: R10.

Madar Research (2006) 'Madar Research Reports 70 Percent Growth in Arab Mobile Phone Subscription in 2005', press release, Dubai, 29 July.

Madden, M. (2008) 'Online video', *Pew Internet and American Life Project*. Online. Available www.pewinternet.org/PPF/r/219/report_display.asp (accessed 20 August 2008).

Madden, M. and Jones, S. (2008) 'Podcasts Proliferate, But Not Mainstream', *Pew Internet and American Life Project*. Online. Available http://pewresearch.org (accessed 28 August 2008).

Madden, N. (2008) '*Ugly Betty* Looks Very Attractive to Unilever in China', *AdAgeChina*, 16 April. Online. Available http://adage.com/china/article.php?article_id = 126395 (accessed 5 August 2008).

Magder, T. (2006) 'International Agreements and the Regulation of World Communication', in J. Curran and D. Morley, eds *Media and Cultural Theory*, London: Routledge, 164–76.

Malas, N. (2008) 'Democratizing the Arab Screen', *Middle East Broadcasters Journal*, 16: 12–17.

Malouf, D. (2003) 'Made in England: Australia's British Inheritance', *Quarterly Essay*, 12: 1–66.

Manchanda, U. (1998) 'Invasion from the Skies: The Impact of Foreign Television on India', *Australian Studies in Journalism*, 7: 136–63.

Mandler, R. (2007) 'The Future of Television Advertising', panel discussion at the Future of Television Conference, New York City, November. Audio online. Available www.televisionconference.com/audio2007.shtml (accessed 12 July 2008).

Mankekar, P. (1999) *Screening Culture, Viewing Politics: An Ethnography of Television, Womanhood and Nation in Postcolonial India*, Durham, NC: Duke University Press.

Marchand, R. (1985) *Advertising the American Dream: Making Way for Modernity, 1920–1940*, Berkeley, CA: University of California Press.

Marques De Melo, J. (1988) *As Telenovelas de Globo*, São Paulo: Summus Editorial.

—— (1992) 'Brazil's Role as a Television Exporter within the Latin American Regional Market', paper presented at 42nd Conference of the International Communication Association, Miami, May.

Mattelart, M. and Mattelart, A. (1990) *The Carnival of Images: Brazilian Television Fiction*, New York: Bergin & Garvey.

May, A. and Ma, X.-L. (2007) 'Hong Kong: Changing Geographies of a Media Capital', *Media International Australia*, 124: 156–65.

McLelland, M. (2008) 'Race on the Japanese Internet: Discussing Korea and Koreans on "2chaneru"', *New Media and Society*, 10(6): 811–30.

McMillin, D. (2001) 'Localizing the Global: Television and Hybrid Programming in India', *International Journal of Cultural Studies*, 4(1): 45–68.

—— (2002) 'Choosing Commercial Television's Identities in India: A Reception Analysis', *Continuum: Journal of Media and Cultural Studies*, 16(1): 123–36.

—— (2007) *International Media Studies*, Malden, MA: Blackwell.

McMurria, J. (2007) 'A Taste of Class: Pay-TV and the Commodification of Television in Post-war America', in S. Banet-Weiser, C. Chris and A. Freitas, eds *Cable Visions*, New York: New York University Press, 44–65.

Media Matters for America (2008) 'Tipping the Scales: Cable News Channels Dedicate More Coverage to RNC's Scheduled Programming during Peak Hours than to DNC's', Online. Available www.mediamatters.org (accessed 20 August 2008).

Media Plan Institut (2000) 'Dossier', *Novosti o medijima*, 66, Sarajevo, 31 August.

Mehta, N. (2006) 'India as a New Media Capital: The Global and Regional Impact of Indian Television', paper presented at AusAID-Asia Pacific Research Futures Research Network Conference, Canberra, 25–26 September.

Mikos, L. (2008) 'Aesthetic Difference in National Adaptations of *Ugly Betty*', paper presented at Television without Borders conference, University of Reading, June.

Miles, I. and Green, L. (2008) *Hidden Innovation in the Creative Industries*, NESTA, July. Online. Available www.nesta.org.uk/hidden-innovation-in-the-creative-industries (accessed 8 August 2008).

Milivojevic, S. (2000) 'The Nationalization of Everyday life', in N. Popov, ed. *The Road to War in Serbia*, Budapest: CEU Press, 608–29.

Miller, T., Govil, N., McMurria, J. and Maxwell, R. (2001) *Global Hollywood*, London: British Film Institute.

Ministry of Trade and Industry (MTI) (2008) *Growing Our Economy: Competitiveness of the Economy*, updated May 2008. Online. Available http://app.mti.gov.sg/default.asp?id = 487 (accessed 12 August 2008).

Miro TV, Internet television site. Available www.getmiro.com (accessed 29 August 2008).

Mishra, S. (1999) 'Dish Is Life: Cable Operators and the Neighbourhood', in C. Brosius and M. Butcher, eds *Image Journeys: Audio-Visual Media and Cultural Change in India*, New Delhi: Sage, 261–77.

Mitchell, G. (2008) 'The "Online Campaign" – Election 2008 – Rolls On', *Editor & Publisher*, 6 September. Online. Available www.editorandpublisher.com (accessed 8 September 2008).

Mladina (2008) 'Seselj ovira sojenje', 10 August.

Moran, A. (1982) *Making a TV Series: The Bellamy Project*, Sydney: Currency Press/AFI.

—— (1985) *Images and Industry: Television Drama Production in Australia*, Sydney: Currency Press.

—— (1998) *Copycat TV: Globalization, Program Formats and Cultural Identity*, Luton: University of Luton Press.

—— (2005) 'Configurations of the New Television Landscape', in J. Wasko, ed. *A Companion to Television*, Malden, MA: Blackwell, 291–308.

—— (2008) 'Cultural Power in International TV Format Markets', in J. Wasko and M. Erickson, eds *Trans-border Cultural Production: Economic Runaway or Globalization?* New York: Cambria, 333–58.

Moran, A. and Keane, M. (2003) *Television Across Asia: TV Industries, Program Formats and Globalization*, London: Routledge.

Moran, A. and Malbon, J. (2006) *Understanding the Global TV Format*, Bristol: Intellect.

Morley, D. (2000) *Home Territories: Media, Mobility and Identity*, London: Routledge.

—— (2004) 'At Home with Television', in L. Spigel and J. Olsson, eds *Television After TV: Essays on a Medium in Transition*, Durham, NC: Duke University Press, 303–23.

Morrissey, B. (2008) 'The New Gold Standard: Why Data – and the Ability to Use It – Will Change the Way You Do Everything', *Adweek*, 4 February.

Mother Jones (2007a) 'Fight Different', July–August: 27.

—— (2007b) 'Politics 2.0: The Big Idea', July–August: 28–37.

Murdock, G. (2000) 'Talk Shows: Democratic Debates and Tabloid Tales', in J. Wieten, G. Murdock and P. Dahlgren, eds *Television Across Europe: A Comparative Introduction*, London: Sage, 198–219.

Murdock, G. and Halloran, J.D. (1979) 'Contexts of Creativity in Television Drama: An Exploratory Study in Britain', in H.-D. Fischer and S.R. Melnick, eds *Entertainment: A Cross-cultural Examination*, New York: Hastings House.

Museum of Broadcasting Communications, China (2008) Online. Available www.museum.tv/archives/etv/C/htmlC/china/china.htm (accessed 20 July 2008).

Musil, S. (2008) 'Olympic Games Take the Gold in the Workplace', *CNet news*. Online. Available http://news.cnet.com/8301-1023_3-10016938-93.html (accessed 13 August 2008).

Neumann, W.R. (1991) *The Future of the Mass Audience*, Cambridge: Cambridge University Press.

New Straits Times (2000) 'Special Role Media Play in Singapore', 30 September. Online. Available www.singapore-window.org/swns.htm (accessed 3 March 2008).

New York Times (2008) 'Conventions: CNN Claims Ratings Milestone', *New York Times* TV Decoder blog, 29 August. Online. Available www.tvdecoder.blogs.nytimes.com/2008/08/29/conventions-cnn-claims-ratings-milestone (accessed 3 September 2008).

News Corporation (2008) 'Sky Brasil serviços Itda'. Online. Available www.newscorp.com/management/skyla.html (accessed 18 June 2008).

Nielsen Media Research (2006) 'Nielsen Media Research reports television's popularity is still growing', 21 September. Online. Available www.nielsenmedia.com/nc/portal/site/Public/menuitem.55dc65b4a7d5adff3f65936147a062a0/?vgnextoid = 4156527aacccd010VgnVCM100000ac0a260aRCRD (accessed 3 March 2008).

—— (2008a) *Nielsen's Three Screen Report*, May. Online. Available www.nielsen.com/pdf/3_Screen_Report_May08_FINAL.pdf (accessed 31 July 2008).

—— (2008b) 'Nielsen Reports TV, Internet and Mobile Usage among Americans', 8 July. Online. Available www.nielsenmedia.com (accessed 3 August 2008).

—— (2008c) 'Anytime Anywhere Research'. Online. Available http://a2m2.nielsen.com (accessed 20 August 2008).

Ninan, S. (1995) *Through the Magic Window: Television and Change in India*, New Delhi: Penguin.

Nordicity Group (2006) 'Analysis of Government Support for Public Broadcasting and Other Culture in Canada'. Online. Available www.nordicity.com/reports.html (accessed 30 June 2008).

Norton-Taylor, R. (1999) 'Allies Target Serbian "Nerve Centre"', *Guardian*, 22 April.

O'Hagan, A. (2008). *The Atlantic Ocean: Essays on Britain and America*, London: Faber & Faber.

Ohm, B. (1999) 'Doordarshan: Representing the Nation's State', in C. Brosius and M. Butcher, eds *Image Journeys: Audio-visual Media and Cultural Change in India*, New Delhi: Sage, 69–96.

Ong, A. (1999) *Flexible Citizenship: The Cultural Logic of Transnationality*, Durham, NC: Duke University Press.

—— (2006) *Neoliberalism as Exception: Mutations in Citizenship and Sovereignty*, Durham, NC: Duke University Press.

Ortíz de Urbana, A. and López, A. (1999) 'Soaps with a Latin Scent', *UNESCO Courier*, May. Online. Available www.unesco.org/courier/1999_05/uk/connex/txt1.htm (accessed 18 August 2008).

OSI: Network Media Program (2005) *Television Across Europe Report*, 'Regulation, Policy and Independence in Serbia'.

Oxford English Dictionary Online. Available http://dictionary.oed.com/cgi/entry/00302205?single = 1&query_type = word&queryword = marketization&first = 1&max_to_show = 10 (accessed 20 April 2008).

Palmer, S. (2008) 'Ben Silverman's Comments on Margins vs Ratings Signal the End of Broadcast Television', *Huffington Post*, 24 July. Online. Available http//:www.huffingtonpost.com/shelly-palmer/ben-silvermans-comments-o_b_114225 (accessed 10 August 2008).

PARC (2007) *Harvest Y2007*, Dubai: Pan Arab Research Centre.

Patel, J. (2007) 'Innovations That Are Shaping the Future of Television', panel discussion at the Future of Television Conference, New York City, November. Audio online. Available www.televisionconference.com/audio2007.shtml (accessed 12 July 2008).

Petersen, S.M. (2008) 'Loser Generated Content: From Participation to Exploitation', *First Monday*, 13(3). Online. Available www.uic.edu/htbin/cgiwrap/bin/ojs/index.php/fm/article/view/2141/1948 (accessed 12 April 2008).

Pew Research Center (2005) *The Internet and Campaign 2004*. Online. Available www.pewresearch.org (accessed 12 August 2008).

—— (2007) 'Campaign Internet Videos: *Sopranos* Spoof vs *Obama Girl*', 12 July. Online. Available www.pewresearch.org (accessed 12 August 2008).

Pirie, D. (1973) *A Heritage of Horror: The English Gothic Cinema 1946–1972*, London: Gordon Frazer.

Politika (2005) 'There Are 755 Broadcasters in Serbia', 2 July: A9.

Pouwelse, J., Garbacki, P., Epema, D. and Sips, H. (2005) *IPTPS 2005*, LNCS 3640, Berlin/Heidelberg: Springer-Verlag, 205–16.

Power, C. (2005) 'Look Who's Talking', *Newsweek International*, 8 August.

PQMedia Data (2006) 'Exclusive PQ Media Data: Media Companies to Come out Winners as 2006 Political Media Spending Heads for Record Books', 2 November. Online. Available www.pqmedia.com (accessed 20 August 2008).

Press Reference, Taiwan Press, Media, TV, Radio, Newspapers. Online. Available www.pressreference.com/Sw-Ur/Taiwan.html (accessed 23 July 2008).

Preston, M. (2007) 'Political Television Advertising to Reach $3 billion', CNN.com, 15 October. Online. Available www.cnn.com (accessed 12 March 2008).

Project for Excellence in Journalism (2005) *The State of the News Media: An Annual Report on American Journalism*.

Pun, N. (2005) *Made in China: Women Factory Workers in a Global Workplace*, Durham, NC: Duke University Press.

Rainie, L. and Horrigan, J. (2007) 'Election 2006 Online', *Pew Internet & American Life Project*, 17 January. Online. Available www.pewresearch.org (accessed 12 August 2008).

Rajagopal, Arvind (1993) 'The Rise of National Programming: The Case of Indian Television', *Media, Culture & Society*, 15(1): 91–111.

Rasiej, A., Sifry, M.L. and Weinberger, D. (2008) 'Who Will Be America's First Tech-president?' Online. Available www.techpresident.com (accessed 23 July 2008).

Rawnsley, G.D. and Rawnsley M.-Y. (2005) 'Public Television and Empowerment in Taiwan', *Pacific Affairs*, 78(1): 23.

Rêgo, C. and La Pastina, A. (2007) 'Brazil and the Globalization of Telenovelas', in D.K. Thussu, ed. *Media on the Move: Global Flow and Contra-flow*, London: Routledge, 99–115.

Rizzo, T. (2007) 'Programming Your Own Channel: An Archaeology of the Playlist', in A. Kenyon, ed. *TV Futures: Digital Television Policy in Australia*, Melbourne: Melbourne University Press, 1087–1131.

Robbins, B. (1998) 'Actually Existing Cosmopolitanism', in P. Cheah and B. Robbins, eds *Cosmopolitics: Thinking and Feeling beyond the Nation*, Minneapolis: University of Minneapolis Press, 1–19.

Robison, R. (2006) 'Preface', in R. Robison, ed. *The Neo-liberal Revolution: Forging the Market State*, New York: Palgrave.

Rofel, Lisa (2007) *Desiring China: Experiments in Neoliberalism, Sexuality, and Public Culture*, Durham, NC: Duke University Press.

Roncagliolo, R. (1995) 'Trade Integration and Communication Networks in Latin America', *Canadian Journal of Communication*, 20(3): 335–42.

Rothenbuhler, E.W. (1989) 'Values and Symbols in Orientations to the Olympics', *Critical Studies in Mass Communication*, 6: 138–57.

Roudometof, V. (2005) 'Transnationalism, Cosmopolitanism and Glocalization', *Current Sociology*, 53(1): 113–35.

Roy, A. (2008) 'Bringing up TV: Popular Culture and the Developmental Modern in India', *South Asian Popular Culture*, 6(1): 29–43.

Sakr, N. (2001) *Satellite Realms: Transnational Television, Globalization and the Middle East*, London: I.B. Tauris.

—— (2007) *Arab Television Today*, London: I.B. Tauris.

—— (2008) 'Oil, Arms and Media: How US Interventionism Shapes Arab TV', *Journal für Entwicklungspolitik* 24(1): 57–81.

Saleh, H. (2007) 'Religious TV Channels Experiencing Financial Crunch', *Asharq al-Awsat English edition*, 31 January. Online. Available www.asharqalawsat.com/english/news.asp?section = 5&id = 7850 (accessed 1 February 2007).

Sartor, T. and Page, D. (2008) 'Big Events Eclipse the Issues', *Project for Excellence in Journalism*, September. Online. Available www.journalism.org (accessed 18 September 2008).

Schiller, D. (2007) *How to Think About Information*, Urbana, IL: University of Illinois Press.

Scott, M. (Managing Director, ABC) (2008) '2020 Unleashed – the Future of your ABC', 17 April. Online. Available www.abc.net.au/unleashed/stories/s2219409.htm (accessed 25 February 2008).

Scrase, T. (2002) 'Television, the Middle Classes and the Transformation of Cultural Identities in West Bengal, India', *Gazette: The International Journal for Communication Studies*, 64(4): 323–42.

Screendigest (2008) 'European Broadband Cable 2008', in *Screendigest Report*, 15 July.

Seneviratne, K. (2006) 'Definition and History of Public Broadcasting', in I. Banerjee and K. Seneviratne, eds *Public Service Broadcasting in the Age of Globalization*, Singapore: AMIC.

Serjeant, J. (2008) 'John McCain Speech Draws Record TV Ratings', *Reuters*, 5 September. Online. Available www.reuters.com/article/wtMostRead/idUSN0439266820080905 (accessed 9 September 2008).

Shan, S. (2008) 'Feature: Problems Conflicts Leave TBS under Scrutiny', *Taipei Times*, 20 May. Online. Available www.taipeitimes.com/News/taiwan/archives/2008/05/20/2003412434 (accessed 28 May 2008).

Shattuc, J. (1997) *The Talking Cure: Talk Shows and Women*, London: Routledge.

Shepard, A.C. (2008a) 'The Millionaire's Media Megaphone', *Center for Public Integrity*, 2 September. Online. Available www.buyingofthepresident.org (accessed 10 September 2008).

—— (2008b) 'The Millionaire's Media Megaphone – Part Two', *Center for Public Integrity*, 3 September. Online. Available www.buyingofthepresident.org (accessed 10 September 2008).

Shrikhande, S. (2004) 'Business News Channels in Asia: Strategies and Challenges', *Asian Journal of Communication*, 14(1): 38–52.

Silverstone, R. (1993) 'Television, Ontological Security and the Transitional Object', *Media, Culture & Society*, 15(4): 573–98.

Simons, J. (2008) 'The Networks' New Advertising Model', *Fortune* online, 5 May. Online. Available http://money.cnn.com/2008/05/02/technology/upfronts.fortune/index.htm?postversion = 2008050507 (accessed 12 May 2008).

Sinclair, J. (1999) *Latin American Television: A Global View*, London: Oxford University Press.

Sinclair, J., Jacka, E. and Cunningham, S., eds (1996) *New Patterns in Global Television: Peripheral Vision*, New York: Oxford University Press.

Skinner, D. (2008) 'Television in Canada: Continuity or Change?', in D. Ward, ed. *Television and Public Policy: Change and Continuity in an Era of Global Liberalization*, Mahwah, NJ: Lawrence Erlbaum.

Smith, A. (2008) 'Politics Goes Viral Online', *Pew Internet and American Life Project*, 15 June. Online. Available www.pewresearch.org (accessed 28 June 2008).

Smythe, D. (1981) *Dependency Road: Communications, Capitalism, Consciousness, and Canada*, New York: Ablex.

Solinger, D. (1999) *Contesting Citizenship in Urban China: Peasant Migrants, the State, and the Logic of the Market*, Berkeley, CA: University of California Press.

Sousa, H. (1997) 'Crossing the Atlantic: Globo's Wager in Portugal', paper presented to the conference of the International Association for Mass Communication Research, Oaxaca, July.

Sparks, C. (2007) *Globalization, Development and the Mass Media*, Thousand Oaks, CA: Sage.

Spenser, G. (2006) Interview with Albert Moran, Imagination, London.

Spigel, L. and Olsson, J., eds (2004) *Television After TV: Essays on a Medium in Transition*, Durham, NC: Duke University Press.

Splichal, S. (2006) 'In Search of a Strong European Public Sphere', *Media, Culture & Society*, 28(5): 695–714.

Sroka, T.N. (2006) *Understanding the Political Influence of Blogs: A Study of the Growing Importance of the Blogosphere in the U.S. Congress*. Institute for Politics Democracy and the Internet, April. Online. Available www.ipdi.org (accessed 10 April 2008).

Steemers, J. (2001) 'In Search of a Third Way: Balancing Public Purpose and Commerce in German and British Public Service Broadcasting', *Canadian Journal of Communication*, 26: 69–87.

Steinberg, J. and Elliott, S. (2008) 'ABC Roster is Heavy on the Already Proven', *New York Times*, 13 May: C6.

Stelter, B. (2007) 'Google and Nielsen Link Up for Better View of TV Ad Watchers', *International Herald Tribune*, 25 October: 4.

—— (2008a) 'In the Age of TiVo and Web Video, What Is Prime Time?' *New York Times*, 12 May: C1.

—— (2008b) '38 Million View Obama's Speech: Highest-rated Convention in History', *New York Times* TV Decoder blog, 29 August. Online. Available tvdecoder.blogs.nytimes.com/2008/08/29/conventions-38-million-view-obamas-speech (accessed 3 September 2008).

Stoneman, P. (2007) 'An Introduction to the Definition and Measurement of Soft Innovation', in *Soft Innovation: Completing the Portrait of the Dynamic Economy*. Online. Available www.nesta.org.uk/soft-innovation-completing-the-portrait-of-the-dynamic-economy (accessed 8 August 2008).

—— (2008) 'Soft Innovation in Creative and Non-creative Industries', in *Soft Innovation: Completing the Portrait of the Dynamic Economy*. Online. Available www.nesta.org.uk/soft-innovation-completing-the-portrait-of-the-dynamic-economy (accessed 8 August 2008).

Strachan, A. (2004) 'Powerful, Frightening: Sex Traffic Must Be Seen', *Calgary Herald*, 10 October: D6.

Straubhaar, J. (1991) 'Beyond Media Imperialism: Asymmetrical Interdependence and Cultural Proximity', *Critical Studies in Mass Communication*, 8: 39–59.

—— (2007) *World Television: From Global to Local*, Thousand Oaks, CA: Sage.

Su, C. (2007) Interview, October 2007.

Sun, W. (2007) 'Significant Moments on CCTV', *International Journal of Cultural Studies*, 10 (2): 187–204.

—— (2008) 'The Curse of the Everyday: Politics of Representation and New Social Semiotics in Post-socialist China', in K. Sen and T. Lee, eds *Politics, Media and Regime Change in Asia*, London: Routledge, 32–48.

—— (2009a) *Maid in China: Media, Morality and the Cultural Politics of Boundaries*, London: Routledge.

—— (2009b) 'Making Space for the Maid: Television Drama, Metropolitan Gaze, and a Semiotic of Power in the Post-socialist Chinese City', *Feminist Media Studies*, 9(1), 57–71.

Tabakoff, N. (2008) 'Free-to-air TV Heading the Way of Vinyl Records, Says Media Expert', *Australian*, 24 March: 27.

Taiwan Broadcasting System website. Available www.tbs.org.tw/index_e.htm (accessed 20 September 2008).

Tarlac, G. (2003) 'Vojaski in politicni turbo-folk', *Mladina*, 12(1). Online. Available www.mladina.si/dnevnik/21-03-2003-vojaski_in_politicni_turbo_folk (accessed 25 June 2008).

Teinowitz, I. (2008) 'Olympic Deal Sealed: Obama Makes $5 Million Buy', *AdvertisingAge*, 23 July. Online. Available www.adage.com (accessed 12 August 2008).

Terranova, T. (2000) 'Producing Culture for the Digital Economy', *Social Text 63*, 18(2): 821.

Thomas, A.O. (2005) *Imagi-Nations and Borderless Television: Media, Culture and Politics Across Asia*, Thousand Oaks, CA: Sage.

Thompson, M. (1994) *Forging War: The Media in Serbia, Croatia and Bosnia and Herzegovina*, London: Article 19.

Thussu, D.K. (2005) 'The Transnationalization of Television: The Indian Experience', in J.K. Chalaby, ed. *Transnational Television Worldwide: Towards a New Media Order*, London: I.B. Tauris, 156–72.

—— (2007) 'The Murdochization of News? The Case of STAR TV in India', *Media, Culture & Society*, 29(4): 593–611.

Times of India (2008) 'Billboards with "Eyes" Find Audience', 21 July. Online. Available http://timesofindia.indiatimes.com/articleshow/msid-3261313,prtpage-1.cms (accessed 20 August 2008).

Tinic, S. (2005) *On Location: Canada's Television Industry in a Global Market*, Toronto: University of Toronto Press.

TNS Media Intelligence (2007) *An Analysis of 2007 and 2008 Political, Issue and Advocacy Advertising*, New York: TNS.

Toff, B. (2008) 'Ratings: Barack Obama, and All the Rest', *New York Times* TV Decoder blog, 29 August. Online. Available tvdecoder.blogs.nytimes.com/2008/08/29/ratings-barack-obama-and-all-the-rest (accessed 10 September 2008).

Trpevska, S. (2003) *Television and Audience Segmentation*, Skopje: Broadcasting Council.

Tsang, C., Wong, S., Li, E. and Pang, S. (n.d.) 'CEPA and Its Impact on the Development of the Telecommunications and Media Industries in China and Hong Kong: Online Cyberlaw and Telecommunications Policy in Greater China'. Online. Available http://newmedia.cityu.edu.hk/cyberlaw/index24.html (accessed 20 September 2008).

Tu, W.M. (1991) 'Cultural China: The Periphery as the Centre', *Daedulus*, 120: 1–32.

Tunstall, J., ed. (1970) *Media Sociology: A Reader*, London: Constable.

—— (2008) *The Media Were American: The US Mass Media in Decline*, Oxford: Oxford University Press.

Turner, G. (2003) *British Cultural Studies*, 3rd edn, London: Routledge.

—— (2006) 'The Mass Production of Celebrity: Celetoids, Reality TV and the "Demotic Turn"', *International Journal of Cultural Studies*, 9(2): 153–66.

—— (2009) *The Demotic Turn: Ordinary People and the Media*, London: Sage, forthcoming.

Turow, J. (1998) *Breaking Up America: Advertisers and the New Media World*, Chicago: University of Chicago Press.

TV Telco Latam (2008) 'IPTV and Pay-TV in Latin America 2002–12', 1 April. Online. Available www.tvtelco.com/nota.aspx?IdContenido = 269&IdIdioma = 2 (accessed 26 May 2008).

TVB.com Limited (n.d.) 'Corporate Information'. Online. Available www.tvb.com/affairs/faq/tvbgroup/tvbi.html (accessed 20 August 2008).

TVMASNOVELAS (2004) Second World Summit of the Telenovelas Industry. Online. Available www.onlytelenovelas.com/Only__2_EEUU.php (accessed 18 August 2008).

Twist, J. (2006) 'The Year of the Digital Citizen', *BBC News*, 2 January. Online. Available www.newsvote.bbc.co.uk (accessed 20 July 2008).

Udovicic, R. (2005) *The Stumbling of the Media in Times of Transition*, Sarajevo: Media Plan Institut.

US Census Bureau (2007) 'Minority Population Tops 100 Million', 17 May. Online. Available www.census.gov/Press-Release/www/releases/archives/population/010048.html (accessed 22 February 2008).

Van Zoonen, L. (2005) *Entertaining the Citizen: When Politics and Popular Culture Converge*, Lanham, MD: Rowman and Littlefield.

vanden Heuvel, K. (2008) 'Just Democracy', *The Nation*, 21–28 July: 31–40.

Waggener Edstrom Worldwide (2008) 'Survey'.

Waisbord, S. (2004) 'McTV? Understanding the Global Popularity of Television Formats', *Television and New Media*, 5(4): 359–83.

Wang, F.-L. (2005) *Organizing Through Division and Exclusion: China's Hukou System*, Stanford, CA: Stanford University Press.

Wang, G.W. (2000) 'A Single Chinese Diaspora?' in G.W. Wang, ed. *Joining the Modern World: Inside and Outside China*, Singapore: Singapore University Press/World Scientific.

Wang, H. (2003) *China's New Order: Society, Politics, and Economy*, Cambridge, MA: Harvard University Press.

—— (2006) 'Depoliticized Politics, from East to West', *New Left Review*, 41. Online. Available www.newleftview.org/?page = article&view = 2634.

Wang, J. (2008) *Brand New China: Advertising, Media, and Commercial Culture*, Cambridge, MA: Harvard University Press.

Wasko, J. and Erickson, M., eds (2008) *Trans-border Cultural Production: Economic Runaway or Globalization?* New York: Cambria.

Watercutter, A. (2008) 'Miley Cyrus Delivers Latest Blow in YouTube Dance Battle', *Underwire Blog*, 11 June. Online. Available www.blog.wired.com/underwire/2008/06/miley-cyrus-del.html (accessed 12 July 2008).

Webb, M. (2008) 'The Web is Where It's at for Youth Vote', *AdvertisingAge*, 25 June. Online. Available www.adage.com (accessed 12 July 2008).

Wei, R. (2000) 'China's Television in the Era of Marketisation', in D. French and M. Richards, eds *Television in Contemporary Asia*, London: Sage, 325–46.

Wei, Y. (2005) *Attack on Supergirl (Paochong Chaoji Nusehng)*, Qiongqing: Qiongqing Press.

Weiss, L. (1998) *The Myth of the Disappearing State*, Cambridge: Polity Press.

Wheeler, D. (2007) 'Mobilization and the Internet in the Arab World: A View from Internet Cafés in Egypt and Jordan', paper presented to the Annual Political Science Association Meeting, Chicago, September.

Whiteley, N. (2003) *Reyner Banham: Historian of the Immediate Future*, Cambridge, MA: MIT Press.

Whitney, D. (2007) 'Building a Blended TV Family', *Television Week*, 10 December: 1.

—— (2008a) 'Digital Dealmakers. In Focus: Tara Walpert', *Television Week*, 27(14): 8.

—— (2008b) 'Mobi-TV Reaches 4 Million Video Subscribers', *RCR News*, 4 August. Online. Available www.rcrnews.com/article/20080804/WIRELESS/267063675/-1/tagged/MobiTV-reaches-4-million-mobile-video-subscribers (accessed 28 August 2008).

Wikipedia (n.d.) 'List of Most-watched Television Broadcasts'. Online. Available www.en.wikipedia.org/wiki/List_of_most-watched_television_episodes (accessed 2 September 2008).

Winston, B. (1998) *Media Technology and Society: A History from the Telegraph to the Internet*, London: Routledge.

Wohlfarth, I. (1998) 'The Measure of the Possible, the Weight of the Real and the Heat of the Moment: Benjamin's Actuality Today', in L. Marcus and L. Nead, eds *The Actuality of Walter Benjamin*, London: Lawrence & Wishart, 13–39.

Wong, M. (2002) 'TiVo Watches Subscribers' Super Bowl Viewing Habits', *Lubbock Avalanche-Journal*, 5 February. Online. Available www.lubbockonline.com/stories/020502/sup_0205020095.shtml (accessed 21 August 2008).

World Factbook, The (2008). Online. Available https://www.cia/gov/library/publications/the-world-factbook/index.html (accessed 18 June 2008).

Xinhua (2007) 'CCTV to Launch French, Spanish Channels'. Online. Available www.news.xinhuanet.com/english/2007–/content_6803368.htm (accessed 30 September 2008).

Xu, H. (2000) 'Morality Discourse in the Marketplace: Narratives in Chinese Television News Magazine *Oriental Horizon*', *Journalism Studies*, 1(4): 637–49.

Yang, J. (2006) 'The Second Cultural Revolution: Super Female Voice, Commercialization and the Chinese State', unpublished MA thesis, School of Journalism, University of British Columbia, Canada.

Yardley, Jim (2005) 'The Chinese Get the Vote, if Only for "Super Girl"', *New York Times*, 4 September. Online. Available www.nytimes.com/2005/09/04/weekinreview/04yard.html (accessed 10 July 2008).

Ytreberg, E. (2004) 'Formatting Participation within Broadcast Media Production', *Media, Culture & Society*, 26(5): 677–92.

Yue, A. and Hawkins, G. (2000) 'Going South', *New Formations 'Culture/China'*, (40): 49–63.

Zang, X. (2008) 'Market Transition, Wealth and Status Claims', in D.S.G. Goodman, ed. *The New Rich in China: Future Leaders, Present Lives*, London: Routledge, 53–70.

Zarkovic, D. (2008) 'Seselj u svakoj kuci', *Vreme*, 7 August: 5.

Zhang, L. (2002) 'Spatiality and Urban Citizenship in Late Socialist China', *Public Culture*, 14(2): 311–34.

Zhao, Y. (1998) *Media, Market and Democracy in China: Between the Party Line and the Bottom Line*, Urbana-Champaign, IL: University of Illinois Press.

—— (2000) 'Watchdogs on Party Leashes? Contexts and Limitations of Investigative Journalism in Post-Deng China', *Journalism Studies*, 1(4): 577–97.

—— (2004) 'Underdogs, Lapdogs and Watchdogs: Journalists and the Public Sphere Problematic in China', in G. Xin and M. Goldman, eds *Chinese Intellectuals between State and Market*, London: RoutledgeCurzon, 43–74.

—— (2008a) *Communication in China: Political Economy, Power, and Conflict*, Lanham, MD: Rowman & Littlefield.

—— (2008b) 'Neoliberal Strategies, Socialist Legacies: Communication and State Transformation in China', in P. Chakravarty and Y. Zhao, eds *Global Communications: Towards a Transcultural Political Economy*, Lanham, MD: Rowman & Littlefield, 23–50.

Zhao, Y. and Guo, Z. (2005) 'Television in China: History, Political Economy, and Ideology', in J. Wasko, ed. *A Companion to Television*, Malden, MA: Blackwell, 521–39.

Zhu, Y. (2008) *Television in Post-reform China: Serial Dramas, Confucian Leadership and the Global Television Market*, London: Routledge.

Zhu, Y., Keane, M. and Bai, R., eds (2008) *Television Dramas in China*, Hong Kong: Hong Kong University Press.

Zittrain, J. (2008) *The Future of the Internet and How to Stop It*, Harvard, MA: Yale University Press.

Index